T0272611

JUST A MERCENARY?

JUST A MERCENARY?

NOTES FROM MY LIFE AND CAREER

DUVVURI SUBBARAO

PENGUIN
VIKING
An imprint of Penguin Random House

VIKING

Viking is an imprint of the Penguin Random House group of companies
whose addresses can be found at global.penguinrandomhouse.com

Published by Penguin Books India Pvt. Ltd
4th Floor, Capital Tower 1, MG Road,
Gurugram 122 002, Haryana, India

First published in Viking by Penguin Random House India 2024

10 9 8 7 6 5 4 3 2 1

ISBN 9780143467298

Typeset in Adobe Caslon Pro by Manipal Technologies Limited, Manipal
Printed at Thomson Press India Ltd, New Delhi

www.penguin.co.in

For my parents who taught me values

Contents

Snippets/Op-Eds

Author's Note

Occasionally, authors have to explain why they have written their book. I believe this is one such occasion.

My previous book—*Who Moved My Interest Rate?*—recounting my experiences as the governor of the Reserve Bank of India (RBI) between 2008 and 2013 came out in 2016, three years after I stepped down from the post. Governors before me had narrated some of their experiences in books, but mine was the first full-length book written by any former governor, covering an entire tenure.

That book was motivated by a sense of purpose for at least two reasons. First, the five years I was at the helm of the RBI marked an unusually turbulent period for the world and for India. I believed the dilemmas and challenges I confronted while leading the RBI through that economic turmoil would be of interest—and hopefully, of some guidance—to policymakers. Second, I felt a strong need to demystify the RBI and explain to the larger public how RBI decisions and actions impact their everyday lives.

To my pleasant surprise, that book found an audience— larger than I expected. Many people who read it, especially youngsters, urged me to write a companion book covering my thirty-five-year career in the Indian Administrative Service (IAS) before I went into the RBI. I didn't warm to the idea for several reasons.

First, civil service memoirs is a crowded genre, and the books span the entire spectrum in terms of quality. The ones that stand out do so because the authors have woven their experiences into the political and economic history of the country and they narrate those experiences in an engaging manner. I was not confident my story would pass muster by those benchmarks.

Second, I joined the IAS in 1972. It was a different world, a different milieu in terms of the challenges of administration and the logistics of administering. A few of my stories may be interesting because they are quaint but beyond that, I was apprehensive whether the larger reading public would relate to my experiences or find any value in them. Would I just be embarking on a hugely egotistic enterprise?

Third, I kept no notes and would have to rely entirely on my memory. Jogging through fifty years of experiences seemed quite daunting; besides, there was the risk of selective memory that would embellish my accomplishments and minimize my failures.

Those calculations changed somewhat during the Covid lull. The initial idea was not a book but just a series of 'notes to myself' of some prominent experiences in my career.

Urmila, my wife, who read most of them, encouraged me to bite the bullet and work on a full-length book.

It wasn't easy-going. Whereas I had written the RBI book in a span of eight months amid the unhurried and conducive atmosphere of the National University of Singapore, this one was interrupted by several personal and professional commitments as Covid receded and the world reopened. Also, the misgivings I had about writing my 'memoirs' started resurfacing on occasion, ebbing my enthusiasm.

What you are reading is the product of that laboured endeavour. I prefer classifying this book as 'notes from my life and career' rather than 'memoirs' because there was no attempt to weave all my experiences into a comprehensive framework. This book is more in the nature of recalling experiences on the go, arranged in a roughly chronological order.

The book starts with a chapter on my early life, education and entry into the IAS to give a context of my origins and upbringing. The bulk of the book is devoted to my IAS career from 1972 until I superannuated in 2008 when I was appointed governor of the RBI. There are also two chapters at the end devoted to my RBI tenure, which should be interesting to those who haven't read my earlier book. Even those who read the earlier book will, I hope, find that with the lapse of time, I am able to look at my RBI tenure more objectively.

No matter what you call it—memoirs or notes—the hero of a book like this is, by definition, the author. These stories are mine and I figure in them, but I have made a conscious attempt to situate those stories in the larger context of drawing lessons or explaining policy dilemmas.

I've written about my successes and written also about my setbacks. I've reflected on my mistakes and introspected on my misdeeds. Please do indulge me if you sense any lingering vanity.

Virtually everyone I told about the book asked me who my target reader was. A straightforward answer has eluded me. I've been asked many times, 'How did you get to become the governor of the RBI from the IAS?' If I said, 'Oh! It's just a matter of being in the right place at the right time', I'd come off as falsely modest. On the other hand, if I replied, 'It's a testimonial to my qualifications, proven track record and personality', I'd come across as boorish and boastful. So, I'd finesse my reply combining the two strands, leaving both sides dissatisfied with the conversation. Hopefully, this book will give a more nuanced response to that question. And everyone who is curious about my answer to that question is therefore my target reader. I hope there are many more such curious people than I think.

What is the rationale for the book title *Just a Mercenary?*? I've explained this in the last chapter so that the reader can make their own evaluation of whether the title is justified. Here, I only want to say this: a mercenary, as I understand, is someone who goes to fight a war just because he is being paid for it. He has no commitment to any larger cause.

I am quite clear that all through my career, I've tried to do my best. I am conscious too that my best may not have been good enough on occasion. But the question that constantly runs in my mind is what motivated me. Was it just a sense of duty—an obligation to do your best just because you were getting paid for it? Or was I driven by a higher calling—the need to give back to society for all that I have received? In short, was I just a mercenary or was I more? The answer will perhaps elude me forever.

It is customary for a preface to end with a vote of thanks. My thanks, therefore, to all the people who over the last several years asked me if I was writing a book on my IAS career, thereby unknowingly encouraging me to get started.

No one except the editors has read the full draft. But friends who were kind enough to give me feedback on specific chapters were, in alphabetical order: Syed Akbaruddin, Amitabha Bhattacharya, Sheela Bhide, Chandra Gariyali, Shyamala Gopinath, Vijay Jagannathan, Sunil Khatri, Alpana Killawala, Bhaskar Krishna, K.P. Krishnan, Mahendra Kumawat, Anil Kutti, T. Nandakumar, Gulzar Natarajan, Sudha Pillai, V.G.S. Rajan, M. Ramachandran, G.R. Reddy, Mrityunjay Sahoo, Sadhana Sahoo, Shivangi Sharma, L.V. Subrahmanyam, Usha Thorat and Venky Venkatesan.

The improvement from my first drafts to the final version that you are reading is owed to the comments and feedback from all the above. My thanks to them. I may have inadvertently missed out some and I hope they will forgive me. The standard caveat that I remain responsible for the final version applies.

I am grateful to the team at Penguin—Manasi Subramaniam, Karthik Venkatesh, Ralph Rebello, Shreya Dhawan, Gunjan Ahlawat, Neeraj Nath and indeed all of their teammates for leading me through this difficult project with passion and professionalism.

Many authors say that their families have been their harshest and also most helpful critics. I can now vouch for that. My wife, Urmila, sons, Mallik and Raghav, and daughters-in-law, Rachita and Aditi, who have grown to be more than the daughters we didn't have, have all been my most discerning and caring critics. Their love and care are my most prized blessings.

Career Trajectory

1972	Joined the IAS
1972–74	IAS training in Mussoorie and field training in Nellore District, Andhra Pradesh
1974–76	Sub-Collector, Parvathipuram, Andhra Pradesh
1977–78	Study leave, Ohio State University, USA
1979	District Collector, Khammam, Andhra Pradesh
1980–82	Executive Director, Andhra Pradesh Small Scale Industries Development Corporation
1982–83	District Collector, Prakasam, Andhra Pradesh
1983–84	Humphrey Fellow at Massachusetts Institute of Technology (MIT), USA
1984–86	Executive Director, Andhra Pradesh Industrial Development Corporation
1986–87	Officer on Special Duty, arrack bottling (Andhra Pradesh)

1987–88   Managing Director, Andhra Pradesh State
             Finance Corporation
1988–93   Deputation to Government of India—
             Director/Joint Secretary in the Ministry of
             Finance
1993–98   Finance Secretary, Government of Andhra
             Pradesh
1999–2004   Lead Economist, the World Bank
2005–07   Secretary, Economic Advisory Council to
             the Prime Minister
2007–08   Finance Secretary, Government of India
2008–13   Governor, Reserve Bank of India
2013–23   Various academic pursuits, Visiting Fellow
             at several universities

1

My Life, My Career

A Few Snapshots

Indian Administrative Service (IAS) results day

Kanpur
1 May 1972

A blazing summer afternoon—hot enough to roast birds alive. I was sleeping in my room—Room 213-G, Hall V—in the Indian Institute of Technology (IIT) in Kanpur. I was in the final semester of MSc Physics. All the written exams were done. I had gone 'night out'—to use IIT lingo—working the entire night in the lab completing my project. I skipped breakfast, wrote and handed in my project report and went through the mandatory viva, notorious for the grilling your adviser puts you through with sadistic pleasure. Having completed all the requirements for the MSc degree, the overwhelming sense was more of relief than fulfilment. I slowly trudged back to the hostel on my ramshackle cycle, sleep-deprived and exhausted, had a quick lunch and hit the sack.

At around 4 p.m., someone banged on my door to say that I had a telephone call from Delhi. Incidentally, in IIT hostels, gently knocking on the door was unheard of. In an era when phones were a rarity, IIT Kanpur, which at that time was the largest American-aided educational programme anywhere in the world, took pride in the fact that the entire campus was connected via a telephone system, which was good for in-campus as well as external calls. Each hostel had a phone installed in the common room. I was irritated by this disturbance of my well-earned sleep; nevertheless, I ran the nearly 100 metres downstairs to the phone wondering who could be calling from Delhi.

It was Rau, from Rau's IAS Study Circle, wanting to tell me that I had topped the all-India merit list for selection to the Indian Administrative Service (IAS) and Indian Foreign Service (IFS). Between the screeching on the phone and Rau's habitually mumbling voice, it took a minute for me to understand what he was saying. Rau kept repeating that I had topped not just the IAS list but also the IFS list. The difference was non-trivial. In those days, the IFS interview carried 400 marks as against 300 marks for the IAS interview with the result that marginal differences in the order of merit were possible.

Once the news sank in, I was ecstatic. I had given the IAS written examination some seven months earlier, in October 1971, and had appeared for the Union Public Service Commission (UPSC) interview—personality test as it is called—in March. I had a sense that I had done well in both, but there was no way of telling how well. Unlike the closed class of twenty-five to thirty students that we were used to in IIT, the IAS is an open competitive examination, so you have no idea what the competition is like, and it is impossible to guess where you stand vis-à-vis others. Besides, I had never met an IAS officer to assess myself in comparison.

Those days, very much unlike today, the IAS was not on the career radar of IIT students. So, my 'thumping success' was no big news on the campus. My close friends were, of course, happy for me, gave me bumps till my body was sore and demanded a treat. I promised one, of course, but asked them to hold off till the next day.

My priority was to contact my father back in Eluru in Andhra Pradesh. Since there was no phone in our house in Eluru, I tried to call him on the phone in the neighbours' house but couldn't connect.

In those dark ages with no Internet, no cell phones and no social media, the All India Radio (AIR) news at 9 p.m. was the first source of information on the IAS results. It was a practice for AIR to announce the names of the top five candidates in the IAS merit list in their 9 p.m. news bulletin. As it was results season, I knew my father would be listening to the news, not so much because he was expecting to hear my name but for a signal that the full list would appear in the newspapers the following morning. My father later told me that he had heard my name on the news bulletin, was ecstatic but immediately began doubting if he had heard right. He was reassured only after he had seen my name in print in the newspapers the following day.

First day of my first posting

Parvathipuram
15 July 1974

I arrived at Srikakulam Road railway station from Nellore by the Howrah Mail. The afternoon was hot and muggy. An assistant from the office had come in the official jeep to receive me and take me to Parvathipuram, about 50 km away. He had brought lunch in a large tiffin carrier—sufficient for at least five people to feast on—and offered, somewhat hesitantly, to arrange for me to eat in the privacy of the station master's office. I declined, saying that I had already eaten on the train; I didn't fail to notice the disappointment on his face.

It took us nearly two hours to navigate our way to Parvathipuram because the jeep was rickety, the road was narrow, patchy and potholed, and the traffic—buses, lorries, bullock carts, cycles, cattle and people—although relatively light by today's standards, was haphazard. We drove straight to the office, an old, fraying, single-storey stone building with a tiled roof, situated in a corner of a large, leafy but unkempt compound.

The staff of the sub-collector's office, about a dozen of them, were at the entrance to welcome me. We greeted each other awkwardly and subconsciously sized up each other as strangers do. Having worked with several bosses, these people were veterans at adjusting to the work style of a new boss. Even so, they must have been apprehensive about what personality quirks I might bring to work, while on my part I was unsure about how I would team up with these people, figure out how to learn from them and be their boss at the same time.

Even before I could get my bearings, the office superintendent courteously but firmly hurried me in to sign the papers for taking over charge. The haste was so as to get this done before the 'auspicious window' closed. I am not much for astrology, much less a believer in auspicious timings, but I have never resisted other people who do so, as long as it isn't inconvenient, inefficient or inappropriate.

Immediately after the signing was done, I was ushered into a farewell function for my predecessor who was superannuating that day after having served in the government for over thirty-five years. The significance of the occasion—he at the end of his career and I at the beginning of mine—did not escape me. There were about a hundred people at the function—staff from several offices in that small town. I was conscious of being under their intense scrutiny, as they were watching my every move, utterance and gesture. After all, the arrival of a freshly minted IAS officer was an event in that small town!

My last day in the IAS

New Delhi
4 September 2008

Two nights earlier, I was on a flight home after attending a G20 Deputies meeting in Rio de Janeiro. As the plane landed in Delhi in the early morning of 2 September, my phone started beeping incessantly with an unusual flood of messages. I was confused about the congratulations since not one of them contained a clue as to what they were for. I called my wife, Urmila, who gave me the news of my appointment as governor of the Reserve Bank of India (RBI), but also did not miss the opportunity to complain that since the previous evening she had done nothing but field phone calls from literally hundreds of people, many of them not even known to us.

I had been finance secretary to the Government of India for about sixteen months by then—long enough to understand the issues and priorities and set myself goals to be accomplished during the rest of my tenure. And now this most unexpected turn in my career. All through my working life, I had been quite aspirational, but becoming the governor of the RBI had not been on my career calculus. Not because I disdained the job, the opposite actually—I didn't think I had the 'experience' for it. I was delighted of course, but also apprehensive about whether I'd be able to measure up to the job.

Fortunately, I had more immediate concerns, such as preparing for the move from Delhi to Mumbai, which pushed these apprehensions to the background. The next few days were a blur as I rushed to wind up several tasks in the office and tie up loose ends at home.

In the middle of the logistical nightmare of the transition that I was muddling through, Y.V. Reddy, the outgoing governor, who was also from the IAS, called me up from Mumbai to advise that I should seek voluntary retirement from the IAS before assuming office as governor. At the time, I was fifty-nine and still a year away from superannuation. Reddy's reasoning was that I should unequivocally be covered by the code of conduct prescribed for the governor, which may be at variance with the IAS code of conduct.

When I checked, I was informed by the 'rules people' in the Department of Personnel not to bother since I would be deemed to have retired from the IAS as soon as I assumed office as governor. Never in the thirty-five years of my IAS career did I imagine that I would sever links with the civil service, which had nurtured and defined me all through my adult life, so nonchalantly.

As I took an early morning Air India flight from Delhi to Mumbai on 5 September 2008, my thoughts were less on my thirty-five years in the IAS and more on the challenges that lay ahead for me as governor of the RBI.

My first day at the RBI

Mumbai
5 September 2008

My early morning flight from Delhi landed in Mumbai in blinding rain. As always self-conscious about too much protocol, I had requested Grace Koshie, secretary to the RBI board and in charge of protocol at the RBI, to send just one protocol officer to receive me.

On the long ride from Santa Cruz airport to the RBI central office in South Mumbai, a melange of thoughts crowded my mind—about my IAS career that had just ended and the new career at the RBI that was about to begin.

As civil servants, we were trained to be anonymous. This appointment as governor had turned me from an unknown unknown to a known unknown. Over the last three days since the news of my appointment, there had been news coverage of my background and career trajectory, and extensive commentary on my reform credentials and policy biases. There was speculation about where I would stand on the growth-inflation balance and my potential stance on exchange rate management. There were questions about whether, as governor, I would fulfil my dharma of countering fiscal profligacy for which I was—some said—'at least partly responsible' as finance secretary.

One bit of commentary that weighed uppermost in my mind was on whether I would stand up for the independence of the Reserve Bank. There was a view that my familiarity with and sympathy for the government's point of view would help repair the strained relationship between the Ministry of Finance and the Reserve Bank. Others thought that because of my allegiance to the government, I would be nonchalant about preserving the RBI's independence and yield to pressures from the government on policy issues. There were even suggestions that the government was, in fact, dispatching one of its trusted civil servants to the RBI to influence the bank's policy from within.

These questions about my credibility weren't comforting, but there was nothing much I could do in the short term. I would have to prove my credentials by what I said and what I did during my tenure. But I had no complaints. That challenge came with the territory.

As I reached the RBI office, I literally walked into a farewell lunch for Y.V. Reddy, the outgoing governor.

Reddy and I went back a long way. He was eight years my senior in the IAS and we both belonged to the Andhra Pradesh cadre. We didn't have the opportunity to work together while serving in the state, but we overlapped in the Ministry of Finance in Delhi as joint secretaries in the early 1990s. He was handling the balance of payments and played a prominent role in managing the 1991 external payments crisis.

As finance secretary, my relationship with Governor Reddy hadn't been entirely smooth. He was circumspect about some of the reforms we were pushing from the government. Also, during my time as finance secretary over the last year and a half, inflation had been firming up. In a media conference a couple of months ago, I was asked what the government was doing about inflation. I mentioned the steps the government had taken to stem the price rise but also added that the RBI's monetary policy had to be the first line of defence against inflation. I had said that quite innocuously although Reddy seemed to have interpreted that as the government instructing the RBI to act.

One happy thing though is that these differences had not impaired our friendship. At the farewell meeting, I, in fact, emphasized how over a four-decade career, Reddy had served the country with dignity and distinction.

At a brief ceremony in the RBI board room at 3 p.m., Reddy signed off and I signed on. Reddy suggested that I briefly meet the media waiting outside the room for a photo opportunity. When questioned about what my immediate priority as governor would be, I said quite unhesitatingly that it would be bringing inflation down.

Little did I know that my priorities would change dramatically in just a few days!

My last day at the RBI

Mumbai
4 September 2013

My last day as governor of the RBI—marking an end to five turbulent years at the helm of that great institution.

Real-life events do not respect leadership transitions. The last couple of months of my tenure had gone completely off-script. I thought that would be the time when I would travel around and visit the Reserve Bank's regional offices across the country and walk around the central office departments to reminisce and rejoice with others over our time together. I particularly wanted to reach out to the middle- and junior-level staff of the Reserve Bank, who usually operate below the governor's radar but whose ideas, insights and perspectives had influenced me more than they realized. In the event, I was so preoccupied with managing the exchange rate crisis triggered by the 'taper tantrums' that my last day in office had arrived almost as abruptly as my first day as governor.

At 11 a.m., I spoke to the entire Reserve Bank staff across the country via a video link-up and told them that I would carry many, many pleasant memories of my association with the bank. The challenges and anxieties we had navigated and the joy and fun we had had together would be enduring memories. I pointed out that in a full-length feature article on the Reserve Bank in 2012, *The Economist* had said: 'The RBI is a role model for the kind of full-service central bank that is back in fashion worldwide.' I hoped, I added, that in a few years from then, everyone watching and evaluating central banks around the world would say: 'The RBI is a role model for the kind of knowledge and ethical institution that a central bank should be.'

There was a lunch that afternoon to bid me farewell and welcome the new governor, Raghuram Rajan. Gathered there were the directors on the board of the Reserve Bank, serving senior management and retired senior officers of the Reserve Bank, CEOs of banks and financial institutions, other financial sector regulators—about 200 people in all. There was the expected round of speeches—nostalgic, emotional and touching.

I kept my own remarks deliberately light-hearted. I told the gathering that there were many things I would miss about being governor, but most of all I would miss being important. Once I stepped down, I would enjoy the freedom to open my mouth without the pressure of having to say something profound every time I spoke and that I would freak out on going to a matinee show of *Chennai Express*. I gave some advice to Raghu. He could, I told him, comfortably delegate to his senior management less important tasks like setting the interest rate and issuing bank licences, but that he ought to retain with himself important decisions like the menu for lunches to be hosted by the governor, gifts to be given to visiting dignitaries and seating arrangements at meetings.

At a brief ceremony at 3 p.m. that afternoon, I signed off and Governor Rajan signed on. Minutes later, I walked out of the office, went down eighteen floors in the elevator—with hundreds of Reserve Bank staff present on the ground floor to see me off amidst the clicking cameras of the assembled press photographers—got into my car and drove away, past Flora Fountain, on to Marine Drive and Chowpatty and into my post-career life.

Signing off on the manuscript of this book

New Haven, Connecticut
7 October 2023

It is a glorious New England autumn day here in New Haven, Connecticut. Just this morning, I signed off on the full manuscript of this book. I am aware there is still a lot of grunt work ahead, but the main writing part is now behind me. So I hope, anyway.

I've been at Yale for a few weeks now, as a senior fellow at the Jackson School of Global Affairs. My deliverables include, among other things, teaching a graduate course on central banking in emerging economies. Over the last ten years since stepping down as governor of the RBI, I've dabbled in academia and taught at several places in India and outside. This is the first time, though, that I am taking on the responsibility of teaching a full course.

Over the last couple of months, I've spent a considerable amount of time putting together the syllabus for the course, researching the reading material and preparing the lecture notes. It was heavy work but less daunting than I had feared. It was, of course, a rewarding learning opportunity.

And as I sign off on this book draft, typing away in my apartment on Chapel Street on the edge of the Yale campus, my thoughts are also on the course I am teaching. We are midway through it now, and I am eagerly awaiting the student feedback at the end of the course in December.

Being continuously challenged, anxious about whether I am being diligent enough and craving for success in everything I do has become a way of life.

2

Make Your Bed Every Morning

School, IIT, IAS

I was born in Kovvur, a mofussil town on the banks of River Godavari, in November 1949, a few years too late to be one of midnight's children. My father, a lawyer, was serving in the state government as an assistant public prosecutor. My mother had been married off before she completed high school, and much of her education came from what she learnt in life rather than what she had learnt in a school.

I was the fourth of seven children, and looking back over seven decades later, I realize how many sacrifices my parents must have made to bring us all up on my father's meagre salary, although back then I was quite happy with our lower middle-class lifestyle and never really missed anything. Like all parents in our socio-economic class, my parents never compromised when it came to giving us an education even as they must have been unsure of our prospects amidst all the uncertainty, scarcity and gloom of the 1950s and 1960s.

A few years after I was born, my father got a promotion, and we moved to Eluru, the headquarters of West Godavari district in Andhra Pradesh. I went to a municipal elementary school at the end of our street. When I finished Class V, my father took me to the municipal high school at the other end of the street to admit me there in Class VI. The headmaster took one look at my birth certificate and said that I was too young for Class VI. I started howling and screaming right there. Seeing my anguish, the headmaster, known to my father, suggested that he could find a workaround if we got a certificate from the elementary school that I had completed Class V there. So off we went down the street. Tragedy unfolded as the headmaster there couldn't find my name in his records even after repeated searches, although he admitted that he saw me in the school every day.

What had happened was that when I was about four years old, I began accompanying my elder sister, a year older than me, to school, sat next to her and moved up class by class with her for five years. The informality of schooling in those days was such that no teacher ever thought to ask who I was and what I was doing there. Even my parents forgot that I had not been formally enrolled. The result of this fiasco was that I had to continue in the elementary school for one more year.

Admission to Sainik School

When I was twelve and in Class VIII, my father saw a notification for admission to Sainik Schools. They were a new government initiative, and the plan was to set up one in each major state. What attracted him was the offer of scholarships to meritorious students. Encouraged by his suggestion, I took the countrywide entrance examination and did well enough to earn a scholarship.

So, in January 1962, I was admitted to Class VIII in Sainik School, Korukonda, in Visakhapatnam district in north coastal Andhra Pradesh. Korukonda is a small village about 50 km from Visakhapatnam. The reason the Sainik School allotted to Andhra Pradesh was set up there was that the erstwhile royal family of Vizianagaram had a palace there that was lying unused. The maharajas were known for their patronage of education and arts, and the then heirs to the palace, P.V.G. Raju, a minister in the state cabinet, and his brother Vizzy, who was a noted cricket radio commentator, had generously donated the palace for setting up the school.

Moving from a lowly endowed municipal school to a Sainik School with relatively generous funding from the Ministry of Defence was a big leap for me in many ways; abruptly shifting from Telugu medium to English medium was just one of them. Since Sainik Schools were enjoined to prepare students for entrance to the National Defence Academy (NDA), the school curriculum was predominantly oriented towards that goal—drill, PT and sports, and extracurricular activities aimed at personality development received as much attention as classroom instruction. For many of us from lower-middle-class backgrounds, it was a privilege to be in a Sainik School, but as the first cohort of students, we also had to put up with all the teething problems of a new institution. It didn't help that our teachers were as new to the system as we were. The Sainik Schools had all the positives of a good public school without the elitist status. On the whole, school was fun, but for the food. But of course, does a hostel exist anywhere in the world whose food is liked by the inmates?

The moving force behind the school was our principal, Commander Trevor de Almeida of the Indian Navy, who built the school from a green field as it were with untiring determination, enthusiasm, thought and intelligence. He focused not just on personality development but also on character building. Virtually every aspect of this school— the curriculum, discipline and, most importantly, the values governing our school life carried Commander Almeida's imprimatur.

In later years, I've been asked several times: 'Who was your best teacher?' The name that invariably flashes in my mind is that of Commander Almeida. He taught me some of life's most valuable lessons.

'Focus on whatever you are doing' used to be his most common exhortation. He would elaborate to make the point. 'Eat while you eat, study while you study, play while you play.' Do one thing at a time, and give it all your attention, was his forthright message.

This might sound simplistic, inane even, but practising it, as I realized, can be a severe test of discipline. And the dividends it pays by way of efficiency gains and positive outcomes can be surprisingly large.

I was tested, of course. In many of my IAS assignments, I was often forced into situations where I had to do several things all at the same time. Actually, that's an understatement. I was often required to firefight on several fronts simultaneously. Modern management science tells us that the answer to this challenge is multitasking. My own experience has been that multitasking is a no-go. It might give you an illusory satisfaction of efficiency, but the net result will be worse than if you had attended to each task with undivided attention.

As I moved on in life, I also learnt to interpret this lesson in a broader sense. What Commander Almeida was telling us was to give everything and anything we do not only our undivided attention but also our best. No task is too small nor too routine—whether it's making your bed first thing in the morning or polishing your shoes the night before to be ready for the next day—to deserve less than your wholehearted commitment, enthusiasm and effort. This inculcates discipline that prepares you for the big challenges of life.

Commander Almeida taught us by example. In how many schools in the country, I wonder, do principals personally take on the task of teaching students to sing the national anthem with such energy, enthusiasm and commitment? He would insist that we stand at attention, heads held high, chest up, shoulders straight and sing with pride and gusto. For him, if you were singing the national anthem, then for those few minutes, you had to do it as if singing the national anthem was the sole purpose of your existence.

He taught us not only to be disciplined but also to enjoy being disciplined. Even today, nearly half a century later, making my bed as soon as I get up gives me a magical sense of accomplishment that mentally prepares me for the challenges that lie ahead in the course of the day.

My failed NDA bid

A condition attached to accepting a scholarship in a Sainik School was that you were required to write the NDA entrance examination, and if selected, you were mandated to join. By the time it came to my turn to write the NDA entrance test in the summer of 1965, I had become quite keen on joining the air force. Helped by the school curriculum oriented to the NDA examination, I did quite well in the written test as well as in the follow-up physical fitness and personality tests, ranking fourth in the all-India merit list. However, I could not make the grade because of a congenital eye problem, which the medical board thought could impair my vision in the future.

I was disappointed, but only temporarily. Sainik Schools also prepare their students on a parallel track for the Indian School Certificate (ISC) examination, which I passed in 1966. Although I topped my class, my grades were fairly unimpressive. This was in part because of the relative neglect by the school, at any rate in those early years, of the ISC in comparison to the NDA examination, but no excuses.

Going to IIT for want of a choice

I have been asked several times in later life, and by many, many people, why I wanted to join the IAS and when exactly I decided to try for it. It's difficult to give a precise answer. My father, who served under several IAS and Indian Police Service (IPS) officers, used to tell us children about them, how smart and intelligent they were and how they solved people's problems. He used to say that I must work hard to try and get into the IAS. Over time, the IAS became my career choice by default. But there was no guarantee that I would get into the IAS, and what I would do if I didn't make it did cross my mind. But I consciously decided to defer agonizing over that until the IAS chapter was closed.

The eligibility requirement to write the IAS examination is just a college degree—any college degree. In the early 1970s, the conventional wisdom was that if you wanted to write the IAS, you had to study the liberal arts. But I was more interested in the sciences and decided to go that route even at the risk of being disadvantaged in the IAS examination. As to which college to go to, I didn't have many options. My father was keen that I join any of the leading colleges in the country in one of the metro cities—Delhi, Mumbai, Kolkata or Chennai—so I would get a wider exposure. But none of them would accept me because of my poor ISC grades.

Simultaneously, I also applied for the IIT Joint Entrance Examination (JEE). In the mid-1960s, IITs were still in their formative years, just about establishing a reputation for excellence; it would not be until the 1990s that they would acquire an impressive global brand equity. The JEE was certainly stiff even then but was admittedly less competitive than it is these days.

Not realizing that the JEE would be my lifeline to a good college, I didn't prepare seriously for it; even so, I was lucky to secure a high enough rank to choose any branch in any of the IITs. It was only during the counselling that helps you make a choice that I learnt that IIT Kharagpur was also offering a three-year BSc (Hons) course, and after agonizing only briefly, I opted for it. My decision was motivated not only by my interest in physics but also by some vague calculation that a science degree would help me more than an engineering degree in the IAS examination. I topped my class in BSc (Hons) at the end of three years. Since I was still not old enough to write the IAS examination, I moved to IIT Kanpur in July 1969 for post-graduation in physics.

Although both were IITs, the Kharagpur and Kanpur IITs were different in some respects. The Kharagpur IIT was the first to be set up. It had technical assistance from UNESCO but the funding was entirely indigenous. The campus as well as the academic facilities were modest. Kharagpur was, and still is, mainly a railway town and did not have much to offer students by way of off-campus dining or entertainment. The only decent cinema hall in the town was the South Institute—popularly called SI— of the Railways and the only decent food joint was the BNR Canteen on Platform No.1 of the Kharagpur railway station. The campus therefore had to become self-contained out of necessity with the result that there was a vibrant scene of sports and extra-curricular activities throughout the year. The result was that students received a more rounded education.

The Kanpur IIT, on the other hand, was much better endowed. Until the mid-1970s, it received substantial US technical assistance and had gone on to become the largest American-aided education project anywhere in the world. The workshops and laboratories were better equipped, the campus was better laid out and most faculty members had doctorates from US universities. It was at that time also one of only two academic institutions in the country, the other being the Tata Institute of Fundamental Research (TIFR) in Bombay, to have a mainframe computer.

Getting thrown off a train

There are many reckless things that we do in our youth that give us shivers in hindsight in later life. One such incident for me was getting thrown off a train in the middle of the night when I was at IIT Kharagpur.

Making railway reservations to go home during the holidays was a project that took weeks. When advance reservation opened a month before the holidays, hundreds of IIT students would rush to the Kharagpur railway station, creating a virtual stampede there. When in the midst of that chaos, confusion and jostling, you eventually reached the booking window, each transaction took over ten minutes because the reservation clerk had to write a telegram in each case to Howrah station where the train originated. And we would make several trips to the railway station after that to check if the reservation had been confirmed.

On one trip home, my best friend Venky got a confirmed reservation, but I didn't. Without a second thought, we decided to share that one berth. Sometime in the middle of the night, a TTE (travelling ticket examiner) came to check our tickets, scolded me for travelling unreserved and ordered that I get off the train at the next station. Both of us pleaded for mercy but the TTE remained hard-hearted!

So, at around 2 a.m., the Madras Mail stopped at Bhadrak in Odisha. Venky gave me a tearful farewell as I jumped off the train and made a dash for the unreserved bogie somewhere in the front of the train. The platform was dark and eerie, it was drizzling lightly, the guard whistled and the train started. I ran desperately and caught the unreserved bogie just as it was moving off the platform. The door was locked from the inside. The drizzle had turned into a light rain, the train was picking up speed and the flickering lights of Bhadrak were fast fading away. In desperation, I banged on the door, and maybe twenty seconds later, an old man opened it with a frown on his face and let me in.

Forty years later, when I was governor of the Reserve Bank, I adopted Jalanga, an off-the-road village about 8 km from Bhadrak, as part of my village immersion programme. As it happened, I went to Jalanga four times in the five years I was with the RBI. On each visit, I would pass by the Bhadrak railway station, by now bigger and busier of course, and each time a chill would go down my spine as I recalled those, possibly the longest, twenty seconds of my life from forty years ago.

The IAS project

There were about eighteen of us in the MSc physics class at IIT Kanpur. It used to be said of IIT Kanpur at the time that as soon as you set foot in the institute, you had half a leg in the US. About fifteen of my classmates were applying to US universities for a PhD. When I used to tell my friends in the science and engineering streams that I was planning to write the IAS, the instant reaction was surprise if also some disdain. Some of them who were slightly familiar with the IAS told me that if I wanted to write the IAS, I should have gone to a university in Delhi or Allahabad, implying that an IIT was decidedly the wrong choice if your aim was the IAS. In a way, quite unintentionally, I was a trailblazer in the sense that the flow of IITians into the civil services, which was a trickle during my time, became a stream in the 1980s and then a flood by the 2000s.

The IAS/IFS was a one-step examination then unlike the two-stage prelims and mains now. The examination comprised, then as now, compulsory papers as well as optionals. In the 1970s pattern, candidates had to take five optional papers. The choice was wide enough to allow me to pick all five papers from the science and mathematics streams. But whether I should do so was not a straightforward decision.

When I went to Delhi for an inter-college debate competition, I used the opportunity to meet Rau of Rau's IAS Study Circle and consulted him on how to prepare for the IAS, and in particular on the choice of optional. Rau discouraged me from taking only science and mathematics papers, saying that it might be too risky and suggested that I take at least two liberal arts papers. I was diffident about this since these would be entirely new subjects; could I prepare on my own and compete with students who studied these subjects in a college classroom? But in the end, I decided to defer to Rau's advice, and after working out some permutations and combinations, zeroed in on physics, higher physics, pure mathematics, British history and British constitutional history as my optionals.

In the 1970s, we were allowed only two chances at the IAS/IFS examination. To utilize the two chances effectively, I could have waited till I completed my MSc to take the examination. I decided, however, to take the plunge as soon as I was eligible age-wise. In this decision, I was encouraged by the flexibility in IIT Kanpur's education curriculum, which mimicked the American system of allowing students to drop out of a course in the middle and rejoin later on, if they so wished. Taking advantage of this, I dropped the last semester of my MSc and went home to study for the IAS examination.

I prepared on my own for a few months and then in the summer went to Delhi to Rau's IAS Study Circle for coaching. I enjoyed studying British history and British constitutional history, and for all my misgivings, scored the highest marks in British constitutional history and somewhere in the top ten in British history. The coaching at Rau's helped but even more helpful was the opportunity it provided of meeting and interacting with other candidates. It was oddly comforting to see that many, like me, had their share of apprehensions and doubts about making the grade. But of course, there were a few who were super confident they would make it.

After the IAS examinations were over, I went back to IIT Kanpur in January 1972 to complete the fourth semester of my MSc.

The IAS interview—from Moharram to Existentialism

The IAS written results came out in mid-January, and I had cleared the cut-off. A few days later, I got a call from the UPSC for an interview, which was scheduled towards the end of February. I took an overnight train from Kanpur to Delhi, arrived there by about 5 a.m., went to my friend's house in R.K. Puram, showered and changed, pressed my new suit and wore it, had the breakfast so lovingly prepared by my friend's mother and was all ready by 8 a.m.

My interview was scheduled for 9 a.m., the first slot for that morning. Delhi used to be quite cold even in late February in those days, and at 8 a.m. it was still semi-dark, and there was a lot of fog. On any other day, I would have taken a bus to the UPSC, but thinking that it might look odd to get into a bus all suited and booted, I had thought of upgrading myself to an auto for this very special occasion. But my father, who was understandably anxious that I should arrive for the interview neat and tidy, had insisted that I should take a taxi. I deferred to him if only to contain his anxiety. So, there I was, wearing a suit for the first time in my life, sitting in a taxi, also for the first time in my life, going for the UPSC interview with a syncretic combination of nerves and confidence.

I arrived at the UPSC on Shahjahan Road by about 8.40 a.m., well in time. The staff checked my papers and seated me in the waiting room. I was called in by around 9.10 a.m. Here is a reproduction from my memory of the first two minutes of that interview.

Me: Good morning Sir, good morning Sir (*I looked all around and made eye contact with all five members seated across the table on either side of the chairman. Yes, there was no ma'am on that side*).

Chairman: Good morning. Please sit down.

Me: Thank you, Sir.

Chairman: Are you still at IIT Kanpur?

Me: Yes, Sir.

Chairman: So, when did you get to Delhi?

Me: Early this morning, by an overnight train, Sir.

(*The chairman turned to a member seated on his far left.*)

Member: Do you read newspapers, Mr Subbarao?

Me: Yes, Sir. I do.

Member: Which one?

Me: *The Statesman*, Sir.

Member: So, did you look at this morning's paper?

(*I had not, and I was quite flustered at being caught like this even before we got off the block. Thankfully, the chairman came to my rescue.*)

Chairman (*to the member*): Look, it's still cold and dark. I'm not sure you've seen this morning's paper. Why do you ask him? He's just arrived in Delhi and was all tied up preparing to come here. I don't think he would have had the time.'

Member (*turning to me again*): All right, tell me then, did you read yesterday's paper?

Me: Yes, Sir.

Member: Do you remember the front-page picture of yesterday's *Statesman*?

(*Today, if anyone were to ask me that question, I would draw a blank. Whatever I see in a newspaper is just a fleeting memory. But being younger then, I fortunately remembered what I had seen in the previous day's paper.*)

Me: Yes, Sir. It was a picture of Muslims celebrating Moharram.

Member: (*with what seemed to me like a hint of glee on his face*): Celebrating? Is Moharram a festival to be celebrating?

(*I was ashen-faced, for the second time in one minute.*)

Member: Moharram is not a festival. It's a day of mourning. It is mourning for the grandson of the Prophet who was martyred. (*And he added, for good measure*) You've lived in Kanpur for two years, which has a sizeable Muslim population. I thought you'd know this.

(*My instinct was to plead an excuse, something like the IIT campus was secluded, far away from the city and didn't provide an opportunity to be exposed to the city life of Kanpur. Thankfully, I didn't blurt that out not so much because of the good sense not to be defensive but rather because I was shell-shocked at how my interview was crashing so early in the game. Not happy enough with the reprimand he had given me, the member persisted.*)

Member: Okay, tell me which sect of Muslims observes Moharram?

Chairman (*looking at me and then at the member with slight irritation*): He doesn't even know what Moharram is. Why do you press the issue?

The interview by which I had set so much store had just blown up spectacularly in my face in the first two minutes. I was shattered. I expected the members would now merely go through the motions of interviewing me and dismiss me in fifteen minutes. In the event, the interview lasted a full forty minutes, the quality of the conversation improving markedly over that period. We covered a wide canvas—a comparison of the two IITs at Kharagpur and Kanpur, the growing rift between the Centre and states and the constitutional provisions for the protection of states from Central hegemony, Nixon's China visit and the philosophical implications of Heisenberg's uncertainty principle in quantum mechanics.

I still vividly recall a particular topic that came up for discussion in the interview. I had written in my application that I was on the IIT debating team. 'What was the latest topic you debated on?' a member asked me. That happened to be: 'Man is condemned to be free', a statement from the existentialist philosophy of Jean-Paul Sartre. The interview board pushed me into interpreting that statement. Here is a precis of what I told them:

One of the tenets of existentialist philosophy is that we are forced to make choices as we go through our lives no matter that life itself is absurd. Not knowing which way to go, we look for anchors to guide us in our choices. We will realize, though, that trying to find anchors is a futile endeavour; it is just not possible to avoid the burden of decision-making by artificially constraining our choices, nor is it possible to learn from other's experiences. Every person has to make choices by falling back on their own experience. In short, man is condemned to be free.

I must admit it didn't exactly go as fluently as that, and to this day I wonder if the wise men on the board were impressed by my deep insights into philosophy or put off by a cocky twenty-two-year-old pontificating on what is arguably one of the most abstract concepts in the history of ideas.

But why did this topic from my interview linger in my mind whereas much of the rest of the conversation had faded away? Possibly because the truth of this came back to me several times in later life, both in personal and professional contexts. Oftentimes, we wonder if we should have made a different choice, a different decision. Should you have accommodated a minister a little more by giving his constituency priority in the housing programme by bending your allocation formula instead of being rigidly fixated on the formula? Would having him on your side have helped achieve the larger objective?

But in making choices like this, you have no rules to guide you, nor can you learn from someone else's experience. You are condemned to be free!

By the time the interview ended, I had the distinct sense that I had sailed along quite well. I could see it from the faces and body language of the interview committee. Of course, I fumbled in some of the responses, and virtually everything I said, I could have put across better. But overall, it was an encouraging experience, especially given the fiasco at the start. In fact, I scored 75 per cent in the interview, and my recall is that only two others—Sudha Khanna (later Sudha Pillai) who ranked second in the All-India merit list and Prahlad Mahishi—scored better than me.

In the crosshairs of the police

About a fortnight after my interview, sometime in the second half of March, a police constable knocked on my door in the IIT hostel. My initial reaction was more of surprise than apprehension since we hardly ever saw any police on the campus. And to the best of my knowledge, I had not committed any crime!

The constable showed me a newspaper photograph of IIT students protesting at the main gate of the IIT a few weeks earlier. I was one among about fifty-odd students in the picture, but the camera angle had caught me prominently. The constable simply asked if it was me in the picture, and when I said yes, he only asked that I report to the police station a kilometre away from the campus the following morning.

I was more confused than worried. The photo was a few weeks old, why did the police single me out from all the students in the picture, even leaving out the protest leaders? I pressed the constable but all that he offered was that he had been sent by his boss, the police inspector, to do a preliminary check and that it was in response to a reference from the Government of India regarding my selection for the IAS.

I was now able to vaguely connect the dots. I knew that it was routine for the police to conduct a verification check of all candidates who qualified for the interview. There was no cause for joy since it was by no means an indication that you had made the grade. On the other hand, there was cause for concern since I had heard that in the past, some candidates had been disqualified for selection to the service because of adverse political antecedents.

The background to that picture is as follows.

Sometime in late 1971, Prime Minister Indira Gandhi was travelling to the US on an official visit. Kenneth Keating who was then the US ambassador to India had failed to show up at the Delhi airport to see her off as protocol demanded. This glitch came at a time when Mrs Gandhi was riding high on popularity as a war with Pakistan on Bangladesh was imminent. When Keating was questioned by the media about this insult to India, he begged off saying that his alarm did not go off. I recall that in subsequent days, the US embassy in Delhi was flooded with alarm clocks gifted by people from across the country so that the 'ambassador did not oversleep'.

Just a few weeks after that alarm glitch, IIT Kanpur had invited Ambassador Keating to be the convocation speaker, mainly as a gesture of thanks for American support to IIT Kanpur, which was winding down. Hundreds of IIT students were unhappy with this decision and decided to organize a protest at the main gate to prevent the chief guest from entering the IIT campus. The protest folded together a host of causes—Keating's 'alarm clock insult' to the nation, American imperialism around the world, the Vietnam War and poaching IIT talent from India. The protest fizzled out in fifteen minutes, and Keating had a successful visit to the IIT. But a photograph of the protesting students was captured by the media and landed me in a soup.

Soon after the constable left, I panicked. Would my selection to the IAS be derailed by this misadventure? Distraught, I ran to Professor Jacob Tharu, the dean of students, explained the situation to him and requested his help. Calmed a little by his assurance that he would sort things out, I went, as instructed, to the police station the following morning. I was pleasantly surprised when the police inspector received me with due deference, offered me not only a chair but also tea and biscuits, and even before I began explaining, told me that they had already sent a clear report on my antecedents.

I went to Professor Tharu to thank him. He told me that he had spoken to the superintendent of police (SP). Evidently, the police had suspected extremist activity on the campus, but Tharu had assured the SP that I had no such links and that my joining the protest was more youthful enthusiasm than any overt extremist leanings. Tharu's reply solved the mystery of why the police inspector saw me as a potential IAS officer rather than a die-hard Naxalite.

Switch from IFS to IAS

After the euphoria of topping the merit list had ebbed, I had to make an important choice—whether to join the IAS or the IFS. In the UPSC application, I had given IFS as my first choice, but the UPSC allowed candidates to switch preferences within ten days after the publication of the results.

In a typical batch with an intake of a hundred, there would be about fifteen slots for the IFS and the balance eighty-five for the IAS. In the early 1970s when I qualified, most of the toppers on the list opted for the IFS unlike now when the choices of the toppers are more mixed. In fact, some candidates were so set on the IFS that if they didn't make the grade, they would opt out altogether and write the examination again even if that entailed the risk of not even making the IAS in the second attempt.

In opting for the IFS, I was going more with the flow rather than making an informed choice. My father, however, had an express preference for the IAS. He had seen many young IAS officers as his bosses, and seeing their son in that position had an enormous emotional appeal for my parents. My father wrote me a letter persuading me to choose the IAS without, of course, pressuring me in any way. After agonizing over it, I decided to switch my preference and accordingly sent a telegram to the UPSC within the ten-day time limit.

The choice between the IAS and the IFS is an intensely personal one. There are positives and negatives on both sides. Looking back after fifty years, though, I am glad I chose the IAS. For sure, the IFS offers an interesting and challenging career, and IFS officers play an important role in pursuing and promoting India's interests around the world. But for me personally, nothing tops the sheer variety of jobs and opportunities of an IAS career.

Make your bed every morning

I wrote about the values and discipline that Commander Almeida taught us in the Sainik School. Many, many years later, I came across a commencement speech given by Admiral William H. McRaven at the University of Texas at Austin in May 2014.* In the speech that went viral, Admiral McRaven spoke about ten lessons he had learnt during the SEAL training when he was commissioned into the US Navy—lessons that are helpful to anyone wanting to change the world and/or deal with life.

The first of Admiral McRaven's lessons is: Make your bed every morning. Here is what he said relating to this first lesson.

---

* 'Adm. McRaven Urges Graduates to Find Courage to Change the World', UT News, 16 May 2014, available at: https://news.utexas.edu/2014/05/16/mcraven-urges-graduates-to-find-courage-to-change-the-world/.

Every morning in basic SEAL training, my instructors, who at the time were all Vietnam veterans, would show up in my barracks room and the first thing they would inspect was your bed. If you did it right, the corners would be square, the covers pulled tight, the pillow centered just under the headboard and the extra blanket folded neatly at the foot of the rack—that's Navy talk for bed.

It was a simple task—mundane at best. But every morning we were required to make our bed to perfection. It seemed a little ridiculous at the time, particularly in light of the fact that we were aspiring to be real warriors, tough battle-hardened SEALs, but the wisdom of this simple act has been proven to me many times over.

If you make your bed every morning you will have accomplished the first task of the day. It will give you a small sense of pride, and it will encourage you to do another task and another and another. By the end of the day, that one task completed will have turned into many tasks completed. Making your bed will also reinforce the fact that little things in life matter. If you can't do the little things right, you will never do the big things right.

And, if by chance you have a miserable day, you will come home to a bed that is made—that you made—and a made bed gives you encouragement that tomorrow will be better.

If you want to change the world, start off by making your bed.

I can relate to this lesson. Making your bed every morning can feel like a useless chore and a burden. Its value can seem trivial. But once you internalize the protocol of making your bed every morning, the sense of accomplishment can be a big motivation for seizing the day. As Admiral McRaven elaborated in his book[*] where he expanded on the ten lessons of his speech:

Making my bed correctly was not going to be an opportunity for praise. It was expected of me. It was my first task of the day, and doing it right was important. It demonstrated my discipline. It showed my attention to detail, and at the end of the day it would be a reminder that I had done something well, something to be proud of, no matter how small the task. Throughout my life in the Navy, making my bed was the one constant that I could count on every day.

[*] Admiral William H. McRaven, *Make Your Bed*, Michael Joseph, UK, 2017.

3

Whatever the Assistant Collector Pleases . . .

IAS Training

I reported for training at the National Academy of Administration in Mussoorie on 15 July 1972.

Mussoorie was my first exposure to a hill station, and it was a strange and enchanting experience. These days the country is so homogenized by increased mobility and communication that if you were airdropped, you wouldn't be able to tell the difference between say, Hyderabad and Lucknow. It was different in the early 1970s—cities and towns had their own distinct and unique features. The hilly terrain, narrow winding roads, scattered dwellings dotting the hill slopes, low-intensity traffic, cold and damp weather and most of all, the hardy and charming hill people gave Mussoorie a distinct character and an endearing personality.

IAS batches—then and now

We were 142 in our batch of the IAS, and together with a hundred-odd from IFS, IPS and other allied services such as the Indian Revenue Service (IRS) and the Indian Audit and Accounts Service (IA&AS), we were about 250. The pattern of training then was a three-month-long foundation course for all civil services together, after which other civil services trainees went away to their specialized training institutions while the IAS trainees remained in Mussoorie for a year-long professional course.

We were a heterogeneous group drawn from across the country with our different languages, cultures and backgrounds. There were a few who came from privileged backgrounds and had studied in some of the elite colleges of the country. The vast majority, however, came from modest backgrounds and had studied in local colleges and universities. But of course, we were all united by the uniquely privileged service we were entering.

As I compare our IAS batch of fifty years ago with a typical batch today, I can see some distinct differences. Firstly, back then, the age range for entry was twenty-one to twenty-four years, and we were allowed only two chances at the examination except for scheduled caste and scheduled tribe candidates. Compare that with the upper age limit of thirty-two years and six attempts these days. In my batch, most of us, as many as 80 per cent, according to my rough reckoning, wrote and cleared the bar in the first attempt while the remaining 20 per cent did so in their second attempt. The ratios are reversed today. Only about 20 per cent make it on the first attempt, and the top rankers are typically candidates in their fourth or fifth attempt. Also, quite obviously, the average age of our batch was twenty-three years whereas today it would be about thirty.

The second difference between then and now pertains to the proportion of women among qualified candidates. In the early decades after Independence, women candidates were just a trickle; even by 1970, women made up just 9 per cent of those entering the IAS. That trickle turned into a steady stream beginning in the early 1970s; our IAS batch of 142 in 1972 comprised twenty-two women—15 per cent. The proportion of women kept rising steadily thereafter to a maximum of 31 per cent in 2020. Currently, 21 per cent of serving IAS officers are women, showing that the gender gap is being bridged, albeit not rapidly enough.

What matters when talking about gender parity is not just the entry-level statistics but also the average career profiles of male and female IAS officers. In what would now be seen as a grotesque case of gender bias, in the first three decades after Independence, it was quite common not to post women as district collectors, the defining job of an IAS career. They lost, of course, but the nation lost more.

There has since been a gradual attitudinal change. In February 2022, of the fourteen districts in Kerala, ten had women serving as district collectors.[*] Some time ago, there was a charming picture in the media of a young IAS officer, a nursing mother, who brought her infant to the office.[†]

---

[*] '10 out of 14 districts in Kerala to have women collectors', mathrubhumi. com, 25 February 2022, available at: https://english.mathrubhumi.com/news/ kerala/10-out-of-14-districts-in-state-to-have-women-collectors-1.7292447.

[†] Ria Das, 'Corona Warriors: IAS Officer Returns to Work with Infant Baby', shethepeople, 13 April 2020, available at: https://www.shethepeople.tv/ news/srijana-gummalla-ias-officer-returns-work-infant-baby/.

Many women now occupy high-profile jobs across the country, several have been chief secretaries of states and secretaries in the Central government. We have yet to get a female cabinet secretary though, the highest civil service position in the country, to confirm that the male bastion has been fully blasted.

The third difference between then and now as I look back, albeit through a heuristic prism, is that a significant number of my batchmates were children of civil servants whereas today that proportion would be much smaller. Is it the case that children of civil servants become disenchanted with the civil service after watching their parents? Or is it because of more attractive opportunities beyond the civil service?

The layout of the Mussoorie academy

The Mussoorie academy is set up in the erstwhile Charleville Hotel of colonial vintage, which boasted of having played host to royalty on occasion. In 1904, the famous Mussoorie brewer MacKinnon bought it and turned it into the Happy Valley Club. After Independence, the government acquired the property and established the National Academy of Administration in the premises in September 1959 by merging the IAS Training School, Metcalf House, Delhi, and the IAS Staff College, Shimla. The academy was rechristened in 1974 as the Lal Bahadur Shastri National Academy of Administration (LBSNAA) to honour the memory of the late prime minister.

Contrary to my mental image of a neat, well-laid-out campus, no doubt shaped by seeing a few universities and public sector undertakings, the academy campus had a makeshift look and feel. The planning and layout were dictated by the hilly terrain, with facilities scattered all over, making the best of what was possible rather than any logistic efficiency. The result was that we had to walk quite a lot across the undulating terrain in the course of the day, but we were all in our twenties and I don't recall anyone complaining about it. In fact, more people, especially South Indians, complained about the cold than the daily strain of walking.

When I visited the academy thirty years later, I found that the landscape had changed quite a lot. A fire had gutted the dining hall and the central hall. That became the trigger for replacing the old cement and wooden structures with stone constructions; the only structure to survive the refurbishing is the iconic 'Charleville' post office building. The academy now boasts of a modern dining hall, two large auditoriums, a spacious library and a gym. It's more functional possibly, but the old-world charm of Charleville is gone.

Foundation and professional courses

During the foundation course, I found the academy to be an unremarkable combination of an elite public school and a mediocre college—PT and horse riding in the morning, eating in a well-appointed dining hall and being attired in suits for much of the day. We had classroom instruction in law, political science, public administration and the Constitution, subjects quite new to me. Although this gave me a passing and much-needed familiarity with these subjects, the lectures themselves were banal and failed to arouse my curiosity.

The professional course, with its emphasis on field issues and challenges, was more focused. This was to a large extent because of B.N. Yugandhar, a 1962 batch IAS officer of the Andhra Pradesh cadre, who was the course director. Soon after taking over as course director, Yugandhar spoke to us—a motley group of trainees with inflated egos and exaggerated notions of self-importance. I distinctly remember what he told us: 'My job is to prepare you for the rough and tumble of field postings in the first ten years of your career. No complaints or grumbling about overwork, odd hours, having no time for relaxation, etc. That's how it's going to be in the field, and that's how this training is going to be.'

In a sense, Yugandhar defined the quintessence of the IAS—the challenge and opportunity of working on the frontlines. He believed passionately in plunging headlong into the field—to see, listen, talk and experience. Whether it was freeing bonded labour or providing drinking water facilities in villages, he believed that the only way a civil servant could be effective was by going out and dirtying her hands.

Yugandhar visited me later when I was sub-collector, Parvathipuram, my first posting after training. We went on an intensive three-day tour of tribal villages by jeep and occasionally by foot. I had already visited dozens of these villages earlier but travelling with him and seeing the empathy and enthusiasm with which he interacted with tribal people was a rewarding learning experience. At the end of the tour, he asked me if I had camped overnight in a tribal village and was disappointed that I had opted for the relative comfort and convenience of travellers' bungalows.

Gallivanting in Mussoorie

Sunil Khatri, whom I got to know when we were both taking coaching for the IAS exam at Rau's and who has remained my friend and well-wisher all through the years, introduced me to all the happening places in Mussoorie—the Savoy, Whispering Windows, the Library Point and all the momo joints.

One of my fondest memories of the Mussoorie days is the weekly jaunts to Kulri for a breakfast of aloo puri and jalebi. If today anyone asked me to walk over 5 km just for breakfast, I would baulk at the suggestion, but it seemed so effortless and fun in those youthful days! We were usually a foursome—Sudha Khanna, Gopal Pillai, Veena Sriram and I. It was during those outings that love blossomed between Sudha and Gopal. They got married while we were still under training; Sudha Khanna became Sudha Pillai and transferred from the Punjab to the Kerala cadre. All of them distinguished themselves in the service—Sudha was member-secretary of the Planning Commission, Gopal was home secretary and Veena retired as secretary for the Development of the North-East Region (DONER).

Prime Minister Indira Gandhi visits us

A highlight of our training in Mussoorie was then prime minister Indira Gandhi's day-long visit to the academy in April 1974.

The first major event on her programme for the day
was the unveiling of a statue of Lal Bahadur Shastri, her
predecessor, after whom the academy was being renamed.
She seemed a bit startled when she saw the statue. The
reason became clear when she spoke briefly after the
unveiling. Statues, she said, should be life-size if they are
in the open and a bust, if indoors. Shastri's statue was the
wrong combination—a bust on the lawn in the forecourt
of the director's office. What soured the mood was what
she added: 'I wish senior officers in the government knew
this much.'

Ms Gandhi seemed clearly disenchanted with
Rajeshwar Prasad, the director of the academy at the time.
The grapevine among the trainees was that it was because
Prasad was earlier principal secretary to Lal Bahadur
Shastri.

The disenchantment became even more evident when
she later addressed us. The director, who spoke before
her, welcoming the prime minister, said that he hoped the
government would take an early decision on whether the
academy would be shifted to Delhi or retained in Mussoorie
because further development of facilities in Mussoorie was
on hold due to this uncertainty. The speculation at that
time was that the buildings that were coming up in what
is now Jawaharlal Nehru University (JNU) in Delhi were
actually planned for the IAS training academy.

Indira Gandhi was clearly miffed by this remark.
Evidently, because of pressure from K.C. Pant and other
Congress leaders from the hill regions of what was then the
larger state of Uttar Pradesh, she had decided to abandon
the proposal to move the academy to Delhi, but the decision

hadn't flowed down through the bureaucratic channels. In her address to us later, she ticked off the director once again, saying she didn't understand why senior officers of the government kept raising issues that had already been settled. For sure, it wasn't a good day for Rajeshwar Prasad!

There was nothing particularly remarkable in the prime minister's address; it went along hackneyed lines—how the IAS was the steel frame and how much the government depended on the IAS as its most critical delivery arm. She spoke about values, ethics and discipline—all the usual spiel—nothing original in content or delivery.

It was what happened later that has stuck in my mind. After she finished her address, it was the turn of an officer trainee to deliver the vote of thanks. That privilege went to M. Ramachandran, the president of the Mess Committee (PMC) at the time. Ramu, who later served in Uttar Pradesh, Uttarakhand and in the Government of India with great distinction, began with the usual cliché: 'On behalf of the entire academy, I thank the prime minister for taking time out of her busy schedule ...' Even as Ramu was in mid-sentence, Ms Gandhi got up, returned to the podium, gently nudged Ramu aside and started speaking once again. This, in a nutshell, is what she told us:

'Every time I go to an event, people thank me for attending the event "in spite of my busy schedule". Yes, I am busy. But I choose to go to events like this because it's part of my work, and I shouldn't be thanked for what I am doing as part of my work.'

She went on to add:

> A couple of weeks ago, I went to Lucknow to call on
> an ailing uncle of mine (I think she was referring to
> B.K. Nehru, ICS). He called me to his bedside and said,
> '*Beti*, you are the prime minister of the country now.
> But I am sure you are not as busy as I was when I was a
> district magistrate'.

Ms Gandhi continued, 'I don't know how busy IAS officers
are because I've never been one myself. But I can tell you
this that as prime minister, I still get time to read a couple
of books every month, write a letter every week, have
dinner with friends and see a movie occasionally.'

More than her banal address, it was this important
message of Ms Gandhi on work-life balance that stuck in
my mind far into my career.

District training

Under the sandwich pattern of training, the professional
course ran in Mussoorie for six months after which the
trainees left for a year of district training. They then
returned to the academy for a three-month summing
up training.

For my field training, I was posted to Nellore District
in coastal Andhra Pradesh. Nellore was agriculturally
prosperous, and the Reddys, the dominant community
of the district, had a progressive outlook. They were
trailblazers in the state for first-generation agriculturists
because they began investing their savings in industry.

They were also quite liberal in spending money on luxurious houses and cars. The local folklore was that even if all they wanted was a tube of Colgate toothpaste, they would drive in their Ambassador cars to Madras (now Chennai), 200 km away, to buy it from the exclusive Spencer's store there!

In Nellore, the collector was K. Obayya, a 1960 batch IAS officer, and the joint collector was H.K. Babu of the 1968 batch. They were polar opposites in personality and work style. Obayya was steady, subdued, disciplined, if also a bit self-conscious. He would go by the book and not rock the boat. Babu, on the other hand, was a firebrand who instilled fear in subordinates and terror among lawbreakers. He revelled in using his power and authority to catch wrongdoers; it was typical of him to raid rice mills to check if the miller had given his levy—the foodgrain he was to sell to the Food Corporation of India (FCI) under the Procurement Scheme—and cinema halls to check if they were cheating on entertainment taxes. But both Obayya and Babu were very friendly and kind to me. They put me through the paces, and I learnt a lot by seeing them work.

As a trainee officer, I was designated as assistant collector, quite an ego-boosting title!

I was still single then. The collector allotted me a one-bedroom house in the Officers' Colony. It was small and modest but accommodated my limited belongings and met all the needs of my solitary lifestyle. I had an attender-cum-cook who didn't have much to do since whenever I was in town, I had lunch in the office with either the collector or the joint collector. Babu lived across the street from me, and we had dinner together virtually every evening.

What I found most disconcerting about life in the district setting was the constant surveillance of you by your staff out of no motive beyond sheer curiosity. Fifty years ago, being an IAS officer was quite a big deal; the people and particularly the staff looked up to you. They would watch what you did, where you went, whom you met, what you ate and how you spent your time. It's not particularly uncomfortable if you are uninhibited but can be quite constricting if you are shy, self-conscious or if you value your privacy more than the average.

Another thing to get used to was the way people showed deference to you. I found that subordinates rarely spoke to me in the second person. It was never, 'What time will you leave on tour tomorrow?', but 'What time will the assistant collector leave on tour tomorrow?'. When my mother visited me for a week, the cook asked her first thing in the morning, 'What will Madam have for breakfast today?' My mother was taken aback wondering if a 'madam' had entered my life unbeknown to her, only to calm down after I explained to her how addressing someone in the third person was their way of showing deference.

The district training went as per a well-honed timetable. It started with attachment to a village for four weeks, moving up the hierarchy thereon to a *firqa, tehsil*, subdivision and district level. There was also attachment to various district offices such as education, health, agriculture, industry, etc. Since there were no department manuals, much of the learning had to happen by asking questions and through a process of osmosis.

Village life

Keeping in view Yugandhar's advice, I tried to understand village life as much as possible. The sociology of a community where everyone knew everyone else was quite different from an urban setting defined by anonymity and aloofness. The caste system was part of village life and there was no awkwardness or secrecy about it. The scheduled castes lived in their settlements, but there was by and large no discrimination in the use of public spaces or utilities. There were cases of rape, harassment and exploitation, but those were isolated instances rather than systemic.

By the early 1970s, the affirmative action policy enshrined in the Constitution towards scheduled castes and scheduled tribes was sufficiently internalized, and there were several government programmes to uplift their socio-economic status. A flagship programme was the assignment of government land to landless scheduled castes and scheduled tribe households. Although the numbers regarding assignments were flattering on paper, the ground reality told an altogether different story. If a plot of assigned land was cultivable, it was invariably already occupied by a landed farmer, and evicting him to give possession to the assignee was always a challenging proposition. Either the assignee was scared to ask for possession or if he indeed did get possession, the evicted big farmer would grab the land back. Alternatively, the land would be barren, full of boulders and rocks, and the cost of clearing it to make it fit for cultivation was far beyond the means of the assignee.

Politics was all-pervasive. While there was relative harmony in some villages, most were faction-ridden with cleavages along caste or party lines.

Learning the basics of agriculture

Charan Singh, who was prime minister during 1979–80, is reported to have said derisively of Indira Gandhi, his political rival, that she couldn't tell a wheat crop from a rice crop. That could be more of an embarrassment for a young IAS officer; she has to, at the minimum, be able to identify crops grown in the district. I tried to learn that as also the relative economics of different crops and the factors that influenced the farmer's choice of what crop to grow.

The government had a massive programme going at that time to popularize high-yielding varieties (HYVs) of rice. There was resistance from farmers drawing from both fact and myth. The plain fact was that HYVs were more input-intensive—they required more water, fertilizer and pesticides, which small farmers couldn't afford. There were several apprehensions too—that HYVs were not nutritious because they stayed in the ground for a shorter duration than the traditional varieties, the volume of cooked rice for a given volume of raw rice was smaller, the rice was more perishable and therefore unsuitable for keeping overnight and eating as breakfast in the morning as was their practice and so on. HYVs are now well entrenched, but convincing farmers to shift from traditional varieties of rice to HYVs in the early 1970s was an uphill task. It was for me a valuable lesson on the journey of an idea or a trend from awareness to acceptance and then to adoption.

The perils of an exalted status

Among the district-level staff, the IAS enjoyed an exalted status, the stereotypical view being that 'an IAS officer knew everything'. It was an ego booster all right, but it was also a big obstacle to learning. Subordinate officials at the district level who were supposed to train you thought it would be presumptuous on their part to 'teach' an IAS officer. A trainee IAS officer therefore had to make an extra effort to disabuse his trainer—whether it was a village officer or the district education officer—of this notion and put him at ease so that he would be confident enough to 'teach' you.

I remember that this 'exalted status' thrust on me once landed me in an awkward situation. An IAS officer posted as sub-collector or collector is also an executive magistrate charged with the responsibility of maintaining law and order, if necessary, by using magisterial powers under the Criminal Procedure Code (CrPC). As per the training manual, a trainee IAS officer has to try a minimum of twelve criminal cases in order to be eligible for being vested with the required magisterial powers under the CrPC by the time she assumes independent charge of a subdivision.

Most of these cases are trivial in relative terms like people fighting on the village street and causing a nuisance, minor theft, cheating and so on. In a regular magistrate's court, these cases rarely go to the trial stage. Chastened by the harassment of attending the court for repeated adjournments, the parties typically compromise, file a petition accordingly and the magistrate discharges them.

This illustrates the adage that 'the process is the punishment' that we associate with Indian judicial dispensation.

For the purpose of IAS training though, such summary disposal did not count. The training manual laid down that the cases should be contested and the assistant collector had to actually record statements of the accused and witnesses and pass a judgment. Only then would the trainee get the credit for it.

I realized as I was coming to the end of my district training that I had done only ten cases and was two short of the requirement of twelve cases. I therefore accelerated the pace of the trial. In one case where two people were accused of fighting in public and disturbing public order, after I had done all the recording of evidence and related paperwork, the parties filed a compromise petition. I was disappointed and irked by this because a case settled through a compromise like this would not count towards my target of twelve. On the advice of my camp clerk, I requested the lawyers of both parties to continue to contest the case. The parties agreed on the tacit understanding that I would, 'after considering all the evidence', conclude that no offence had been committed and let them off.

But after completing the trial, it looked to me like the two men had, in fact, committed affray (a public order offence in law). It would have been a simple matter for me to let them off with a warning. That would be legally valid—indeed appropriate—and still count as a 'contested case' for my target of twelve.

Instead of following that straightforward option, I wondered if I could award them a penalty. Once again, I turned to my camp clerk for advice on whether I could break our gentleman's agreement with the lawyers on discharging the parties. The camp clerk, Krishnayya, a burly man in his mid-fifties and a calm, silent type, was one of those who believed that an IAS officer could do no wrong. He said, 'If the assistant collector pleases, he may award punishment to the parties.'

And so I did—sentenced both parties to a month of imprisonment for the grave crime of affray! Such stiff punishment for affray was possibly unheard of in the judicial history of Nellore. When I handed out the judgment, the lawyers were outraged by this breach of trust on my part. They complained to the district judge who in turn informed Collector Obayya. The collector gently reprimanded me and told me to take that judgment off the record and rewrite it.

So much for IAS officers knowing everything and being able to do whatever they please!

Where do you draw the line?

No IAS officer gets trained to be honest. Early in my district training, when we were once travelling in a car, Obayya told me, 'Subba, this training period is your year of freedom. Once you are in a regular posting, you will be under constant scrutiny—what you do, where you go, whom you meet, how you demarcate your personal and professional space will all be under watch. People will form perceptions about your character and integrity. The only advice I want to give you is that during this one year under training, mix freely with everyone, those in power and authority and those without, test the waters and draw your own line.'

Notwithstanding that advice, every IAS officer struggles with the challenge of remaining clean and being seen to be clean all through her career. There are no template answers to where you draw the line on probity and how you tailor your work style and lifestyle to enforce your own standards.

The only guide is your conscience.

The tahsildar and his dog

Because of the power and prestige of their jobs, many people—politicians, corporates, professionals—try to befriend IAS officers. Some of these friendships are innocent while some can be a nuisance and some even potentially burdensome. Here's a parable on what IAS officers should know about friendships and adulation.

A childless *tahsildar* had a pet dog. He was very fond of the dog, so many of the people who came to see him made a big show of cuddling the dog and sometimes even bringing gifts for him. And then one day, the dog died. The entire town joined the funeral procession.

A few years later, the tahsildar himself died. No one joined the funeral procession!

Where Do You Draw the Line on Probity?

To be effective, IAS officers must not only be clean and impartial but should also be seen to be so. Everyone is bound to be tested, and everyone struggles with where to draw the line on probity. There are many temptations to go off the straight and narrow path, and the penalty for not bending can be costly, at any rate in the short term. What complicates matters is that there are no template solutions to real-world dilemmas, and every officer has to draw their own line and tailor their behaviour and lifestyle to conform to that.

Hardcore corruption—gratification in any form with a clear quid pro quo—is, of course, a no-no. But what about soft corruption, which comes in many forms and where the quid pro quo is more diffuse?

Say you are looking to buy an apartment and an acquaintance with whom you've had official dealings offers to get you an allotment from the developer's quota at a 10 per cent discount. There might indeed be a developer's quota available at a discount, and what you are getting is not out of line, but why indeed should he be giving it to you?

Let me give another illustration. Say, you are renting out your house and someone you know only through your work offers to take it on rent at the market rate. Do you agree with that? After all, you are getting no more than the market rate. Should a prospective tenant be rejected just because he knows you? The answer depends on where you draw the line and your ability to handle a potential conflict of interest.

The late T.L. Sankar (TLS), an outstanding IAS officer by any reckoning, was principal secretary, industries, in the Andhra

Pradesh government and was my boss for many years. We both happened to travel together to Delhi once. As we were exiting the airport, I noticed that there were two corporate cars lined up for TLS. The corporate liaison officers told him that they had also booked hotel accommodation for him. TLS was clearly irritated, walked past them brusquely and sat in the government car sent by the Andhra Pradesh Bhavan.

TLS had just taken over as principal secretary, industries, and the corporates were testing him. Evidently, some of his predecessors had not only accepted such hospitality but had even demanded it. Here again, where you draw the line is a personal choice, but perceptions do matter.

Months later, TLS told me in a casual conversation that a corporate had once come to see him in the Andhra Pradesh government guest house in Delhi, and while leaving had given him a suit piece as a gift. That company was in the textile sector, and the suit piece was their standard compliment. TLS told him politely: 'Look, I know this suit piece is a small thing for you. It's a small thing for me as well. But I will feel more comfortable if I don't take it since I can then decide on your case with a clear conscience.' I believe that sort of honest dealing helps avoid a lot of complications.

When I was a joint secretary in the Ministry of Finance in Delhi, an exporter had once invited me to a party at his house, and for good measure dropped the names of some senior officers who routinely attended his parties. I didn't go. The following month, he invited me again, which I again ignored. When this happened a third time, I took the TLS approach and told him: 'Look, I have regard for you. I am by no means disdainful of all the others who attend your parties. But I feel uncomfortable attending a party in your house when I have official dealings with you. Please do not press the invitation.'

It's certainly not the case that I didn't go to parties or dinners. I did, but only when hosted by people whom I knew at a personal level and was comfortable that they would not in any way misuse the connection with me.

Walking the straight line in field jobs is a more complex proposition because questions of pecuniary integrity get layered over by caste and political affiliations. The practice I followed was to be friendly with everyone but to make sure that official contacts didn't spill over into the personal space. This meant no socializing at a personal level. The only exception I made was to attend weddings, but I did so formally and briefly.

It's important not to carry this to an extreme level. Almost invariably, if you go to a village, people there offer you tea or coconut water. This happens in the open, not in anyone's house. I always accepted it, even if on many occasions only to sip in order not to hurt the hosts. There was a colleague who always declined this hospitality on the grounds that it would impair his image of impartiality. His boss, the collector, who happened to be with him on a village visit, asked him: 'Is your price a cup of tea?'

I am, of course, oversimplifying the issue. There is a lot of grey area and officers have to seek their own comfort level. Walking this line without being seen as too stiff and sanctimonious at one extreme or too loose at the other extreme is difficult and tricky. Being consistent is challenging but greatly comforting.

How one negotiates this balance over an entire career is a test of character and personality.

4

Chasing the Monsoon

Sub-Collector, Parvathipuram

After completing the second phase of my training at Mussoorie, I was posted as sub-collector of the Parvathipuram subdivision, which was then part of the Srikakulam district in north coastal Andhra Pradesh. This was my first independent posting, and I was both excited and apprehensive.

When I arrived on a hot muggy afternoon to take charge, even before I could get my bearings, the office superintendent courteously but firmly hurried me in to sign the papers. The haste was so as to get this done before the 'auspicious window' closed. I am not much for astrology, much less a believer in auspicious timings, but I have never resisted other people who do so, as long as it isn't inconvenient, inefficient or inappropriate.

Immediately after the signing was done, I was ushered into a farewell function for my predecessor who

was superannuating that day after having served in the
government for over thirty-five years. The significance
of the occasion—he at the end of his career, and I at the
beginning of mine—did not escape me. There were about a
hundred people at the function—staff from several offices
in that small town. I was conscious of being under their
intense scrutiny, as they were watching my every move,
utterance and gesture. After all, the arrival of a freshly
minted IAS officer was an event in that small town!

Parvathipuram was a large subdivision with five tehsils
(called *talukas* in Telugu) and two sub-tehsils.* It comprised
over a thousand villages and three small towns; it had hills
and plains, wet and dry cultivation but no industry save
for a lone jute mill in the private sector. It also had 'agency
areas'—tribal tracts so designated since colonial times
where special laws—called regulations—applied. The
purpose of these regulations was to protect tribals from
exploitation by the 'wily' non-tribal plains people. All in
all, Parvathipuram, I gathered from the IAS folklore, was a
good opportunity to get a breadth of experience.

Touring villages

Every new posting puts you on a steep learning curve; the
curve is obviously even steeper in your very first posting.
The field training helps, but being on your own is a
combination of adrenaline, apprehension and uncertainty.

---

* A district is divided into subdivisions, which are further subdivided into
tehsils. A district is headed by a collector, a subdivision by a sub-collector
and a tehsil by a tahsildar.

There is a lot of learning by doing and improving as you go along.

Whenever I had a doubt, I would unhesitatingly ask my staff and they would explain things with a charming combination of deference, eagerness and authority. But I soon realized that while they were good at explaining how things were done, they weren't very good at explaining why they were done the way they were. Oftentimes I was impressed by the efficacy of the systems and practices codified through years of experience but sometimes also irritated and perplexed by the procedures. I tried to change some of these practices, which in my view were not adding value but typically faced stiff resistance. It was difficult to break the staff's commitment to what was written in the book.

There is no unique way of administering a subdivision, and officers typically devised their own styles. At one extreme, you can stay put in your office and wait for people and work to come to you. At the other extreme, you can be touring constantly, seldom available in your headquarters for your staff or the public to come and see you. Our deputy director at the Mussoorie academy, B.N. Yugandhar, had repeatedly told us that if we wanted to be effective administrators, there was no alternative to touring and interacting with people intensely. Partly inspired by his exhortation, I veered towards the latter model, although not the extreme version (see tailpiece: Mary's room).

I set myself the goal of visiting every village in my subdivision at least once within my first year and decided that I would target four days of touring every week, or four days of being on 'camp', which was officialese for touring.

A back-of-the-envelope calculation showed that I would have to visit on average four to five villages every day I was on tour to meet my self-prescribed target. I was conscious this would be a difficult regimen to maintain given all the unanticipated work commitments that would inevitably come my way, but the broad plan did give me a sense of direction.

I looked for a report that would give me a comprehensive overview of the subdivision. There were a few, but ironically the most succinct and comprehensive turned out to be the District Gazetteer compiled during the colonial administration, which captured in one place considerable information on the area, including economic details and the culture and sociology of the people. Whatever may be our complaints and grievances about colonial exploitation, we still have to give the officers of the Raj high marks for the diligent effort they put into understanding the people and places they administered.

Even for me, born and brought up in the state, understanding village life was difficult; imagine how much more difficult it would have been for colonial administrators from another background to comprehend an alien culture and a strange society. What is remarkable is that not only did they put immense effort into understanding the area and people, but they also codified it, and did it so well that even decades after they left, improving on what they had compiled as district gazetteers proved to be a daunting task.

Visiting villages was undoubtedly a rich learning experience; it was also a lot of fun. A sub-collector's visit—whether planned or unplanned—was an event in the village as it raised hopes about some of the long pending grievances being resolved. As the jeep entered the village, dozens of children who would be playing on the streets would run after it. Typically, we would gather under a tree, and within minutes about fifty to sixty people would show up.

Compared to today when children are reasonably healthy and well clad, fifty years ago, many children were skinny and malnourished. Boys did not typically wear a shirt; girls wore torn clothes, and their hair was straggly and unkempt. Rashes, fungus and bruises on the skin were common. I'd ask the parents why they were not sending their children to school. The typical reply would be just a giggle from the mothers. If I pressed, the parents would push forward a boy and say that he went to school but still had no job. Most of the boys who did go to school could not complete their Class X.

Unfortunately, the lesson the parents and children took from this was that schooling was a waste of time. If even after all that schooling, the boy couldn't land a government job, what was the point of learning? The tragedy was that once a boy went to school, he would no longer do manual work in the field since he was now 'educated'. The result of schooling, at any rate from the parents' perspective, was to turn a child from being a helping hand on the farm to becoming an extra mouth to feed.

As an aside, I must add that the progress we, as a country, have achieved in schooling over the last fifty years must rank as a remarkable success. Education experts say that there are three challenges in primary schooling—enrolment, retention and achievement levels. I believe we have cracked the first one with almost 100 per cent enrolment, thanks in large part to the midday meal programme, which incentivizes parents to send their children to school. Given research findings that nutrition is critical for children to learn, especially in their formative years, India's nationwide midday meal programme arguably ranks among the most successful development initiatives anywhere in the world. We have been successful on the retention dimension as well with almost the entire cohorts of children going from primary to secondary schooling. The high dropout rate of girls has been arrested by attention over the last two decades to building toilets for girls. Achievement levels remain a formidable challenge though. In 2022, the Annual Status of Education Report (ASER) compiled by the Pratham Foundation found that only a quarter of the children in Class V could do a division and just over 40 per cent could read a Class II text.*

Dealing with petitions

Once word got around of my village visit, people would come with petitions about their grievances—land disputes, requests for regularization of land they had occupied and had been cultivating, requests for house sites, but most of all, requests for jobs. Initially, I would inquire into these petitions with energy and enthusiasm but very soon this turned out to be a frustrating experience simply because my success rate was low. An overwhelming number of these petitions were from youngsters who had done a few years of high school and wanted 'government jobs'. Government jobs were few

---

* Annual Status of Education Report, Pratham Foundation, 2022, available at: https://asercentre.org/aser-2022/.

even back then. More importantly, recruiting anyone into the government directly was beyond my pay grade.

As for petitions about land disputes, I realized that where occupation by the landless poor could be regularized, it had largely been done. The outstanding petitions were for the regularization of objectionable occupations such as road margins or foreshores of irrigation tanks. If, in fact, you took cognizance of these requests, you had to evict these people. The best course, I figured, would be to ignore such requests.

The unintended popularity I gained for inquiring patiently into petitions soon landed me in a problem of sorts. As word got around, people from distant villages would trek or take a bus to come to my office, sometimes accompanied by their women and children, to hand over petitions. Since I was typically 'away on camp' at least half the time, they would wait, often even for a couple of days, in my bungalow compound for me to return.

Imagine the scenario and the dilemma: I'd return typically around 9 p.m. after several days of intensive touring, physically tired and mentally exhausted, only to encounter scores of petitioners, all eager to tell me their tale of woe. If I did not see them right away, they would have to wait another night, and that would weigh heavily on my mind. On the other hand, knowing full well that I couldn't resolve most of their requests, it was difficult to summon up the enthusiasm to listen to their grievances till late into the night.

I soon realized that this reputation for receiving petitions also entailed a moral hazard—I was being gamed! Factions within villages would use poor people to petition against their rival faction, making me a pawn in village politics.

After about six months of this experience, I decided to discourage individual petitions simply because it was turning out to be an inefficient use of my time. In an ideal world, one would want to dispense administration at the individual or household level but in the far-from-ideal world we were inhabiting, the costs of doing this exceeded the benefits. I was spending far too much time on individual petitions and delivering very little by way of results. I decided that I'd be better off following what they call in management 'the 80:20 formula'—solving problems at the aggregate level, like clearing a hundred-acre tract of fallow land of shrubs and assigning it to the landless, for example.

All this was fifty years ago—a different era, a different context. I am not aware if the pressure of petitions is as intense in field jobs today. Nevertheless, my struggle with petitions illustrates a broader lesson of administration—follow the Bentham utility principle: greatest happiness of the greatest numbers. It is possible some individual grievances will remain unresolved but that is the price to pay for this.

Naxalites on my job chart

As it happened, I landed in Parvathipuram at an interesting time—when the extremist movement that had ravaged the agency tracts for nearly a decade was ebbing. The Naxalite movement, many would recall, originated in the 1960s in the Naxalbari area of West Bengal as a backlash against the exploitation of peasants by landlords. It soon spread to college campuses in Kolkata (Calcutta, as it was then called) as a broad anti-establishment revolt with Marxist overtones. Many students went 'underground', and the prestigious Presidency College was closed for several months to quell the unrest. In some sense, Kolkata was echoing the 1960s counterculture youth rebellion in the West, defined by anti-Vietnam war demonstrations on college campuses across the US, and student protests in Sorbonne, France, and across much of Europe against conformism, patriarchy and materialism.

At home in India, the Naxalite movement, which originated in Bengal, hopped over Odisha and found anchor in the hilly agency tracts of Parvathipuram. What made this remote tribal area particularly hospitable to a movement like this? Economists and sociologists explained this as the tribals finding an outlet in the movement for their pent-up anger and frustration at decades of exploitation by non-tribals.

The tribals in the agency tracts typically practised 'podu' cultivation—spraying seeds on hill slopes just after the first rains and returning a few months later to collect whatever meagre produce grew. During the intervening months, they collected minor produce from the forests such as tamarind, mohua seed and soapnuts and sold it in the market. Since their incomes were uneven, they borrowed from non-tribals—typically shopkeepers. In the event of default, which was the case much of the time, they would lose their land to the lenders, or worse, become bonded labour in their own homestead. It was this historical injustice and frustration that made them particularly vulnerable to 'capture' by the extremists.

The leaders of the Naxalite movement were, paradoxically, not tribals, but socially conscious non-tribal men and women of typically middle-class backgrounds who had sacrificed the comfort of their homes and livelihoods to fight the cause of the tribals.

Police intelligence reports of the time said that the Bengal leaders of the movement—Charu Mazumdar and Kanu Sanyal—had camped in the Parvathipuram agency tracts for months together to train local leaders and indoctrinate the second rung of followers. In fact, in 1970, it was from this area that Kanu Sanyal was captured and convicted in the Parvathipuram Conspiracy Case for which he served a term of seven years in the Visakhapatnam district jail. It is widely believed that Vempatapu Satyam and Adibhatla Kailasam, the fiery local leaders of the movement, were killed by the police in a fake encounter in July 1970.

The movement was by no means all black and white—both the authorities and the extremists operated in the shadows of the law. There were quite a few cases of extremists raiding the homes of landlords at night and beheading entire families. From the other side, there were allegations that police and forest officials would kill the leaders of the movement as well as foot soldiers in 'encounters'. After a lot of violence and bloodshed on both sides, the movement was cooling by the mid-1970s when I went there on posting.

As the agency villages were slowly settling down to 'peace' times, folklore, laced with romanticism, started shaping the narrative around the movement. The blazing heroism and fiery defiance of Satyam and Kailasam were the stuff of several tales. During my tours, the local staff would recount those stories, point to hilltops where peoples' courts had been held to dispense instant justice, to hideouts where bloody encounters had taken place and to houses where entire landlord families had been executed by the extremists.

Shaken by the experience, the state government reacted predictably, launching several programmes to improve tribal livelihoods so as to wean them away from extremist influence. Roads to their villages, encouraging them to shift from podu to settled cultivation, drinking water facilities, special residential schools for tribal children and health centres to provide care, especially against malaria, were all part of the umbrella reconstruction programme. Drawing, I believe, largely from this Srikakulam experience, the Central government launched the Integrated Tribal Development Agency (ITDA) Project on a pilot basis in six districts of the country, Srikakulam being one of them. Banks were enjoined to allocate a specified share of their total lending to tribals for livelihood support like milch cattle and sheep or for drilling a well on their land.

My job as a front-line administrator was to oversee the implementation of this massive welfare and economic support programme. Needless to say, we were all on a steep learning curve because there was little collective understanding in the local administration of the tribal way of life.

Notwithstanding all that I heard and saw, I was still surprised by the historical exploitation of tribals. In theory, this shouldn't have been possible—simply because there were laws in the statute book to protect tribals from such exploitation. In particular, there was the Land Transfer Regulation (LTR), which held that any transfer of land by a tribal to a non-tribal was illegal. Similarly, there was the debt relief regulation according to which no tribal could owe any money to a non-tribal no matter that the tribal did indeed borrow money from the non-tribal. All it required was for the tribal to petition the sub-collector that his land had been taken away from him or that he was being coerced to repay a loan. The sub-collector could then pass an order restoring the land to him or cancelling his debt. The protective legislation, a legacy of colonial times, was notable for its remarkably positive bias towards the tribals, its extraordinary clarity of purpose and simplicity of procedure.

Yet why did so much exploitation take place right before the administration's eyes? If the protective legislation did, in fact, instil fear in non-tribals, the Naxalite movement should have been a non-starter.

The solution to arresting the exploitation of tribals seemed obvious; use the teeth of the law to prevent injustice to them. So, in the early months of my posting, I went around from one tribal hamlet to another, talking to tribal households, inquiring about their land, livelihood, debt and welfare. I encouraged them to petition against the land they had lost or the debt they owed to non-tribals. I assured them that I could restore their lands and cancel their debt just by my signature. I even told them that my staff would write their petitions; all they had to do was just tell us.

Carried away by my own evangelism, I expected to be flooded with petitions.

In the event, nothing happened! To my surprise, frustration and despair, I got no more than a dozen petitions in the first six months.

And then, I discovered the answer. It wasn't exactly an epiphany; the realization dawned on me only gradually. The tribal-non-tribal relations were intertwined in an intricate ecosystem. The non-tribal moneylender was the tribal's lifeline. If his child fell ill and he had to take her to a doctor in the dead of the night, the only person who would lend money then was the local 'sahukar'. He was the one who lent them money if their crops failed, their animals died or they had to celebrate weddings or perform funerals. They could petition me and have their debt written off, but then they would make an enemy of the local moneylender. Who would come to their rescue when they next landed in a dire situation? The protective legislation was not going to work unless we also developed alternatives to the moneylender.

The lesson was clear. We could deliver welfare and secure tribal livelihoods only if we built safety nets for them, in particular by helping them build savings. This was not ironclad protection, but it would insure them against exploitation by way of loss of assets, indebtedness and bonded labour. Drawing from this lesson, going from one bank to another, encouraging and cajoling them to lend to tribals for income support became part of my job chart.

This experience taught me an important lesson for success in public policy: keep your ear close to the ground.

The Emergency

The Emergency* was declared in June 1975, about a year after I arrived in Parvathipuram. There were news stories,

* The 'Emergency' is part of independent India's history, and this is not the place to go into its causes and consequences. But for those not familiar

through censored media of course, of how office discipline had improved across the country, trains were running on time and the government was functioning like clockwork. In our small ecosystem of a semi-urban setting, nothing much changed. Our offices were small, our staff were already quite disciplined and punctual, and whatever petty corruption there was, I suspect, continued.

The most enduring memory of the Emergency at the field level is of forced family planning operations. As it turned out later, that was mostly a north Indian phenomenon. We too conducted family planning camps with great vigour and enthusiasm, of course, but there was no coercion, mistreatment or compromising on safety standards to meet targets.

There was some sense—possibly because of osmosis from what we read in the papers and heard on the radio—that the Emergency required us to take our regulatory and policing function seriously. I took to this quite enthusiastically, driven more by youthful arrogance than a sense of purpose.

Typically, on a tip-off, I would arrive in a village by surprise and raid the house or godown of some big farmer suspected to have hoarded paddy without giving the procurement 'levy'. We would swarm into homes and break open godowns. As the drama unfolded, scores of villagers would gather, many gleeful that at last the big landlord who had been mistreating or exploiting them was being brought to justice even as the farmer or his

with it, it was a period when Indira Gandhi, then prime minister, invoked an extraordinary provision in the Constitution to cancel elections and suspend civil liberties.

family members pleaded or argued that there was nothing illegal in the foodgrain stock they held. After my staff counted and took stock, we would do the necessary paperwork, seal the godown, unmindful of the entreaties of the farmer, sit in our vehicles with a sense of heroism and go away.

The procedure in such cases was for us to complete the paperwork and file a case before the appropriate authority. Quite often, the delinquent farmer would manage to get an interim order from the court releasing his stocks. Once that was accomplished, with no skin in the game, he would prolong the case hearing for months, if not years. Pursuing the case in those circumstances meant a penalty for the administration by way of additional work.

Because our success rate if we went by the book was so low, I thought I'd beat the system. Typically, the day after the raid, the big farmer would come to your office to plead his case and explain his innocence. After some stonewalling, I resorted to summary justice. I would demand that the farmer pay some stiff amount into the Prime Minister's Relief Fund as a condition for me to release his stock. I took care to do this negotiation in the presence of at least a couple of my staff members so as to cover my own back. After we settled on a sum and the farmer showed us the receipt of his payment into the PM's Fund, I would release the stock and destroy the paperwork.

The summary justice I was dispensing was clearly wrong. Had I been caught, I would have been subject to serious disciplinary proceedings. But my youthful arrogance and enthusiasm blinded me to those risks.

The Kotia question

Early in my tenure, the collector, my boss, alerted me to the sensitive problem of the Kotia group of villages along the Andhra Pradesh-Orissa (now Odisha) border, which are claimed by both states. These are sixteen remote hilltop villages with a population of about 5000 Kondh tribals, situated in an area rich in minerals like manganese, bauxite, graphite and limestone.

The border dispute dates back to 1936 when Orissa was carved out of the Madras Presidency. All the villages of the erstwhile Jeypore Estate except these sixteen villages were included in Orissa. Although Orissa never acquiesced in this exclusion, the Madras Presidency continued to administer these villages. Curiously, when Andhra Pradesh was carved out of the composite Madras State post-Independence in 1956, these villages were not included in Andhra Pradesh either.

As a result, this group of villages became stateless, and both Andhra Pradesh and Odisha continue to claim them to this day. I understand the dispute is still pending in the Supreme Court as also awaiting a Parliament resolution on clear demarcation. A curious result of this border dispute is that both states continue to woo these villages with goodies, and the Kondhs too have become adept at playing off one state against another.

A facelift for the haunted house

The sub-collector's bungalow on the outskirts of the town was a colonial-era relic—a large two-storey building with a tiled roof and wooden flooring, huge verandas, wide balconies with wooden railings and two rickety staircases. It was situated in the middle of a large, open ground dotted with huge trees and shrub jungle. Over the decades, successive occupants had made alterations to the interior of the bungalow to suit their taste and convenience with the result that the bungalow had lost some of its character without becoming particularly convenient to live in.

The sub-collector's office was a more modest single-storey stone structure, situated in an adjacent compound, also huge and scruffy. In fact, there was only a narrow private alley separating the two compounds, which together formed an ecosystem of their own. At one edge of the combined compound ran the railway line, which saw a single passenger train go in either direction around midday. The rest were all goods trains, roughly one every two hours. The lone passenger train became in some sense my emotional connect to the outside world.

Since there were no residential colonies in the vicinity, the whole area turned quite eerie after dark. There were the inevitable tales of the bungalow being haunted. There were many versions of this story, but all of them involved either the lady of the house or the mistress of a bygone sub-collector having committed suicide and her spirit still wandering in the house.

I typically slept upstairs in the covered veranda while a lone night watchman slept downstairs. I discounted the stories about ghosts, but I have to admit that in the dark of the night with the tree branches swaying in the gentle breeze, it did not require much imagination to 'see' a woman in white with her feet slightly above the ground moving around gently on the creaking wooden floors.

I made several requests to the local Roads and Buildings (R&B) Department, which looked after the maintenance of government buildings, to carry out some repairs to the bungalow. After some persuasion, they obliged me, but not fully, pleading shortage of funds.

And then a godsent opportunity came my way. Chief Minister Vengal Rao was visiting Srikakulam District, and his tour programme included lunch and rest in Parvathipuram. The local Inspection Bungalow was decrepit, and Collector Munivenkatappa asked if I would 'spare' my bungalow for the chief minister's use that afternoon. He didn't have to plead much; I was delighted, and not just for the opportunity to host the chief minister. The R&B Department miraculously produced funding and worked day and night for a week to give a substantial facelift to the bungalow.

That was the 1970s. Today, when the norm is for chief ministers to travel by special planes and helicopters, I don't believe a chief minister staying in an Inspection Bungalow, much less in a sub-collector's house, is even within the realm of possibility.

Lord, give me my daily bread

There was no bakery in Parvathipuram in those days. If I wanted to have bread for breakfast, my cook would arrange with a bus driver the previous evening to buy a loaf of bread from a bakery in Visakhapatnam (Vizag), 100 km away. The following morning, the cook would wait on the roadside, sometimes for over an hour, to collect the bread from the driver on his return trip.

There were other experiences too that would appear quaint to twenty-first-century sensibilities. Photocopying had yet to arrive in India. We did manage though. One of the staff in my office was designated as a copyist. If someone wanted an authenticated copy of a title deed or government order, they would pay a small fee and apply to the sub-collector. The job of the copyist was to hand-copy the document, which would be verified word for word by another clerk chosen at random by the head clerk. It would then be signed by me by way of authentication.

The telephone—a dubious lifeline

Those were the dark ages of telephones—a far cry from today's near-universal connectivity. As the sub-collector, I was the prized owner of not just one but two phone connections—one each in the office and at home. They functioned around half the time. To make a call, you had to lift the receiver and wait for the operator to come on line and ask for the number you wanted to be connected to. You were completely at her mercy, and if her magical voice did not materialize, there was no way to make a call.

If I had to speak to my boss—the collector, who was in Srikakulam, just 60 km away—I had to book an 'urgent trunk call'. Typically, the operator would call every three to four hours thereafter to report that the call wasn't materializing and did I want her to keep it pending? It became a common practice for me to speak with my collector around 10 p.m. when the 'traffic' was lighter. There was a provision to make a 'lightning call', which had overriding priority. We were warned by finance department circulars not to make lightning calls except in an emergency. The finance department need not have bothered; the telephone lines did not recognize any lightning!

A tragic consequence of this poor connectivity that still haunts me is the destruction wrought by fire accidents. Since phones did not work, the only way to contact the fire station was for the village headman to send a messenger, who would cycle all the way to the fire station to report an accident. Entire villages used to be gutted before the fire engines arrived.

Can we please come to the office on Sundays also?

Since the office and the bungalow were in an integrated compound, and since I was living alone, the lines between office and personal space became comfortably blurred. It was quite common for me to go to the office on Sunday mornings not so much to do any office work but to read the Sunday papers or a book. I would also be out of the way of the maid while she cleaned.

Early on, I found that some staff too began showing up at the office. Not wanting to ruin their weekly day off, I told them that they need not come to the office just because I was there. I assured them that I'd let them know if I needed them. They could all go home. They disbursed without a word. A couple of Sundays later, I again found some staff in the office and I again packed them off.

When this happened a third time, I got irritated and told them in a rather firm tone that their coming to the office on my account was causing me distinct discomfort. Would they please go home? Then one of the staff made bold to ask, in deferential third person, of course, 'Sir, if the sub-collector doesn't mind, can I tell him something?' I was curious. He said, 'Sir, our houses are small and inconvenient. The children are crying, the wife is sending us on errands, etc. We come here to escape that and spend time together. Besides, here there is the office boy to fetch us tea and refreshments.' Yet another lesson for me in seeing things from another person's perspective.

Don't wreck smooth correspondence

The language used in official correspondence was grammatically correct if also stilted and verbose. Initially, I would correct the drafts given to me by my staff in an effort to make the language lighter and every letter self-contained rather than referencing all previous correspondence by long chains of letters, numbers and dates, which resembled computer code.

My enthusiasm in this endeavour was punctured by a service colleague who told me bluntly that it was all a waste of time. He said, 'Subba, sure, the letter is from you to the boss in the other office, but it's your clerk who is writing it this side and his counterpart clerk who is reading and responding to it from the other side. Why do you unnecessarily interfere in that process, which has stood the test of time?' Sound advice although the compulsive urge to edit everything that comes my way has not left me even a half-century later.

As I write this (July 2023) another thought strikes me. Large language models (LLMs) like ChatGPT are all around us, arousing both fear and curiosity about how they will change our learning, understanding and communication. Almost certainly, they will come to be used in government correspondence. When asked to write an official letter, it will be interesting to see whether these chatbots will mimic and write letters in the clerical English that we are used to or whether they will resort to plainer English. If it's the case of one chatbot on one side writing to another chatbot on the other side, will it make any difference anyway?

What caste do you belong to?

Caste and politics were part of village life. One wanted to operate above those fault lines, but that didn't mean one could remain indifferent to them. In fact, I realized that understanding those tensions was important to doing my job well.

It's unfortunate that caste continues to rule politics in the country. One would have thought that as income and education levels improved and mobility increased, caste consciousness would recede into the background. On the contrary, exactly the opposite has happened: caste continues to have a dominant influence on our economics, politics and indeed, our entire way of life.

If south India is bad, north India is worse. I had first-hand experience of this when I was sent to the Deoria constituency in eastern Uttar Pradesh as an election observer in the 1991 elections. I landed there as an unknown quantity, and my name was too neutral to give any indication of my caste. Within hours of getting there,

I found that everyone I interacted with—both officials and non-officials—was distinctly uncomfortable until they could put me in a caste slot. Since directly raising the issue was out of the question, a barrage of questions would follow: had I been a vegetarian all my life, did I do puja at home, did I know any Vedas, etc.? I enjoyed myself by giving confusing replies to their questions.

In the late 1990s when I was finance secretary in the Government of Andhra Pradesh, there was a widespread agitation in the state for job and education reservations for backward castes. The government, ill-advisedly in my view, decided to launch a special caste census. Teachers in schools in particular were asked to do a caste enumeration of the students. Our two boys, then aged about fourteen and twelve, came and asked Urmila: 'Amma, what caste do we belong to?' This innocent question filled us with pride for bringing up our children with caste agnosticism.

That pride may have been misplaced. In later years, I became sensitive to what Dalit activists point out—that not knowing one's caste is an 'upper' caste luxury that is not available to them because the world never lets them forget where they belong.

The Indian Civil Service (ICS) and I

Living and working in an erstwhile Presidency subdivision was a constant reminder of my Indian Civil Service (ICS) predecessors and the life I imagined they lived. As I said earlier while talking about the protective legislation for tribals, while one might have grouses about the colonial rulers, they did attempt to introduce systems into administration. For example, they carried out permanent settlement of land—in other words, every inch of land was surveyed, classified and recorded. The District Office Manual, which introduced the Tottenham system of filing and correspondence, was still the system in use. The method by which they classified irrigation sources was still the best practice.

The ICS folklore hit me in real time when I encountered the tiger problem some six months after I went to Parvathipuram.

It was a cold wintry December evening. I was in my office doing 'files' at the end of the day when a group of villagers came and reported to me in evident panic that a tiger was running amok; it had taken away a calf the previous week and an infant the previous day. Even as the villagers were talking to me, my subconscious recalled a story once related to me of one of my predecessor sub-collectors who, when told that an elephant had crashed into the office compound, immediately asked the staff to look up the Board Standing Orders (BSOs) on what was to be done under the circumstances. The story is probably apocryphal, but it nonetheless illustrated the faith in field offices that the BSO would provide guidance for every contingency in the universe.

I assured the villagers that I would take action and urged them to go back home. But I was quite clueless about what to do next. Even as I was stressing about my next steps, imagery flashed across my mind of what any of my ICS predecessors would have done. He would probably have picked up his gun, driven straight to the village, kept vigil and shot the tiger dead inside of an hour, acknowledged the admiring villagers in stiff half gestures, sat in the jeep nonchalantly and returned home for a late-night drink and dinner. Within a week, the tiger's head and skin would have become yet another trophy on the walls of the sub-collector's bungalow!

Such glory clearly beyond me, I resorted to more mundane options. It took me an hour to get the district forest officer on the phone. He assured me that he would send a squad of forest guards to the village but that would be possible only the next day. Meanwhile, I picked up the local deputy superintendent of police (DSP) and drove to the village. There was not much we could do but I felt I had to go there if only to honour my promise to the villagers. We returned after chatting with the villagers for an hour.

The forest guards went to the village the next day, camped there for three days and eventually captured the tiger.

Alas, no ICS heroism for me!

The daffedar in the white turban

The sub-collector's personal staff were an endearing lot, defined by loyalty, discipline and stoicism. Since I was single and living alone, there was not much work for any of them to do, but I was touched by the effort they put in to make my life comfortable. Among the personal staff was the 'daffedar' who was with the sub-collector all through the office hours and always accompanied him on camp. Daffedars were typically the strong and silent types. Parisi Naidu was always dressed in an immaculate white cotton dhoti and shirt, and I never ever saw him without his white turban. We seldom spoke; we so easily fell into an efficient working relationship that verbal communication between us seemed not just unnecessary but even redundant.

One morning we were to set off on tour at 7 a.m. I got into the jeep, expecting Naidu, as per standard operating procedure, to jump into the back immediately. But he remained standing, hesitating to get in. Very uncharacteristically, his shirt was dishevelled, his eyes were droopy and he had not shaved, but of course, he still had his turban on. I looked at him quizzically with mild irritation at this unusual slacking. And then he told me: 'My wife died at 4 a.m. If *doragaru* (saheb) permits, I will not come on camp today.'

Being a private person, I am not given to tearing up easily, but my throat choked at the man's stoicism and sense of duty. His wife of thirty years had just died, and he had come to seek my permission to go and perform her cremation! I took him in the jeep, drove to his house, paid my respects to his departed wife, left him behind, sent instructions to the office head clerk to provide support to him for the last rites and set off on my way. I wonder if they come like that any more.

On another occasion, on a tour of agency villages that had no road access, we left the jeep on the roadside one early morning and set off walking. We returned to the jeep late in the evening, physically and mentally exhausted, after having walked maybe about 25 km. Since he was over fifty, I asked Naidu as we were getting into the jeep if he was tired. I expected him to be pleased by my considerate inquiry; instead, I sensed that he was hurt. Hurt, not that I was harbouring doubts about his stamina but that I was

harbouring doubts about his sense of duty. He said, in as
firm a voice as his sense of propriety permitted, 'If *doragaru*
permits, I will go back right now and retrace today's walk.'
There couldn't have been a more effective put-down!

Education on leprosy

A few months into my tenure, Dr Thangaraj came to see
me one morning. He was the superintendent of the leprosy
hospital run by the Telugu Baptist Mission in Salur, another
small town within my subdivision. I had met him a couple
of times, and he enjoyed a good reputation in the area
for his work on leprosy eradication. After a few minutes
of pleasantries, he said, 'I understand you are hesitating
about posting a former leprosy patient as your jeep driver.'

I was taken aback by this interference by an outsider in
my official decisions, especially from such an unexpected
source. But within a few moments, I made the connection.
My jeep driver, Appalaswamy, was retiring at the end of
the month. The next in line to succeed him was Sreenu, who
was fully qualified, with a driving licence and sufficient
experience. Unfortunately, he had contracted leprosy
earlier but was now cured. The rest of the office staff
nevertheless ganged up to protest, telling me, courteously
but firmly, that they would tolerate him in the office,
but he could not be posted to the 'prestigious job' of the
sub-collector's jeep driver. In all honesty, I must confess
that I too had misgivings about having him handle the jeep.

Dr Thangaraj told me: 'Look, this is an excellent
opportunity for you to set an example, to show that leprosy
patients can be integrated into society.' What he left unsaid

was that it would be a shame if someone like me were to perpetuate the stigma against leprosy.

Minutes after Dr Thangaraj left, I asked the office superintendent to issue orders posting Sreenu as my driver, a job in which he continued for the next ten years until he retired. I believe none of my successors had any complaints.

Leprosy was rampant in my subdivision—the incidence of the disease was about four times the national average. When I visited him next, Dr Thangaraj explained to me that contrary to popular perception, most forms of leprosy weren't contagious except by chronic contact. He took me around his hospital and encouraged me to shake hands with his patients. I was apprehensive initially, but my confidence grew over time until there came a time when I pumped hands with leprosy patients almost unconsciously.

There wasn't any specific government scheme for supporting the welfare of those affected by leprosy. Many of them were capable of working but were ostracized because of stigma. They also had problems enrolling their children in schools. I encouraged the local Lions and Rotary Clubs to build rehabilitation colonies for people afflicted with leprosy by providing government land.

I was quite proud of this accomplishment until Dr Thangaraj mildly reprimanded me. He said this approach of building separate housing colonies for leprosy-afflicted people was actually strengthening the stigma attached to the disease. Thanks to his guidance and counsel, from then on, I made every effort to integrate leprosy-afflicted people into society, in particular ensuring that their children went to regular schools.

Admittedly, my success was limited. To fight a social norm so deeply ingrained in people was an uphill task, but I tried my best.

Proud owner of a car

I bought a car after about three months in Parvathipuram. Actually, I didn't need one. I couldn't take it on tour; most roads were too rough even for a jeep. And I had nowhere to go privately. But Sheelabhadra Banerjee, a close friend and a service colleague a year senior, said to me: 'Subba, if you ever want to own a car, the time is now. After a few years, you wouldn't be able to afford one.'

This advice was, of course, prompted by the modest salary of a junior IAS officer and the steep hike in petrol prices the previous year (1973) after the OPEC oil shock. I took a loan from the government and bought a used Ambassador car for the princely sum of Rs 13,000! All I could do with it was go for a spin around town after dinner in the evening. I sold the car after a year for Rs 8500, thankful that I got even that much.

Chasing the monsoon

I learnt—and unlearnt—many lessons during my tenure as sub-collector that would serve me well in my later career. By far the most important was 'chasing the monsoon'—a totally different appreciation of the rains. Not having been exposed to village life in my growing-up years, I looked forward with delightful anticipation to the first rains after the intense heat of the summer only to regard the continual rains in the subsequent months as a plain nuisance. But after just a few months in the subdivision, I realized how the economic and emotional well-being of a billion Indians depended on rainfall.

The intimate connection between rainfall and our well-being as households, as communities and as a nation stayed with me all through my career, no matter what my job at the time involved—promoting rural industries, managing the balance of payments or handling state and Central finances.

The governor looks to the sky for guidance

Fast forward three and a half decades when I was over a year into my tenure as governor of the Reserve Bank. In the summer of 2010, I was in Thiruvananthapuram for the RBI board meeting. Because of the drought the previous year, there was nationwide anxiety about how the monsoon might turn out that year. This was also the time when we, in the Reserve Bank, were engaged in exiting from the accommodative policies triggered by the 2008 financial crisis. The exit path acquired additional urgency since inflation was picking up momentum. Adjusting interest rates to subdue inflation and stimulate growth can be a tough job at the best of times but can get much tougher when the monsoon—some 60 per cent of India's farms are rainfed—fails.

In the media interaction following the board meeting, there was the inevitable question about whether the Reserve Bank would tweak its 'exit path' in view of the monsoon prospects. Instinctively, my mind went back to my Parvathipuram days, and to a book I had read several years ago—*Chasing the Monsoon* by Alexander Frater*—a fascinating account of the New Zealander's journey across the Indian subcontinent in close pursuit of the monsoon. Frater's romantic adventure, quite expectedly, starts in Thiruvananthapuram because that is where the southwest monsoon starts its journey across India. Quite by coincidence, we happened to be in Thiruvananthapuram at the time.

In answer to the question on the monetary policy stance, I replied that like millions of farmers across the country, we in the Reserve Bank too were chasing the monsoon.

In hindsight, I think my response could have come off as evasive or even arrogant. But the media decided that I had answered their question. Perhaps they liked the imagery of the RBI governor sitting alongside farmers under a village tree, looking skywards for guidance on the interest rate policy.

Here is a citation from a feature story, 'RBI's Subbarao Chases Monsoon', in the online edition of the *Wall Street Journal*:

> All RBI governors face this problem [of inflation caused by rising food prices on account of weak rainfall]. But it has a special resonance for Mr. Subbarao, as he discussed with reporters last week . . .
>
> District collectors and sub-collectors play an important role when it comes to rains and water. They assess the ground situation to decide whether to declare

---

* Alexander Frater, *Chasing the Monsoon: A Modern Pilgrimage through India* (Picador, 2017).

a drought or to declare a flood—two events often generated by the monsoon rains, or lack of them.

It was during that time that Mr. Subbarao realized 'my emotional well-being, my career prospects depended on rains,' he said at the RBI function.

Nearly four decades later, he remains hostage to the monsoon.

'Now at the end of my career as the Governor of Reserve Bank, I realize that (my) entire performance will depend on the monsoon and not what I do about interest rates,' Mr. Subbarao quipped. 'If there is good monsoon, it is ok. Otherwise, the Governor of the Reserve Bank is to be blamed.'*

Villagers sitting under a tree with anxiety writ large on their faces looking skywards for signs of clouds remains my most enduring memory of those early days of my career.

Down memory lane

One risk of a nostalgia trip is that your recall of a quiet, quaint place will be shattered by the inevitable changes over time.

Nevertheless, I took that risk and went back to Parvathipuram in August 2022, some forty-six years after I had left it. I was delighted that I did; it was a wonderful trip down memory lane.

---

* 'Durga Raghunath, RBI's Subbarao Chases Monsoon', 26 May 2010, *The Wall Street Journal,* available at: https://www.wsj.com/articles/BL-IRTB-1828.

I happened to be in Vizag for a speaking commitment and decided on a whim to take an early morning bus to Parvathipuram. I didn't inform anyone that I was coming, and no one was waiting for me at the other end; it was a liberating feeling.

A lot had changed, of course. The highway to Parvathipuram was world-class, save for patches still under construction. The roadside villages that we passed looked prosperous, and there was brisk economic activity. Thatched huts and crumbling dwellings had given way to solid constructions and even some swanky multi-storey structures. The most heart-warming sight undoubtedly was to see healthy, neatly dressed girls riding bicycles to school—a far cry from the ragged, malnourished girls of my time.

As we approached Parvathipuram, I saw that the town had grown and expanded. The main road was wider, the shops were full, and restaurants and hole-in-the-wall eating joints dotting the road were doing brisk business. Most of all, contrary to the impression etched in my mind from decades ago, there was no one sitting idly on the roadside! Everyone was engaged in doing something.

As we approached the bus stand, I counted at least five bakeries, giving the sub-collector of today a choice of at least five varieties of bread compared to the stale bread from a far-off bakery in Vizag transported by special arrangement during my time. Parvathipuram had certainly moved up on my personal 'bakery index'.

I got off the bus and walked the nearly kilometre to the sub-collector's office. It was blazing hot, but I avoided taking an auto so I could experience the sights and smells of this town that has such a special place in my heart and my career.

I sent in my business card and announced myself to the sub-collector—quite apprehensive that s/he might be irritated by this unexpected intrusion into their work schedule. What happened next was heart-warming. Bhawna—a freshly minted IAS officer of the 2019 batch—my successor forty-six years later—came breezing out and invited me in with an open heart and open arms.

We spent the next five hours together exchanging notes, both of us eager to learn from the other's experience. Since my time, Parvathipuram had become a separate district. Bhawna took me to call on the collector (Nishant Kumar) and joint collector (Anand Orikapat) and then took me home for a delightful home-cooked lunch.

I was sad to see that the stone building that had housed the sub-collector's office for decades had crumbled. The office had now moved to a new two-storey steel and concrete structure built in the same compound. The furniture and fixtures were modern, and computer terminals were ubiquitous. The old rickety jeeps had given way to swanky air-conditioned SUVs, while videoconferences had replaced physical meetings. Most communication now happened via the cell phone. Procedures had been simplified and there was much greater responsiveness at the front-end than I had thought possible.

The sub-collector's bungalow had been upgraded to the collector's bungalow. Collector Nishant Kumar and his wife were kind enough to allow me to peep into their home. The living quarters had been upgraded with modern furniture and fittings but without changing the character of the building. The large, unkempt shrub jungle from my time was now a manicured garden even as the shady trees in the compound continued to stand.

Almost everyone whom I had associated with—office staff, peons, drivers, acquaintances—had all passed on, save for Venkat Rao, the peon-cum-driver, who came rushing to see me as soon as he heard that I was visiting. I was touched by his affection and concern, and we exchanged notes about our lives and families, including our respective grandchildren. Bhawna was kind enough to drive me through the town, including to the Thotapalli reservoir, 10 km away.

I had arrived in Parvathipuram that morning alone. When I took the train back to Vizag at seven that evening, there were at least twenty-five people, including local railway and police officials, to bid me goodbye. Bhawna teared up, and I nearly did.

Mary's room

Imagine that there lives in a room a brilliant neuroscientist named Mary. The peculiarity of the room is that it is completely black and white—no colour. Not just the room, but everything inside it as well. The walls are painted black and white; the furniture is black and white and even the display on the computer screen is black and white.

However, even though Mary herself hasn't experienced colour, she knows everything there is to know about it. She knows about cones and rods and how light travels from the retina to the occipital lobe through the optic nerve. She also knows about the variations in frequency and wavelengths that make up different colours. She is an expert in colours without ever having experienced them.

One day, her computer screen malfunctions, and it shows her an apple that is red in colour. Now, remember that Mary already knows everything about the physics and biology of colours. Do you think consciously experiencing colour adds anything to her knowledge of colours?

This is a thought experiment put forward by philosopher Frank Jackson in 1982. According to Jackson, even with all the knowledge about colours, Mary will still learn something new when she first experiences colour.

Like most philosophical questions, Mary's room is hotly debated; it has no settled answer. But in my own lived experience, it has a definitive answer. You can learn all you can about village life by reading, listening and even seeing videos. But there can be no substitute for actually experiencing it!

5

A CIA Agent?

The Long Road to a PhD

One January morning in 1976, some eighteen months into my sub-collectorship, I received orders in the post—*tappal* as we called it in Andhra, and *dak* as it's called in the north—transferring me as project officer of the Small Farmers Development Agency (SFDA), Srikakulam. In effect, this was a transfer to a different post within the same district. The transfer was a surprise and a disappointment. I was getting familiar with the issues and challenges of Parvathipuram, had set myself a number of goals and was really enjoying the job. I was expecting to serve at least the normal tenure of two years, and now this transfer!

The puzzle behind this unexpected transfer was solved in a week. The chief minister at that time, Vengal Rao, by far the most apolitical chief minister that I had served under, had family interests in the Bobbili area, which fell within the Parvathipuram jurisdiction. Before he joined politics, Vengal Rao had served as a manager in the Bobbili raja's estate and obviously had regard for the erstwhile zamindars. The rajas and their extended families had a variety of business interests in the area—cinema halls, jute mills, shops, bus transport, etc. Some of them fell victim to my surprise inspections and had to pay penalties, and on occasion, their businesses even faced closure. This was not just a loss of money but also a loss of face for the erstwhile royal family. Obviously irked by this, they took their grievance to the chief minister.

A junior IAS officer flies well below the radar of a chief minister, but in this case, Vengal Rao was vaguely familiar with me because I had hosted him in my sub-collector's bungalow for a few hours during his district visit a few months earlier. To solve the Bobbili question, he seemed to have asked the chief secretary to nudge me out but to do so without hurting me. Hence this transfer within the same district and that too with jurisdiction over the entire district, making it look like an out-of-turn promotion!

I was already familiar with the work of SFDA because I had become good friends with K.S. Sarma, the outgoing project officer. Sarma used to stay with me when he was in my area, and we even toured quite a lot together. The SFDA, the precursor to the present-day DRDA (District Rural Development Agency), was in pilot mode at that time, and Srikakulam was one of about forty districts in the country chosen for the pilot run. The pilot nature of the project allowed for a lot of flexibility and innovation. Notwithstanding my initial misgivings, I found the job interesting and challenging.

The four-year study itch

Many of my classmates from IIT who had gone to the US for graduate studies were getting their PhDs around this time, some of them from pedigreed universities. Slowly and unconsciously, a thought crept into my mind: Why don't I get a PhD too? These days, a few of the IAS entrants are already PhDs, and many more get a doctorate in the course of their careers. But fifty years ago, an IAS officer with a doctoral degree was a rarity.

To determine that you have to pursue a PhD in economics if you want your higher studies to help your IAS career was a no-brainer. I was aware of the challenge of venturing into a new subject but felt confident of being up to it. I was aware also that American universities were flexible about admitting graduate students into academic disciplines that they had not studied earlier provided the applicant could demonstrate the intellectual capability to foray into the new field. I did the usual GRE and TOEFL examinations; in addition, to prove my preparedness for higher studies in economics, I did the subject GRE in economics as well, for which I prepared for a couple of months by working late into the night like in my IIT days.

The application process was excruciating—and expensive. Unlike now, we had hardly any access to foreign exchange at that time, and at each university, you had to seek an exemption from the application fee. Most allowed it on the condition that you would pay it if you were granted admission but getting that conditional waiver was an anxious and time-consuming process.

One had to attach transcripts of prior education to the application. There were no photocopying machines within a 100-km radius of Parvathipuram, and I had to wait until someone from my staff or within my circle of acquaintances was going to Vizag and request them to get photocopies made. The copies were invariably of poor quality, and I worried that my application might be rejected on these grounds alone.

Getting recommendation letters, an integral part of the application process, was the most taxing part. My IAS bosses would write them if I requested but would an academic institution attach any weight to their assessment? I could request my professors back at IIT Kanpur, but they were physics teachers. Even in the unlikely event that they remembered me from four years ago and agreed to write a recommendation, would their recommendations count for studying economics? In any case, since I didn't have much of a choice, I tried a mix of both.

I ended up applying to six universities altogether, got rejected by four and was accepted by two. Of the latter, only Ohio State University (OSU) offered me financial aid—a research assistantship to work on a project in agricultural economics. Evidently, they attached some weight to what I was doing in the SFDA. Being the only acceptance with financial aid, it meant a lot to me.

A CIA agent?

Little did I realize at the time that the path ahead on this journey for higher studies was going to be much more arduous than the path I had already traversed. Here's how it unfolded.

The IAS conduct rules allowed officers to apply to foreign universities for higher studies without prior permission but required that they obtain clearance before accepting an offer. When I applied for permission to accept this offer of admission, the state government cleared my request quite expeditiously and sent it to the Central government for final clearance. It was getting Central clearance that proved to be a harrowing experience.

In Delhi, they raised every objection possible. Note this was the Emergency period, and the government was trolling for CIA agents within the system. How did I, a student of physics, get admission into an economics course, that too with financial assistance? I must surely be a CIA agent! To verify that I had no CIA links, they asked for copies of my application and all the transcripts. They wanted to see copies of the recommendation letters too but that was privileged and confidential communication between the referee and the university, and I had no access to them.* Convincing the Government of India that the university would not release the recommendation letters turned out to be a nerve-racking experience.

I was asked to write a note on why I believed higher studies in economics would help the country's administration, a question no self-respecting undersecretary would ask today! That was easy since I had to write a statement of purpose as part of my application. Mind you, I was doing all this long distance, through the intermediation of the

---

* These days, most universities allow the applicants to see the recommendation letters unless the applicant herself waives that privilege.

state government and via snail mail, which was the only mode of communication available at that time.

I suspect some investigative agencies were put on the job of checking my antecedents, but I couldn't be sure. Meanwhile, one deadline after another slipped away; at my request, the university was kind enough to allow me a deferment for six months. Finally, the under-secretary in the Department of Personnel in Delhi hit the limits of his imagination and ran out of queries to raise. In a rare mood of generosity, he certified that my application was in the clear, that I was not a CIA agent and the file travelled up the hierarchy and I got the final permission—some ten agonizing months after the process started.

The Nizam Trust in Hyderabad had a scheme of travel grants to deserving students. Because of the benevolence of a senior IAS officer, Hashim Ali, who was one of the trustees, I applied for, and was granted, a one-way travel grant, which would be given on a reimbursement basis. Not having enough savings of my own, I borrowed money from my father to fund the travel.

A culture shock

I arrived in Columbus, Ohio, on an early January morning in 1977 in the midst of a mid-Atlantic blizzard with just fifty dollars in my pocket—twenty dollars bought at the airport in Mumbai, the maximum we were allowed at that time, and the balance thirty dollars borrowed from an IIT friend. The journey took over forty hours because air travel was slower during those days—the aircraft had to make stops along the way for refuelling—and because of a botched connection in London. By the time I arrived in Columbus, I was fatigued, sleep-deprived and confused, and, of course, I had lost all sense of time. It didn't help that the handle of my torn, frayed suitcase had given way and I had to carry it under my arm halfway across the campus from the taxi to the International Student Office (ISO), my first port of call.[*]

The ISO was very helpful. They asked me first to help myself to coffee and cookies in the pantry. Cookies? I was too tired for an education in American English. I was ravenously hungry though. I went into the pantry and helped myself to everything that was on offer, never mind what they thought of me.

A student volunteer in the ISO drove me around the campus and surroundings, and within hours, she found me a room in an off-campus rooming house where I boarded with five American undergraduate students—four white and one black. We each had separate rooms, but the bath and kitchen were shared. She helped me shop for some groceries to tide me over until I got my bearings and lent me fifty dollars to get by until I got my first paycheque. By the time she dropped me back at the rooming house, it was some sixty hours after I had left India. I was exhausted and dazed. I collapsed on the bed and slept like a log.

I hadn't cooked before, and even heating packaged food required a huge amount of learning by doing. Settling down in that strange environment, and that too with ambient temperatures averaging -10°C, was a harrowing experience.

---

[*] Suitcase wheels had not been invented then.

A lot of things were unfamiliar, and many things were different. To go up a building, you took the elevator, not the lift. It was still the post office, but you mailed, not posted a letter; you ate fries with food and chips as a snack. You stood in a line, not a queue, and a Coke was also a soda. But there was one thing about American life—it was easy to adjust to. More importantly, no one cared what you did; it was such a liberating feeling.

In some ways, it was a positive culture shock as well. I had to register in the bursar's office before I could register for classes. The admission fee was waived for me as part of the financial assistance, but the girl at the desk said that I had to pay a late fee because I was reporting a week late. I told her the delay was due to the late receipt of the I-20 sent by the university, which had delayed my getting a student visa. I carried the envelope with the post date as proof just in case she asked to see it. But to my astonishment and relief, she said, 'Okay, in that case, I'll waive it.' This wasn't some mid-level official in the office; she was just a student doing a part-time job in the bursar's office. What a contrast from having to prove that you were not a CIA agent!

There were several other experiences in those early days on an American campus to remind me how much that country of plenty and choice was different from the India of scarcity and controls that I had grown up in. Let me give you just one example.

The OSU campus was large, and there was a bus to ferry students from place to place. In my first week, I was waiting at a bus stop along with maybe another twenty-five students. When the bus arrived, with a mindset shaped by my Indian psyche, I pushed aside everyone to get on to the bus, even as I could feel the dirty looks from them. It took me a few days to realize that space on the bus was not a scarce commodity and that the bus would not drive away until everyone had boarded.

A few months later, I went to New York for a visit. I got out of the subway and was confused about which exit to take to the street level. At one of the exits, I asked someone who looked like he was staff of the subway system, an African American, if that was the exit to take for Rockefeller Centre. 'That's cool, man', he said, and I couldn't figure out if he was saying 'yes' or telling me that my trail to the Rockefeller Centre had gone 'cold'.

Is economics like physics?

At the university, I registered for basic graduate-level courses in economics. The learning curve was steep but not unmanageable. Having studied physics earlier, it was inevitable that I would, even if unconsciously, compare economics and physics. At one level, the two subjects were similar, but at another, vastly different.

In both economics and physics, our everyday experiences deviate from the theory. The theory of rational expectations in economics, for example, says that wages and prices adjust instantaneously to changes anywhere because information about that change transmits instantaneously. But such 'instant adjustment' never happens in practice because there is no such thing as perfect information. A parallel in physics is the implication of Newton's theory that the gravitational configuration of the entire universe adjusts instantaneously in response to even an infinitesimal change in the remotest corner of the universe. We now know that this too cannot happen because Einstein's Theory of Relativity, which holds that no signal can travel faster than the speed of light, rules out instantaneous adjustment.

Take another example. The centrepiece of Keynes' theory is the existence of inescapable uncertainty about the future, which implies that risk cannot be measured precisely beyond a point, and that taking uncertainty seriously has profound implications for how one applies economics. Look at the parallel in physics. The foundation of quantum mechanics is Heisenberg's Uncertainty Principle, which puts an irreducible limit on our ability to simultaneously determine the position and momentum of a particle.

Striking as these comparisons are, there is an obvious flaw in this line of thinking. Similarity in a few laws does not mean similarity in the basic nature of the academic discipline. The fundamental difference between physics and economics is that physics deals with the physical universe, which is governed by immutable laws, beyond the pale of human behaviour. Economics, in contrast, is a social science whose laws are influenced by human behaviour. Simply put, I cannot change the mass of an electron no matter how I behave but I can change the price of a derivative by my behaviour.

The short point is that economics cannot lay claim to the immutability, universality, precision and exactitude of physics. Economics is a social science, and its predictive power is at a fundamental level influenced by human behaviour and actions.

Not staying for dinner?

Living the American student life, I learnt a lot of things about American culture and traditions, some of them the hard way. Some six months after I joined, Dick Meyer, my faculty adviser, invited me for 'cocktails' at his house on a summer evening. Gathered there in the large compound of his house were about a hundred guests from across the university community—his friends, colleagues along with their spouses, department staff and, of course, quite a few students. I was having a good time when I saw that another student, a friend of mine, and his girlfriend, approached Dick to say they were leaving, thank you. I was nearby and blurted out, 'Why aren't you guys staying on for dinner?' Both looked askance at me.

And then the penny dropped. I was unaware that unlike in India, 'cocktails' meant just cocktails and did not include a follow-on dinner unless specifically indicated. It was one of those moments when I wished the earth would cave in and swallow me!

OSU was a big football school and the Ohio State Buckeyes, the university football team, enjoyed cult status around the campus. The annual Ohio-Michigan game was an iconic match, and the entire university community would be consumed by the impending event for weeks before the actual game. I didn't become a football fanatic but acquired sufficient familiarity with the game to not be held guilty of heresy.

Abrupt halt to my studies

About a year and a half into my graduate study, I was cruising along in my coursework, doing reasonably well and was even shortlisting topics for my doctoral work when tragedy struck our family. My elder brother, a medical doctor with a postgraduate degree, committed suicide. He had been troubled for some time, but none of us suspected that he would take this drastic step. All of us, most of all my parents, were devastated. I felt I needed to be with them at this difficult time, to give them emotional support. I mulled over the idea of going back home and talked it over with Dick Meyer, my faculty adviser, who was very understanding. He said that the university would keep my candidature for a PhD open for at least five years. Meanwhile, I was allowed to graduate with an MS degree since I had completed all the requirements for that.

So, within a year and a half of my going for higher studies, I was back home in July 1978 with an MS degree in economics.

The marriage milestone

I first met Urmila in the summer of 1976 when she was assistant collector under training in Krishna District. Once when travelling from Srikakulam to Hyderabad on work, I broke journey at Vijayawada to spend half a day with my friend and batchmate Sunil Khatri, and it was there that I ran into her.

I found her vivacious, cheerful and friendly. I can't say it was love at first sight but mutual attraction developed over the next few months. We met in Vijayawada a couple of times and more often in Hyderabad.

And then I went to the US on study leave without making any commitment. The attraction survived the separation, and indeed it was over correspondence during that period that we made a commitment to get married.

The wedding took place six months after I returned from study leave—in December 1978—in Palghat (now Palakkad), close to Urmila's ancestral village in Kerala. Neither of us realized we were setting off a competition between the staff of the Vijayawada sub-collector's office (where she was posted) and the Kurnool joint collector's office (where I was) about which office—the bride's or the groom's—would attend the wedding in larger numbers. In the end, we had a busload of staff along with their families from both places who combined this trip to Kerala, a first for many of them, with pilgrimage and tourism in God's Own Country.

Urmila served in Andhra Pradesh in several posts and in the Ministry of Defence at the Centre. She too won a Humphrey Fellowship (in 1993) and studied at the University of North Carolina at Chapel Hill. When I was appointed to the RBI, she opted for the job of chief vigilance officer in Air India and retired from that job and from the IAS in October 2012.

Another attempt for a PhD

When I was on 'compulsory wait' awaiting a stable posting, a saga about which I will write in a later chapter, I applied for a Humphrey Fellowship, which provided an opportunity to mid-career professionals from developing countries to study for a year at an American university. It was a non-degree programme with a lot of built-in flexibility about how many and what courses one took. Since it was open to the private sector as well, the competition was quite stiff, so I was delighted when I was selected, and even more delighted because I got placement at MIT, an iconic institution with a huge pedigree.

So, in August 1982, I found myself back in an American university after a gap of four years—this time in Cambridge, Massachusetts. MIT was an intellectually stimulating experience—you could feel the gravitas of the place just by walking around the campus. Nobel laureates were sprinkled around the campus, and if you were lucky, you could even be taught by one. In the early weeks of my MIT sojourn, I was once in an elevator with Wesley Leontief, famous for his input-output model, which was the basis of our much-celebrated Mahalanobis model of planning. I realized my brush with a Nobel shoulder only later and pinched myself to make sure that it was real.

Within hours of arriving on the campus, I made acquaintance with Sumantra Ghoshal, who was then in Indian Oil, the only other Indian among that year's fellows. Since we were both looking for accommodation, we decided to make common cause and share an apartment. After checking out a few listings on the campus journal, we zeroed in on a third-floor apartment on the top floor of a rickety, crumbling house in the historic Beacon Hill area of Boston, across the river from the MIT campus. Obviously, we prioritized cost and convenience over comfort. Both of us were married with a son each, and we had both left our families back in India since the fellowship grant was not sufficient to support a family.

Sharing living quarters with Sumantra is one of my happy associations of that one year at MIT. He was undoubtedly brilliant and had clear academic and professional goals and a game plan for achieving them. At the same time, he was fun-loving and friendly with no personality quirks that could have irritated me. In short, we got along famously in spite of living in close proximity. Our conversations over meals spanned the entire universe but mostly we talked of politics at home in India, business trends around the world and we gossiped about common friends and acquaintances.

Without being conscious of it, Sumantra and I started competing in studies. The Humphrey Fellow administrators laid great emphasis on the breadth of learning—encouraging the fellows to experience a wide range of subjects that would expand their horizons. But both Sumantra and I privileged depth over breadth—taking a full load of advanced courses in economics and management. We even cross-registered for some courses at Harvard, which was possible under an agreement between these two iconic institutions.

Classroom instruction at MIT was quite intense. There are stories, possibly apocryphal, of professors writing on the board 'homework for Wednesday' on the very first day of classes even before they uttered a word. The folklore among students was that you were four weeks behind even before classes started!

Harvard and MIT

The rivalry between Harvard and MIT was also part of that folklore. The stereotypical view was that Harvard had an edge in arts and humanities while MIT had an edge in the hard sciences. This was a false perception then and is even more so now. Nevertheless, the imagined dichotomy spawned a number of jokes. A student reportedly was standing in line at a supermarket checkout counter. When his turn came, the cashier looked at him with a faint frown. He was standing in a line designated for 'five items or less' while his cart was overflowing with items. The cashier remarked to the person standing behind him: 'He's obviously a student. If he's from the school up the river, he doesn't know how to read. And if he's from the school down the river, he doesn't know how to count.'

MIT was famously quantitative. If anything could be reduced to numbers, it was. If you asked someone what she was studying, a typical response would be 'Course 6', not electrical engineering and computer science. Similarly, Course 14 was economics while Course 15 was management. I understand this nomenclature has not changed over the years.

On to a PhD?

The Humphrey year flew by before I realized it. Sumantra did exceptionally well in academics; some consolation for me was that I was almost level with him. Both he and I were told informally that should we decide to stay on, MIT would be happy to offer us admission to their PhD programme and give us credit for the courses we had done. Sumantra took the offer, and he urged me to stay on too. I was tempted but decided to head back home because personal circumstances did not permit me to stay away from India.

After his PhD, Sumantra became a professor of international business at the London Business School and won acclaim in the world of business as well as academia for his incisive knowledge and sharp insights. Sadly, he died at a relatively young age in 2004.

At last, a PhD!

That I didn't get a PhD despite twice having gone for higher studies to the US continued to nag at me. A PhD would take at least two years even if I was given credit for all the coursework that I did at OSU and MIT. Pressures on both personal and professional fronts didn't allow me that space.

After I returned from the Humphrey Fellowship in August 1983, I was posted as executive director in the Andhra Pradesh Industrial Development Corporation (APIDC). P.L. Sanjeeva Reddy (PLS), a 1964 batch IAS officer, was the managing director and my boss. One day we both happened to be in Andhra University (AU) in Visakhapatnam for an event. After the event, PLS, who was an alumnus of AU, took me by the arm to the registrar's office and got me registered as a private PhD candidate. It was all done in fifteen minutes.

As per the university rules at that time, a private candidate who had done all the coursework didn't need to put in residence at the university. All that the candidate had to do was write a comprehensive examination whereafter he could go straight into writing a dissertation. I am embarrassed, even ashamed, to say that I didn't take forward my quest for a PhD despite that relatively simple option being available to me. I wish I had a credible excuse.

It was more than ten years later when I was posted as finance secretary in the Government of Andhra Pradesh that I tried to pick up the threads of my PhD. Sometime in 1995, after putting in two years in that job, I requested then-chief minister Chandrababu Naidu for a year's study leave to write my PhD dissertation, but he was in no mood to let me go. When I reiterated the request a year later, he offered helpfully that I could work on my dissertation in the morning and come to the office only in the afternoon. For a finance secretary to not be available for half a day was just not a workable option. He and I both knew it.

But a happy confluence of circumstances came to my help in my pursuit of a PhD. As I will write in a little more detail in a later chapter, sometime in 1995, a World Bank team had initiated a detailed study of the fiscal sustainability of our state public finances. We compiled a whole lot of historical data and collaborated with the World Bank in analysing and interpreting it.

Meanwhile, thanks to the initiation by B.P.R. Vithal (BPRV), then a member of the Tenth Finance Commission, I had developed a keen interest in fiscal federalism. BPRV, who was finance secretary of Andhra Pradesh for over ten years during the 1970s-1980s, was considered a doyen of state finances. He was an untypical finance secretary who proved that to be hard-headed is not necessarily to be hard-hearted. At BPRV's instance, I wrote a paper for the Finance Commission on the implications of the economic reforms initiated in 1991 for our fiscal federalism. I analysed how a shift to a market-based system would alter the vertical balance between the Centre and states and the horizontal balance across states.

When I took stock of all the analysis we had done for the World Bank study and for my Finance Commission paper, I realized that I had material for a full dissertation; all I needed to do was put it together in a cogent framework.

But there was one more hurdle I had to clear—the written comprehensive followed by an oral examination. I revised my economics, working regularly late into the night, and after four months, sat for the comprehensive examination at Andhra University. Having cleared that, I worked on the dissertation for about six months under the guidance of Professor Jagadeeshwar Rao, my thesis adviser. It was a gruelling schedule—office work all through the day stretching into the weekends and dissertation writing at night. It helped a great deal that I had assistants in the office to run the computer programmes and for typing the dissertation. It also helped that for about three months the chief minister was busy electioneering (1998 general elections), which took some pressure off the work.

So, finally, in September 1998, I earned a PhD based on my coursework in the US and the dissertation I wrote on 'Fiscal Reforms at the Sub-national Level: A Case Study of Andhra Pradesh'. It was a fifteen-year endeavour and a fifteen-month effort.

Value of scarcity

The huge anxiety of rushing on to the college bus in my early days on a US university campus—that incident plays back in my mind from time to time. What explains my uncivilized behaviour?

It is, of course, quite easy to rationalize it. My mindset was shaped by my India experience. In India, a seat on the bus is a scarce commodity and therefore I attached a great value to it.

Like almost everything else in economics, Adam Smith explained this phenomenon too in terms of the 'paradox of value'. Consider this. A diamond has no practical use; yet it is immensely valuable and buys a lot of things. On the other hand, water has immense use; we can't survive without it. Yet, water buys virtually nothing. This contradiction can be explained by considering the scarcity value of a commodity. Water costs much less than a diamond because it is abundant and diamonds are scarce. The scarcer water becomes, the more value we will attach to it. In the limiting case, if there was only one glass of water left in the world, we would offer all the diamonds in the world to buy that glass of water.

Much later in life, I came across a more sophisticated explanation of scarcity from the research of Sendhil Mullainathan (Harvard) and Eldar Shafir (Princeton) as explained in their book, *Scarcity: Why Having Too Little Means So Much.*[*]

Why do successful people get things done at the last minute? Why does poverty persist? Why do organizations get stuck firefighting? Why do the lonely find it hard to make friends? Mullainathan and Shafir show that these

---

[*] Sendhil Mullainathan and Eldar Shafir, *Scarcity: Why Having Too Little Means So Much* (Penguin, 2013).

seemingly unconnected questions are all examples of a mindset shaped by scarcity.

Drawing on cutting-edge research from behavioural science and economics, Mullainathan and Shafir show that scarcity creates a unique psychology in people struggling to manage with less than they need. Busy people fail to manage their time efficiently for the same reasons the poor fail to manage their money. The dynamics of scarcity reveal why dieters find it hard to resist temptation, why students and busy executives mismanage their time, and why sugarcane farmers are smarter after harvest than before. Once we start thinking in terms of scarcity and the strategies it imposes, the problems of modern life come into sharper focus.

The book explains not only how scarcity leads us astray but also how individuals and organizations can better manage scarcity for greater satisfaction and success.

6

Make Haste Slowly

My Relatively Short Tenure as a District Collector

Being a district collector is the defining job of an IAS career.[*] Across the vast hinterland of the country, the collector is 'the government'—the only authority that rural folk recognize and acknowledge. There is no other job anywhere in the world that comes close to it in terms of power, prestige, responsibility and most of all, the opportunity to see the results of your work on the ground.

Every year when civil service toppers are interviewed in the media, the standard question they are asked is: 'Why do you want to join the IAS?', and the standard answer is: 'Because I want to change the world.' It's no surprise that both the question and answer are set in the context of seeing

---

[*] The nomenclature varies from state to state. In some states, it is 'deputy commissioner' and in some others, 'district magistrate'. No matter the nomenclature, the post carries unique authority and responsibility.

an IAS career as being a district collector. Notably, in my parents' generation, one didn't become an IAS officer, one became a collector.

District collectors—then and now

In colonial times, the job chart of a collector was narrow and well-defined—collect taxes and maintain law and order. Independent India has moved on from that simple model, and so has the job chart of a collector. Indeed, within the ambit of law, there is nothing a collector can't do. Some of the newsy things that collectors do—disaster management, conducting elections, maintaining law and order during riots, agitations and protests—are widely noticed, but even the everyday work—even if it's not newsy—can be equally challenging, taxing and fulfilling.

The collector has to oversee virtually all government departments in the district, plan and implement all government programmes and is answerable for virtually everything that happens in the district. And in addition to that, she has to be the chief grievance redressal officer—whether it is a woman who is getting beaten up by her drunkard husband or children not having textbooks in school, the first port of call is the collector.

That I did not have a stable tenure as a district collector is therefore one of the disappointments of my IAS career. I was collector altogether for twenty-one months but spread over three districts (Khammam, Visakhapatnam and Prakasam) and interspersed by other postings.*

---

* I gather, entirely from anecdotal evidence, that across states, tenures of collectors are getting longer and more stable. If so, that's a change for the better.

Khammam

I was posted as collector of Khammam District in February 1979 even before I had completed seven years of service. It was a heady feeling. That posting lasted all of nine months.

Khammam District was an amalgamation of the revenue cultures of Andhra and Telangana since two of its revenue divisions had been part of the Nizam's Hyderabad while the third (Bhadrachalam) was part of the erstwhile Andhra State.* It was my first exposure to Telangana since my earlier postings had all been in the Andhra region. But that wasn't much of a problem since by then there was a full-time joint collector to look after revenue administration with the collector having to intervene only at the margin in important matters.

I distinctly recall the day I assumed charge of the job—I signed my joining papers at around 5 p.m. one February evening. Till well past 8 p.m., I was in the office meeting the district officers who came to 'call on' the new boss. Even as that 'meet and greet' process was on, the district medical and health officer (DMHO) wanted to jump the queue and see me urgently. He came in accompanied by a couple of WHO officials to tell me that they had just put in a written request in my office for exhuming the body of an eight-year-old girl who had been buried the previous day in a remote village.

The issue was that WHO, after assiduous scrutiny across the country, had declared India to be smallpox-free two years earlier in 1977. But now, WHO had obtained intelligence that smallpox cases had cropped up again,

---

* This was when Andhra Pradesh was a composite state. It was divided into two—Andhra Pradesh and Telangana—in 2014.

particularly in the Khammam area. They suspected that this girl in question may have died of smallpox. I am talking of 1979, 'the dark ages' from today's digital age perspective. How this suspicion had arisen and why the collector's permission was required to exhume the body were unclear to me. I briefly quizzed the DMHO on whether we were prepared for contingent action should this case turn out to be positive, signed off on the papers and asked the DMHO to inform me should this turn out to be a case of smallpox. In all the rush and excitement of that first day of being a 'district collector', this issue faded from my mind until the DMHO told me a couple of weeks later when we met on some other occasion that the test had been negative.

What if the test had come out positive and the small-pox-free certification for the whole country had been withdrawn based on what had happened in my district? That surely would have been an inauspicious and unsavoury start to my innings as a collector.

Uneventful to eventful

In the nine months I was in Khammam, there were no elections. College students in the district, largely affiliated with communist parties and politically more engaged and agile than elsewhere, were also untypically quiet during that period. The Godavari, which overflowed during the rains every year inundating hundreds of villages on either bank, was unusually well-behaved that monsoon.

In short, by all accounts, my tenure as collector of Khammam District should have been uneventful. It was anything but, and that was my own doing.

Khammam District, like Parvathipuram where I had worked earlier, had large tracts of tribal villages, classified as 'agency areas', where protective legislation operated. In particular, as per the land transfer regulation (LTR), any transfer of land from a tribal to a non-tribal was null and void. In short, any non-tribal owning or cultivating land in the agency area was prima facie suspect.

I found out soon after taking charge that a major portion of agricultural land in the tribal areas was indeed in the occupation of non-tribals. On investigation, I learnt that as irrigation facilities developed in tribal areas, their lands had become valuable. Thousands of landed farmers from the prosperous coastal areas of the neighbouring Krishna and West Godavari districts had sold their lands there and migrated to the 'agency areas', bought land from tribals and settled there.

In my youthful enthusiasm, I decided that this injustice must end, and proceeded to implement the LTR on a mission mode. I called a meeting of the revenue department, and we discussed an action plan for 'expeditiously and effectively' implementing the LTR. Within a week we had a plan ready. Within a month we had hundreds of cases registered and set in motion due process such as issue of notices, etc. Since the adjudication of cases under the protective legislation vested with the revenue authorities, we could accelerate the process without depending on the judicial system.

The backlash was swift and intense—far more than what I had encountered in Parvathipuram. Many non-tribal framers were deeply agitated by the prospect of being evicted from land that they had been cultivating for decades. They took their grievance to the local MLAs who in turn carried the 'tales of injustice' to the state administration in Hyderabad. Soon enough, the ground reports reached the then chief minister Chenna Reddy.

Santhanam, a senior IAS officer and secretary to the chief minister, called me to inquire about the situation, telling me for good measure that he was doing so on instructions from the chief minister. Santhanam was by all accounts my well-wisher. He was earlier the collector of Krishna District, and my wife, Urmila, had trained under him. He and his family had travelled to Palghat to attend our wedding the previous year. I explained to Santhanam what we were doing; he advised me not to rush things, and that was that.

Meanwhile, many non-tribals approached judicial courts and obtained a stay of proceedings. I consulted the government pleader who advised that the jurisdiction of civil courts on proceedings under protective legislation was questionable. So, contesting judicial court orders turned out to be another battlefront.

Because of process delays, our disposal rate was much slower than we had anticipated. Even where orders had been passed, implementing those decisions by way of restoring the land to the rightful tribal owners turned out to be a problem because the tribals were too diffident to assert themselves. In many instances, we had to order police protection, but the local police, who had over the years developed bonds with the non-tribal farmers, showed no enthusiasm for this 'social justice' programme.

I called the superintendent of police (SP) and asked him to instruct his subordinate officials that they 'must' provide protection to tribals whenever a request to that effect was made by the revenue authorities. But he demurred as well. The pent-up anger in the district police establishment over my demands boiled over, and unusually, the subordinate police officers took out a procession in Khammam town protesting against the 'unjust pressure' by the collector, no matter that under the police manual, the collector is, among other things, also the head of the police department in the district.* What rankled even more was that Santhanam called me, again on instructions from the chief minister as he was careful to tell me, and asked for an 'explanation' on why the police had taken out the procession. Whereas I thought it was the SP who should have been taken to task for this unlawful behaviour by the district police, it was I who was put in the dock. I was outraged but managed to keep my cool.

Within a few months, I found myself battling on several fronts—the non-tribals, local politicians, the judiciary, the police, the local media and the state administration in Hyderabad. And all this without much change on the ground. Remaining motivated was becoming a struggle.

It was in this scenario that Chief Minister Chenna Reddy came to Khammam on a two-day visit in October

---

* Although the District Police Act of 1861 is largely unamended, the collector-police relationship has evolved differently in different states. In states like Andhra Pradesh, Telangana, Tamil Nadu and Maharashtra, the police are mostly their own bosses. In Uttar Pradesh and Bihar, in contrast, the police defer to the collector if in part because what (s)he has to say matters for their assessment. A crude characterization is as follows. In UP and Bihar, 'district magistrates' have control, although less than ideal, over the police apparatus; 'deputy commissioners' in Punjab, Haryana and Karnataka have a middling role, while 'district collectors' in Andhra Pradesh and Tamil Nadu have much less control. It is also true that where district postings are concerned, police postings go through a more thorough political filtration process than postings of collectors and joint collectors.

1979, some eight months after I had taken over. When I received him at the railway station, much to my relief, he was quite civil to me. What struck me, though, was that he greeted Somi Reddy, the SP, with great verve and bonhomie. I gathered later that they were old acquaintances—Somi Reddy had been deputy superintendent of police in the Charminar area of Hyderabad when Chenna Reddy, rising through the ranks of politics, had political interests there.

The first day of the chief minister's tour, mostly in the non-tribal areas, went quite well. Chenna Reddy remained in an expansive mood; he even complimented me on occasion for some good work. It was on the second day, as we entered the tribal areas, that things got gradually difficult for me as the day wore on.

Every event where the chief minister cut a ribbon, laid a foundation stone or addressed a local gathering was overshadowed by scores of non-tribal farmers complaining about the injustice being meted out to them. And everywhere, the MLAs and other local politicians joined the chorus—and all this right in my presence. What struck me, though, was that none of them said anything harsh about me—they were only venting their grievance against my harsh actions. I could see that the chief minister's patience was wearing thin, and he was getting increasingly testy. Even as I was travelling in the car next to him, he became stiff and uncommunicative towards me.

By about 8 p.m., after an exhausting road trip of nearly ten hours, we reached the Bhadrachalam Inspection Bungalow (IB) for a brief stop whereafter the chief minister was to go to the railway station and catch the overnight train back to Hyderabad. There were no air-conditioned cars in those days, and we were all quite tired by the heat, dust and grime of the day.

As we approached the IB, we ran into huge crowds, which were swarming the premises—thousands of non-tribal farmers had gathered there to pour out their grievances to the chief minister and to urge him to stop the harsh and 'unjust' implementation of the LTR. Leading these crowds were MLAs, *panchayat samithi* presidents, partymen and politicos of all hues. Nobody needed to say anything; the situation was quite clear to everyone.

As he saw his vote bank evaporating, the chief minister couldn't contain himself. As he stepped on to the veranda of the IB, he looked at me for an explanation in front of that huge gathering. Chenna Reddy was known for his mercurial temper and for dressing down civil servants in front of others. I was quite nervous, worried that he might humiliate me in front of this huge gathering. But even as I began to explain, he stopped me short and snapped: 'If you want to fight me politically, join politics and do so. But don't remain in the IAS and play these games.'

For an IAS or IPS officer, to talk back to a chief minister is unthinkable, more so in a potentially explosive situation like that. In any case, he gave me no opportunity; he turned around abruptly and stormed into his car in a fierce burst of temper. He didn't offer me a seat in his car; I drove behind in the convoy in my own car. Mercifully, the train arrived shortly after we reached the railway station, and the chief minister left without another word exchanged between us. I did 'namaste' to him as the train moved, and it rankled that he ignored me.

The implementation of the LTR didn't stop after the chief minister's visit, but it certainly lost its momentum and enthusiasm. A couple of weeks later, when I happened to be in Hyderabad for a meeting, I called on the chief secretary and explained the situation to him, including the chief minister's outburst against me. I thought he would offer to speak to the chief minister on my behalf; instead, he said it would be far better if I spoke to him myself. I sought an appointment with the chief minister, but it never materialized.

Instead, what I got was yet another telephone call from Santhanam a couple of days later to say that the chief minister wanted me to put all LTR cases on hold since the government was contemplating an amendment to the regulation to address the grievances of non-tribal farmers. I demurred saying that it would hurt my credibility if I stopped the implementation abruptly. I was well within my rights to ask for orders in writing, but I had the good sense not to push it to the brink because no one, not even I, would have come out of it unblemished. That phone call left me with a deep feeling of anger and hurt.

I was quite agitated over how things had turned out. I agonized over the issue for a day, and then called up Santhanam and told him that I was applying for a month's leave; I needed a break to reflect and regroup. My leave was sanctioned within hours, and the government even posted a replacement as collector leaving no one in doubt that I would be reposted.

Within a month of the chief minister's visit, my Khammam collectorship had ended abruptly. I was quite sad to leave. I had traversed the learning curve and had a good understanding of the issues and challenges. I was getting comfortable with the place and people, including my staff. Most of all, I had a great team—Sheela Bhide was joint collector, her husband, Pradeep Bhide, was a project officer of SFDA, Bir Singh followed by Rentala Chandrashekhar were project officers of the Integrated Tribal Development Agency (ITDA) and Anil Kutti was assistant collector under training. R.P. Singh followed by Jannat Hussain were sub-collectors of Kothagudem while Rama Lakshman was sub-collector of Bhadrachalam. And Urmila was administrator of the (Nagarjuna Sagar Left Canal) Command Area, a post in which she didn't have to report to me. Eight direct-recruit IAS officers in one district all at the same time was an uncommon combination, and it was a lot of fun.

I was certainly going to miss Khammam.

Make haste slowly

Today, over forty years after Khammam, and over ten years into my retirement, I am able to look back on that experience more objectively. I made several mistakes.

First, I failed to see the big difference between the Parvathipuram and Khammam agencies. In the former, tribals had historically been exploited, and they lost their land to non-tribals because of indebtedness. There was pent-up anger and resentment over decades of injustice to them by the non-tribals and even by the administration. In the Khammam agency, on the other hand, the non-tribals bought the land from tribals in a market transaction, albeit an informal market. One could argue that the tribals were not paid a fair market price but it's difficult to make a case that they were cheated out of their land.

Second, it's true that tribals in both agencies were poor and many even destitute. But in the Khammam agency, it wasn't as if the non-tribal farmers were landed gentry. Many of them were small farmers themselves, and if thrown out of their land, they would lose their livelihood.

Finally, I acted in haste. I should have taken a little longer to study the problem and understand the sociology of the place before launching into action. Many of the subordinate revenue staff, having operated on the frontlines for years, had a good understanding of the ground situation. Had I solicited their advice, at least some of them would have advised temperance. I sought their suggestions on implementing the action plan but not on whether we should launch an action plan so abruptly. Needless to say, I should also have taken the superintendent of police and the top district police officials into confidence as we were formulating the action plan.

If I had made haste, but slowly, I probably would have had more success on the ground.* Because of my inexperience and overenthusiasm, I lost the battle as well as the war.

The Khammam experience is also a classic illustration of the 'logic of collective action'. The non-tribals who stood to lose their land if the implementation of the LTR went ahead were an organized interest group, able to mobilize and agitate their cause. Pitted against them were

---

* 'Making haste slowly', an oxymoron of sorts, comes from the Latin phrase, *Festina lente*.

tribals, poor, unlettered and too timid to organize into an interest group.

Time, as they say, heals all ill feelings. A decade later, in the early 1990s, Chenna Reddy returned as chief minister of Andhra Pradesh for a second time. I was then on Central deputation in the Ministry of Finance. When Chenna Reddy was once visiting Delhi, the AP Bhavan invited all of us, IAS and IPS officers of the AP cadre working in the Government of India, for a dinner with the chief minister. When we were lined up to be introduced to him, as soon as he saw me, he broke into a broad grin. He put his hand on my shoulder and asked Kumaraswamy Reddy, his secretary who was doing the introductions, if I was still the firebrand that he knew me as. I must also add here that Chenna Reddy is remembered fondly by old-time IAS and IPS officers as one of the ablest chief ministers of Andhra Pradesh.

The interlude in my district postings

During that rough patch in my career, Yugandhar, who was handling many jobs at that time, including that of managing director of the AP Small Scale Industrial Development Corporation (APSSIDC), took me under his wing. He requested the chief secretary to post me as executive director of the corporation. So, at the end of my leave, I ended up in that job in December 1979, my first posting in Hyderabad.

About six months into my tenure in APSSIDC, Yugandhar suggested that I should be out in the districts rather than spending time on a semi-desk job in the

APSSIDC. His point was that field experience is the most important asset of an IAS officer as he moves up the career ladder and I shouldn't forsake that opportunity. He spoke to the chief secretary, and after that suggested that I meet the chief secretary myself and reiterate the request. That I did.

It helped my case that there was a change of guard at the top. Because of factions within the ruling Congress party, Chenna Reddy was replaced by T. Anjaiah as chief minister. Although both were Telangana politicians, they couldn't have been more different. Anjaiah had risen from labour union ranks, was portly and amiable and had a great grassroots political sense—a sharp contrast to Chenna Reddy who was more educated, domineering, short-tempered and, of course, politically savvy.

The agonizing compulsory wait

Little did I realize when I requested the chief secretary for a posting as collector that I was setting myself up for nearly six months of agony, frustration, uncertainty and inconvenience. That story is worth recounting because although a 'compulsory wait' of nearly six months in my case was by happenstance, I learnt that it has now been weaponized by the political machinery to teach 'errant' officers a lesson.

In response to my request, I was posted serially as collector of Nellore, Cuddapah (now Kadapa) and Warangal districts. In each case, the posting remained only on paper because on each occasion, after the order was issued, I was verbally advised not to take charge. The problem was not so much with me per se but with the incumbents wanting to stay on or district politicians lobbying on their behalf. This impasse lasted for about three months. I continued to be on 'compulsory wait', which meant I wasn't getting paid. I would, of course, get all the arrears when I started in a regular post but until then, I was on my own.

The fourth paper posting in that saga was as collector of Krishna District. Soon after receiving orders, with great enthusiasm, I took an early morning train from Hyderabad to Vijayawada. At the Vijayawada railway station, I expected to witness an age-old custom—a motley bunch of about twenty-five staff coming to receive a new collector. Instead, I found a lone deputy tahsildar waiting for me on the platform. His instructions, he told me sheepishly, were to give me the message that my posting as collector of Krishna District was on hold and that I should return to Hyderabad. Helpfully, he had already bought a return ticket for me and put me on the next available train back to Hyderabad. I was back in Hyderabad late that night, tired, angry and frustrated.

As had become a practice by then, I met the chief secretary who I thought would resolve the problem. But much to my vexation, he suggested that I meet the chief minister myself.

Getting an appointment to meet Anjaiah was easy, but actually meeting him was exceedingly difficult. Typically, all through the day, every room in his house would be brimming with friends, followers, favour seekers and politicos of every hue, and he would go from room to room in his dhoti and *jubba* to talk and listen. Even on the rare occasion when you came face to face with him, it was almost impossible to get his undivided attention.

When on one rare occasion, I managed to get a message across to him about my plight, he told me in his typical Hyderabadi Telugu: 'Look, I know you are a good officer. I want to send you as collector. But I am unable to manage that because of politicians. Why don't you go and meet Sundarayya and convince him not to raise objections to your posting as collector of Krishna District?' Sundarayya was a prominent MLA from Krishna District; interestingly, he was not from the Congress party but belonged to the CPI (M).

I couldn't figure out whether this suggestion from a chief minister to a junior IAS officer was a plea of helplessness or an act of political savvy. Was the chief minister trying to use me to move out the incumbent collector, which he very much wanted to do but was unable to because of political pressures? It was, of course, out of the question that I would plead with an MLA to intercede on my posting, no matter that the chief minister himself had told me to.

And so my posting as collector of Krishna District melted away, and the wait continued for another month. Then one day, I received orders posting me as collector of Visakhapatnam. The incumbent collector, C.S. Rao, had gone abroad for a three-month training. The government couldn't keep the post vacant because panchayat elections had to be conducted. Before going to Visakhapatnam to take charge, I asked U.B. Raghavendra Rao (UBR), secretary to the chief minister, if this was a regular posting or a stopgap arrangement until C.S. Rao returned. UBR had a formidable reputation as one of the finest officers of the AP cadre. He looked at me quizzically and said: 'Look, Subba, the CM attaches great importance to who is the collector of Visakhapatnam because of his problems with the local politicians. He chose you specially because he is confident that you will run a balanced administration. Have no misgivings. There is no move to post C.S. Rao back.'

With that reassurance, off I went to Visakhapatnam, took charge as collector, presided over the conduct of panchayat elections, and was promptly posted out after ten weeks when C.S. Rao returned. I learnt later that UBR was indeed being honest. My posting as collector of Visakhapatnam was meant to be a regular one, and C.S. Rao had been informed accordingly. However, the chief minister seemed to have succumbed to pressure from the politically powerful district minister who asked that I be moved out because 'I was too arrogant'.

Prakasam—a short but steady tenure

After another month of compulsory wait, I was posted as collector of Prakasam District. Some colleagues advised that I should rush there and take charge given the bitter experience of the last five aborted postings. I didn't; I waited for a full week to ensure that what was by then the standard operating procedure—verbal instructions from the government to hold on—was not going to roll out. After making sure that the posting survived a week, I prepared to move.

Before going to Prakasam District, I went and met UBR. He came closest to being an *Ajatashatru*, universally liked and respected for his 'efficiency with a human face'. Venting my frustration at these repeated assaults on my district postings, I told him, 'I've learnt my lesson. Once I take charge in Prakasam, I am going to go for a total personality makeover. I will try and please everyone.' UBR, wise man that he was, smiled and said, 'Perish the thought. Don't try to be anything but yourself. And mind you, you are good as you are.'

With that admonition and encouragement, I joined as collector of Prakasam District in August 1981 after a compulsory wait of twenty-six weeks and a paper tour of nearly a third of the state.

Prakasam District was so named to honour the memory of freedom fighter and former chief minister of the composite Madras State, Tanguturi Prakasam Pantulu, who belonged to this district. It was, I was told, the first district in the country to be named after an individual.

Prakasam District had a small coastal belt that was relatively fertile and prosperous, but much of the hinterland was dry, rainfall-dependent and poor. The district was prone to cyclones along the coast and to drought in the interior. Guntur District to the north of Prakasam used to be the hub of tobacco cultivation. But in the 1970s, Guntur farmers had shifted to cotton both because of the growing backlash against tobacco cultivation and the relative shift in economics between tobacco and cotton. Much of the tobacco cultivation had therefore shifted south to Prakasam.

Prakasam could boast of no major industry. The economy was almost entirely agriculture-dependent—farming and some fishing along the coast.

Ongole, the headquarters of Prakasam District, is renowned for the Ongole bull, famous for its strength and aggressiveness, and used for cattle breeding across the country. It is used in bullfights in Mexico and parts of East Africa and is, of course, the standard fare of festival bullfights in Tamil Nadu and Andhra Pradesh. The mascot of the 2002 National Games in India was Veera, an Ongole bull.

I must say I had a fairly good run as collector of Prakasam. It was also uneventful—no elections, no natural disasters, no major law-and-order problems. Most of the politicians of the district—MLAs, MPs, the *zilla parishad* chairman and panchayat samithi presidents were all from the ruling Congress party. That, of course, didn't mean much because they all belonged to different factions, and their rivalries were bitter and occasionally violent. But what worked for me was that I had developed a good rapport with all of them, treated all of them equally and they all believed that I was unbiased and respected me.

Of all my district postings, I travelled the most on average in Prakasam. Urmila was a project officer of SFDA, and Mallik, our older son, was one year old. We used to plan work to be able to travel together to the extent possible, with Mallik in tow. As Sheel Banerjee, my friend and colleague, once remarked, few kids in the country would have put in as much road mileage as Mallik during his infancy.

I was once on the road with Ramakrishna Reddy, the zilla parishad chairman, to inspect drought relief works. We stopped at a roadside IB for a tea break. The walls of the IB were characteristically damp and shabby, and painted in horrendous colours. I remarked to the chairman: 'Why can't our engineers at least choose more pleasing colours for public buildings?' Reddy smiled at me and said: 'Have you seen any of the engineers' houses? Their walls are as tastefully painted as yours and mine.' The point was that when paint companies made paints, they had some sediment left over. They would mix all those leftovers and make a cocktail paint, which they would then sell at an unofficial discount. Our engineers bought those 'sedimented paints' so as to pocket the discount.

No file can teach you lessons of this type.

My cruising innings as collector of Prakasam District came to an end within ten months as I was selected for a Humphrey Fellowship to study at MIT in the US starting in August that year.

Dirtying your hands

District administration, without a doubt, has changed a lot since I was a district collector over forty years ago. Across the rural hinterland of the country, poverty has declined, awareness levels have increased, most villages are connected by road and have a safe and reliable drinking water source, education and health have become more accessible, many have access to toilets and virtually everyone has a cell phone. All this has helped raise people's aspirations and expectations. Importantly, the relative balance between politicians and civil servants has shifted towards the former. Typically, district-level politicians of today rival civil servants in their education and exposure levels, and the public holds them to account much more effectively than ever before.

Even in that change and flux, the district collector remains the kingpin; she can, and indeed should, make a difference. Being a district collector remains the defining job of an IAS career and it is by far one of the most interesting, fulfilling and responsible jobs in the country.

A World Bank friend of mine, a Hungarian, once said to me: 'Subba, if God asked me, "What job do you want?", I'd request him to let me be the collector of a district in India at least for a few years.'

Schrödinger's cat

Schrödinger's cat is one of the most famous thought experiments in physics. It was designed by the Austrian physicist Erwin Schrödinger in 1935 to illustrate a vexing challenge in the interpretation of quantum mechanics.

Imagine a cat locked up in a canister with a capsule of poison gas next to it. If a random event occurs, the capsule will burst open, and the cat will die of poisoning. The question to an outside observer is, 'Is the cat alive or dead?'

In the non-quantum world that we experience in our everyday lives, the cat is either alive or dead. We will know the answer one way or the other if we open the canister and look. In the quantum world, though, the answer is that the cat is both alive and dead. It is our observation when we open the canister and look that determines which of the two possible outcomes has materialized. At the risk of oversimplification, in the quantum world, it is the observation that determines the outcome.

The reason I am citing Schrödinger's cat here is to emphasize the importance of field-level IAS officers going and seeing what's happening on the ground. Young IAS officers I randomly run into these days tell me that they are tied down to their offices because they are always 'on call'. Besides, they say, digital technologies enable them to monitor what's happening on the ground without having to go there. Perhaps I am an old-timer, but I firmly believe that IAS officers in field postings being tied down to their desks is a decidedly unwelcome development. They should remember Schrödinger's cat—it is their going and seeing that makes good things happen and prevents bad things from happening.

7

Racing to the Bottom

Industrial Promotion in the Old World

Is there a formula that determines IAS postings? There doesn't seem to be one. Indeed, it's not even possible to discern a formula by connecting the dots looking back. I'd like to believe that there is an element of career management that goes into posting decisions, but of course, there's a lot of luck too. And IAS officers jostling for glamorous, important and powerful posts is quite common.

That preface is to put in context the opportunity I got early in my career to work in the general area of industrial promotion for five years, albeit in three different postings. I should put this down to happenstance rather than any deliberate career planning by the authorities.

Five years in industrial promotion

In India, the 1970s was the decade of the Green Revolution. Agriculture departments at the state level played an important role in popularizing high-yielding varieties of food grains, particularly wheat and rice, and encouraging farmers to shift from food crops to commercial crops wherever such a shift was feasible. The campaign was led jointly by specialists in the agriculture departments who provided technical inputs and generalist IAS officers who provided coordination.

By the 1980s, by way of development priority, attention at the state level shifted from agriculture to industry for a variety of reasons—jobs, balanced regional development and higher tax revenues. States began to compete in the promotion of medium, small and micro enterprises, which have since earned the moniker of MSMEs. Many aspiring IAS officers wanted to work in the industries domain for the challenge and opportunity it provided. I lucked out in this regard.

My first posting in the industry sector was as executive director in the AP Small Scale Industrial Development Corporation (1980–81) when Yugandhar took me under his wing after my Khammam collectorship ended abruptly. Later, when I returned from the Humphrey Fellowship, T.L. Sankar, who was principal secretary of the industries department, requested the chief secretary to post me as the director of industries. The chief secretary thought that I didn't have sufficient experience for the job and posted me instead as executive director in the AP Industrial Development Corporation (1983–85) so I could apprentice under the managing director. A few years later, I was posted as managing director of the AP State Finance Corporation (1987–88), which I suspect was a 'reward' for the unglamorous job of arrack bottling that I had just completed 'successfully'. Put together, I had worked in the general area of industrial promotion for over five years, and it was a rich learning experience.*

God-like figures dispensing industrial licences

In the pre-1991 reforms period, the entire industrial promotion scenario was governed by a dogmatic faith in licencing. Licencing, it was believed, was necessary to ensure that scarce capital was not wasted in producing unnecessary goods 'like lipstick, for example', as an official of the time put it. Aspiring investors therefore had to make several trips to Delhi to lobby for their applications for licences and permits. Mid-level officials in the Ministry of Industries and the Directorate General of Technical Development (DGTD) who dispensed patronage were, to us, god-like figures. The post of joint secretary in charge of the secretariat for industrial approvals used to be much coveted.

But this was also the time when we were seeing the 'East Asian Miracle' play out and began to realize the heavy price we were paying for our dirigiste regime. The Rajiv Gandhi years in the late 1980s saw some hesitant reforms, possibly to test the political waters, but they didn't go far enough.

Notwithstanding the licence-permit regime, this was still a heady time to be in industrial promotion. In Andhra Pradesh, we couldn't boast of any big industrial houses.

---

* For good measure, I was briefly non-executive chairman of the AP Industrial Infrastructure Corporation for a couple of months much later in my career—a stopgap posting when I returned from the World Bank and was awaiting a posting in Delhi.

Even the few that there were, such as Andhra Sugars, were in traditional agro-based industries like sugar and paper. Even our relatively big farmers who had investable surpluses couldn't think beyond rice mills. Our challenge was therefore to encourage entrepreneurship. We focused mainly on two groups—farmers with surplus income and technocrats in public sector enterprises such as BHEL, HMT and IDPL who wanted to strike out on their own. Both groups were by definition first-generation entrepreneurs. It's gratifying that some of the entrepreneurs of that time have been trailblazers such as Dr Anji Reddy of Reddy Labs who put India on the world pharmaceutical map.

Market for shoes

In entrepreneurship seminars, they tell the story of a mid-level executive of a leading multinational in shoes being sent to a developing country to explore the market for shoes there. He comes back and tells the management that there is no market for shoes there because 'no one wears shoes'. An executive from a rival company sent on a similar mission returns and reports to the management that there is a huge market for shoes there because 'no one wears shoes!' Our task then was to learn to see the positive side for opportunities and convince our entrepreneurs to do so too. It was a huge learning curve for both us and the prospective entrepreneurs.

Today, as multinationals are pursuing a China+1 policy as insurance against overdependence on China, India is competing with other emerging markets to be the +1. Curiously, the biggest complaint of potential investors today, as it was during the 1980s when I was engaged in industrial promotion, is the high transaction costs of doing business in India.

It was quite a common practice at that time for states to try to attract potential investors by offering them incentives such as subsidized utilities, sales tax holidays, government land at throwaway prices and what have you. The states knew that it was a race to the bottom, and ultimately self-defeating, but there was no one willing to call a halt to this. Potential investors lapped up all this and even pitted one state against the other to take advantage of the competition.

I sometimes asked investors in private moments how much weight they attached to these sops. Their typical response: 'All these are welcome. But what matters to us in choosing a location more than all the freebies that the government offers are the rule of law and a conducive environment for business. We don't want your inspectors coming to our factories to nose around. We will send whatever reports they want. We don't want local politicians politicizing our labour unions.'

It's typical of foreign investors also to bargain for better terms by pitting one country against another. Much later, when I was finance secretary in Delhi during 2007–08, potential investors would often seek a meeting with me.

Their typical spiel would go like this: 'We arrived last night from Shanghai.'

'What did the Chinese offer you?' we would ask eagerly.

They would reel off a slew of incentives that the Chinese had offered.

And how long will they take to deliver this package?

'Oh, in six months, max.'

We'd then confer among ourselves just for a moment and say, 'Okay, if the Chinese will give you all that in six months, we will give you an even more attractive package, and in three months.'

And here's typically what would happen. The Chinese, having promised to deliver in six months would deliver in three months. And we, having promised to deliver in three months, would fail to deliver even in three years.

I'd like to believe that over the years our delivery mechanisms have become more efficient and credible. That states compete with one another for investment is a sign of healthy federalism, but that competition must be based not on concessions and incentives but on providing a conducive environment for business activity. The transaction costs for investors are largely incurred at the operational level and are due to the delays and callousness of the front-end bureaucracy. Rolling out red carpets in Delhi or state capitals like Jaipur, Bhopal or Hyderabad won't amount to much if inefficiency and indifference persist at the front end. After all, it's the weakest link that determines the strength of the system.

Industries are sick but industrialists are healthy

Industrial promotion corporations at the state level typically had a slew of schemes to provide seed capital as well as loans to investors, particularly to first-generation entrepreneurs. I used to be quite troubled by the high default rate in loan repayments. Loan defaults arose because of delays in project implementation as also continued losses as the plants went into operation. Rescheduling loans, which

also included topping up existing loans with new loans—
what has come to be called 'evergreening'—to prevent
units from going sick was a big part of our job chart. The
high levels of delinquency often made me wonder if it was
due to a lack of entrepreneurship or if indeed there was
an element of adverse selection in the type of clientele that
approached us for support. Oftentimes I felt that we would
be better off accepting the sunk costs and writing off the
loans rather than putting good money after bad, but that
was not an acceptable public policy.

'Industries are sick but industrialists are healthy' was
the refrain at that time, and possibly so even today. The
most common modus operandi was for promoters to
siphon off their investment during project implementation
itself by inflating costs with the result that by the time the
project went into operation, they had no skin in the game;
they were simply playing around with public money.

As the saying goes, if you default on a Rs 10 lakh loan,
it's your problem, but if you default on a Rs 100 crore
loan, it's the bank's problem. I saw this play out in my own
experience. When small and marginal farmers defaulted on
loans under the DRDA schemes, typically no more than
a few thousand rupees, the lenders would go after them
to attach whatever meagre belongings they had and push
them to the margins of subsistence. But we allowed, and
still do, industrial entrepreneurs who defaulted on loans
worth crores of rupees to get away scot-free.

In the business of industrial promotion, there is, of
course, a need for encouraging risk-taking and to have
mechanisms for dealing with honest failures. But in doing
so, we must guard against the moral hazard of encouraging

dishonest entrepreneurs and wilful defaulters to thrive. Our failure, if I could call it that, was that we didn't have a foolproof mechanism for distinguishing between genuine failures and 'stealing by stealth'.

NTR scowls at me but then apologizes in stealth

In pursuit of loan recovery, we seldom closed a running unit no matter the extent of default in the hope that the operations would improve and we would get our money back with interest. But when a unit was closed because the management ran out of funds even to meet the variable costs, it was quite common for the State Finance Corporation (SFC) to seize the assets of the unit and sell them in an open auction to salvage whatever we could of the loan. Over the years, the SFC had streamlined the drill of following all the legal and procedural guidelines when seizing the assets of a unit and putting them up for sale. Of course, promoters complained that we were being high-handed but that was par for the course. Much of the seizure of assets and their sale happened below the managing director's radar.

One morning I got a call from the chief minister N.T. Rama Rao's (NTR's) office that he wanted to see me urgently. Within about half an hour, I was in the presence of a scowling NTR. Evidently, the SFC had sold the assets of a unit in which a sitting MLA had an interest. The MLA had complained to the chief minister that we hadn't given the management sufficient opportunity to run the unit to generate revenues. Also, if the SFC had agreed to reschedule the loans and give an additional loan, the unit could have been revived. And to top it all, it was alleged that the SFC had sold the assets in a fire sale far below their market value.

Allegations of this nature were standard fare whenever we attached the assets of units but of course, not all of them had access to the chief minister. I tried to explain the SFC's position to NTR. The MLA had embellished the story to make it appear as if the SFC had singled out this particular unit for extraordinary treatment out of vengeance. That was far from the case; seizing the assets of a defaulting unit and putting them for sale in an auction was standard practice in the SFC, and we routinely sold the assets of a couple of units every month. But NTR was in no mood to listen to my version, scowled all through the exchange, and within ten minutes, I was ushered out of the office of a seething chief minister.

Unfortunately, that wasn't the end of the matter. Later in the week, I got a notice to appear before a special session of the Public Undertakings Committee (PUC) to discuss the SFC's operations. Although couched in general terms, the trigger for the meeting was obvious. It was a tense and angry meeting stretching over three hours with members accusing the SFC under my leadership of doing everything possible to destroy the industrial potential of the state. As is common in meetings such as this, we went round and round. Ironically, members questioned the low recovery rate even while accusing us of harsh recovery practices without seeing the apparent contradiction in their positions. The meeting expectedly ended inconclusively. I was angry, tired and exasperated. But on reflection, I realized that this was par for the course. I shouldn't take umbrage at being called to account no matter my feeling that it was unfair.

A couple of weeks after that stormy PUC meeting, quite by coincidence, I got a posting to Delhi as a director in the Ministry of Finance. This was very much on the cards since I had opted for Central deputation. When the file went to the chief minister for approval to release me to go on Central deputation, NTR, who was unaware of these bureaucratic processes, thought that I had engineered a posting to the Centre out of pique at his 'ill-treatment of me'. The secretary to the chief minister, I understand, tried to explain to him that the two developments had no connection, but NTR wasn't satisfied. He asked to see me.

When I met him, short of apologizing directly, he said everything possible in an apparent effort to mollify me. 'Brother, *we* have our political compulsions. But, *we* have nothing against you. You are one of *our* best officers. Why do you want to go away to Delhi? *We* have launched so many projects to develop the state. You should stay and work with *us*.'

He was, of course, using his trademark royal '*we*'. As much as I was touched by this genuine gesture, I was also anxious that he might take this soft pressure too far and not approve my Central deputation. Urmila had already joined the Ministry of Defence on Central deputation two months earlier, and we had pulled the children out of their school in Hyderabad and done some spadework for their transfer to a good school in Delhi. Most of all, I believed a Central deputation at this stage would be helpful career-wise.

I thanked the chief minister and said something to the effect that I belonged to the AP cadre, and in that sense, the state government had ownership of me but added that gaining some experience in Delhi would be helpful to me

and that it would make me a more useful civil servant.
That meeting ended very agreeably, and from NTR's
perspective, we had managed a truce.

A couple of days later, he signed off on my Delhi
deputation.

Queuing for computers

When I was working on industrial promotion in the
mid-1980s, computers were still a rarity. They were still so
much of a wonder that 'The Computer' was *Time* magazine's
'Man of the Year' for 1982. Knowledge of programming was
quite limited. Things like 'we computerized our accounts' or
'our attendance roster is now on computer' used to be big
boasts not just in the government but also in the private
sector. There was a lot of amazement at what computers
could do to ease record-keeping but not enough realization
that computers would not clean our data, and that if we fed
it garbage, we would only get garbage in return.

Computers were still such a novelty that whenever we
acquired a new machine, we would break a coconut and do
a simple puja. Because they were expensive, they had to be
rationed. Officers used to vie for a place in the 'computer
queue' not so much for the computer itself but because
their office would get air-conditioned in order to be able to
house a computer.

If there is no file on your table, you are no good

Files define a bureaucrat; they are an inevitable part of an
IAS life. It's as if we can't get anything done unless we

create a file in the first instance. Raghav, our younger son, used to tell me when he was little, 'What is so great about your IAS job? All you have to do is sign files. Even I can do that.'

In common perception, the more files an officer has on his table, the more important his job and the harder he is working. Equally, officers who feel 'martyred'—sent off on punishment postings to inconsequential jobs because they defied political diktats—defiantly maintain a scrupulously clean desk to show that they have been 'shunted off' to jobs where there is absolutely no work.

There is an entire mythology that has been built around files but here I want to share a cute little story of my own.

In 1988, when I was in the SFC, Vatsala, Urmila's sister, an IAS officer of the Karnataka cadre, stayed with us for a month along with her little daughters, aged seven and five. She had been deputed for a four-week training programme in Hyderabad and opted to stay at home because of the girls.

One evening after dinner, I was at my study table at home working on my files. Kochu, the younger girl, saw me in the act. 'Boys also sign files,' she said in absolute amazement at this role reversal. Up until then, she had only seen her mother 'sign files'.

A lesson to me on how gender stereotyping of everyday tasks such as 'this is a woman's job', and 'this is a man's job' are culturally ingrained rather than innate.

Politically correct either way

N.D. Tiwari was the industries minister at the Centre during 1984–85 when I was in the APIDC. Entrepreneurs from Andhra Pradesh who applied for licences would typically go to him to plead their case for a licence. Tiwari is often reported to have told them, 'Sure, I will give you a licence but why don't you take your project to UP?'

Vengal Rao, who was our chief minister in Andhra Pradesh, later succeeded Tiwari as union industries minister in the Rajiv Gandhi cabinet. When entrepreneurs from Andhra Pradesh went to him to lobby for their applications, he typically told them, 'It's a good project. It'd have been an easy decision for me if your project was not in AP but in UP, for example. On applications from AP, I have to be more careful because people will blame me for being biased.'

N.D. Tiwari and Vengal Rao, both very competent political leaders, had the larger public good in mind but had two different, and arguably valid, perceptions of political correctness.

Azharuddin

Mohammad Azharuddin, captain of the Indian cricket team in the 1990s, was a national celebrity. For us from Hyderabad, he was very special—someone who showcased our wonderful city to the world. A stylish batsman and a debonair personality, his achievements inspired millions of children across the country.

Mallik and Raghav, our two sons, then in their teens, were among his huge number of fans. Needless to say, Azhar's cricketing exploits were a regular staple of our dinner-table conversation, and, of course, arguments.

And then, one day, we spotted him, in flesh and blood. On a Sunday morning, my sons and I had gone to the Begumpet Airport in Hyderabad to receive Urmila who was returning from an official trip to Delhi. As we were waiting, we saw Azharuddin enter the airport along with a group of four or five people, with all the gravitas, self-assurance and flamboyance befitting his celebrity status.

Mid-morning on a Sunday, the airport wasn't very busy. Mallik and Raghav jumped up with excitement at this unexpected turn in their fortunes and insisted with feverish urgency that we should go and greet him. As a mid-level, faceless bureaucrat, I would be a non-entity for him. I was apprehensive that he may not take kindly to this interference.

But in seconds, the situation went out of my control as the two boys rushed towards him, leaving me with no alternative but to follow them. 'Mr Azharuddin, my sons want to shake your hand,' I said sheepishly.

I immediately sensed that we had pushed him into a standard dilemma that celebrities confront—not wanting to offend fans but at the same time unable to suppress irritation at fan adulation at inappropriate moments. With impatience writ large on his face, he quickly brushed his palms with the boys' hands and moved on. For my sons, of course, this was a heady moment. The bragging rights they had just acquired were a treasure they would show off in school the next day.

Azharuddin fell from grace in 2000 as he was found to be involved in a match-fixing scandal.

* * *

Fast forward to 2012. I was Governor, RBI, and Azharuddin was a member of the Lok Sabha from Moradabad in Uttar Pradesh.

Late one evening, I found myself on a bus at Mumbai airport being ferried to the aircraft for a flight to Delhi. The bus was jam-packed with not even standing space left. In that milieu, a middle-aged man elegantly dressed in slacks and a blazer with a smart young man in tow made his way towards me and introduced himself.

'Sir, I am Azharuddin. I am also from Hyderabad,' he said politely. 'Of course, I know,' I replied with obvious delight in my voice. 'My son wants to shake hands with you,' Azhar said, thrusting the young man towards me, and we pumped flesh.

We conversed briefly thereafter. His younger son, Ayazuddin, had died in a road accident the previous year. I condoled with him as he told me with palpable sorrow in his voice about how the motorcycle involved in the accident was one he himself had presented to his son a few months earlier.

In a few minutes, we made it to the aircraft parked on the tarmac and went our separate ways.

As I settled in my seat, I couldn't help but reflect on the dramatic reversal of roles in shaking hands—an inevitable part of the ebb and flow of life.

8

Why Me?

Officer on Special Duty for Arrack Bottling

In May 1986, I was transferred and posted as Officer on Special Duty (OSD) in the Revenue Department. The transfer itself was not a surprise since I had already spent nearly three years as executive director in the Andhra Pradesh Industrial Development Corporation (APIDC), which was longer than the average tenure of IAS postings in the state. What was a surprise though was the abruptness of it all and the post to which I was transferred. An OSD is an intriguing designation that triggers both mystique and suspicion about the person and the job.

The transfer order was sent to me by a special messenger mid-morning on a Monday and shortly thereafter, there was a phone call from the chief secretary's office that I must assume charge in the new post immediately and see him that afternoon.

Being moved out of a job that I had gotten comfortable with—perhaps too comfortable, according to some people—was deeply unsettling. I was flustered and confused. The posting order didn't indicate what the 'special duty' was. Why wasn't it more specific? What job was I getting into? Why did the chief secretary want to see me urgently? Had I done something wrong, and was I being moved out to facilitate an inquiry? My mind was full of questions.

Unsettling transfer

I relinquished charge in APIDC within half an hour of receiving the orders and went to the Revenue Department in the secretariat, just fifteen minutes away, only to discover that Mr Doraiswamy, the principal secretary, was on leave that day. I went to see the joint secretary in charge of administration. He too had not seen the posting order until I showed it to him and was equally clueless on what it was all about. As I sat in his office, bewildered and flustered about the sudden developments, he called the assistant secretary in charge to instruct him on the paperwork. The first thing the assistant secretary said was: 'We don't have space in the department to accommodate an OSD.' Exactly the type of welcome statement I wanted to hear!

The assistant secretary left the room, his demeanour making no secret of his irritation at the additional burden that had fallen on him, and returned an hour later with the paperwork. The signing done, and after hurriedly sharing the frugal lunch that the joint secretary had brought from home, I rushed to the chief secretary's office in the adjacent block of the secretariat.

I didn't have to wait long as Sravan Kumar, the chief secretary, was as eager to see me as I was to see him. As I entered his office, I found that U.B. Raghavendra Rao (UBR), secretary to the chief minister, was also sitting there—evidently waiting for me.* The gist of what Sravan Kumar told me was this.

The chief minister, NTR, known for his strong views that the poor were being plunged into misery because of their problems with alcohol, wanted to impose prohibition in the state. But the finance department pushed back saying that the government simply could not afford to sacrifice the excise revenue on alcohol. If indeed we went ahead, it would be impossible to implement the CM's populist schemes, including his signature 'rice at Rs 2 per kg' scheme. Forced into a Hobson's choice, NTR decided to defer prohibition to a later day.[†]

Not one to accept defeat so easily, though, NTR said, 'Okay, if I can't prevent my poor people from drinking, I at least want to make sure that they don't die drinking adulterated liquor.' The conversation rolled on and within fifteen minutes it was decided that the government would set up liquor (arrack)[‡] bottling plants in every district, supply only bottled liquor to contractors

---

* Unfortunately, UBR (1965 batch of the IAS) died in a road accident in 1987. An officer and a gentleman in the true sense of the term, had he lived on, he was sure to have reached the very top of the civil service ladder.

[†] NTR would go on to impose prohibition in his third term in 1994.

[‡] Arrack is an alcoholic beverage produced by fermenting palm sap, sugarcane or molasses. It is the alcohol of choice of low-income segments.

licensed by the government and mandate them to sell only this bottled liquor.

Impatient as he always was, NTR wanted the bottled liquor programme to be launched by the start of the following financial year—just about nine months away. Within five minutes, it was decided that since this was the chief minister's priority, instead of entrusting the job to the Excise Department, the project would be implemented through a full-fledged OSD housed in the Revenue Department.

For good measure, Sravan Kumar told me that he had suggested to the CM that the best person for the OSD job was Subbarao and that the CM had readily agreed to the suggestion. That discussion with the CM took place early that morning at around 6 a.m., and the transfer order was issued soon after the chief secretary reached his office. Sravan Kumar's final instructions to me were that I must go and see the CM early the next morning at 5.30 a.m.

Several questions bubbled up in my mind about when, where and how to get started on this bewildering assignment, but by then I had neither the energy nor the enthusiasm to raise them.

As it happened, I was consumed by just one question: 'Why me?' In a system where IAS transfer orders were communicated callously, I was deeply conscious, of course, that a briefing of the sort that the chief secretary had just given me—a mid-level officer—was unusual. I was also touched that he tried to pep up my spirits by making it look like I had been specially chosen for a challenging assignment.

But the 'why me' question still raged in my mind. After all, I had not demonstrated any special talent for a project management type of assignment, much less for one involving bottling liquor. I could reel off the names of at least ten officers of comparable seniority who had demonstrated a special flair for such assignments.

It was late afternoon by the time I left the chief secretary's office. Had I been level-headed and efficient, my next step would have been to try and find out more about what the job involved by going across to the excise commissioner's office. But by then, I was so emotionally and mentally drained that I had no mind space for any of that.

I had half a mind to go back to the assistant secretary in the Revenue Department to renew my request for office space but I lacked the courage to face him again. So, I went home brooding and sulking, not knowing whom to be upset with and where to vent my frustration.

Later that evening, I learnt that the government had posted an IAS colleague, D.V.L.N. Murthy, as the MD of APIDC. For sure, Murthy was very well regarded and had a well-earned reputation for integrity and efficiency. Nevertheless, I had grown to believe over the previous couple of years, working at the level of CEO minus one in the same organization, that I was being groomed for this top job. My irrational mind was angry that the government had ignored my experience and credentials for the job although my rational mind was telling me that it was vain on my part to nurture such notions of entitlement.

As I sat at home brooding, I couldn't brush off the thought of 'why me'. My biggest concern was that this assignment was not doable in nine months. I was deliberately being set up for failure, no matter that I couldn't think of any good reason why anyone should want to so set me up. Moreover, this was by no means a career-enhancing job that would burnish my CV. What do you tell family and friends who inquire about your current assignment? How embarrassing to say that you are bottling liquor! You get into the IAS with aspirations of changing the world, and you end up bottling liquor?

Late that evening, as if sensing by some telepathy my despondency and anger, UBR called to say, 'Subba, I could sense that you were very upset and agitated this afternoon in the chief secretary's office. I want you to know that the CM, in fact, rejected a few other names that the chief secretary suggested for the OSD job, but his eyes lit up when your name came up. He has a good impression of you. I think you should take this as a challenge and live up to the confidence he has reposed in you.' No wonder UBR was known as Ajatashatru.

NTR's battle for prohibition

I contemplated the meeting with the CM the following morning with some trepidation. If I had to reach his place by 5.30 a.m., I would have to leave home at the latest by 4.30 a.m. Since the assistant secretary had not yet bestowed his kindness on me, I did not have an official car. So, at 4 a.m., I walked to the Punjagutta junction and took an auto to NTR's house (camp office, as it is known in jargon) in Abids, in downtown Hyderabad.

NTR started his day early, typically by 4 a.m., and also finished early, by 4 p.m. The entire administration had, of course, adjusted to these timings. It was particularly hard on his personal staff who not only had to start early with him but also had to keep going till late in the evening much after he had retired for the day. While it is common for officers to have lunch in the office, UBR typically had his dinner too in the office.

By the time I reached NTR's place shortly after 5 a.m., it was brimming with energy and activity. Ministers, senior officers and public figures were walking in with self-confidence and self-importance while the entrance halls and verandas were choc-a-bloc with an odd medley of MPs and MLAs, party functionaries, minor politicos, public figures, influence peddlers, petitioners, hangers-on and in NTR's case, a sampling of the larger public who just wanted a glimpse of the man whom they looked upon as God. The police and security were in full force, managing the people and the traffic—waving in ministers, senior politicians and senior officers but pulling aside others for vetting and security checks.

Since I was not senior enough by then to be a frequent visitor to the CM's office, the security staff did not recognize me by face. Besides, I had arrived in an auto-rickshaw. So, I was pulled aside for questioning about who I was and why I wanted to see the CM. The questioning was proving to be both embarrassing and vexatious. Thankfully, UBR spotted me just then and took me by the arm to lead me inside, waving off the security.

I was ushered into NTR's inner sanctum shortly before 6 a.m. The chief secretary was there as were the principal revenue secretary, the excise commissioner and of course, UBR. As soon as he saw me, NTR unleashed a charm offensive.

'Brother, as you know we* have a sacred responsibility to protect our poor people from falling prey to the unscrupulous bootleggers who sell adulterated liquor. We have to wean them away from this terrible habit of drinking, which is destroying their lives and livelihoods. That will take some time. Meanwhile, we must eliminate adulterated liquor. We have therefore decided to supply only bottled liquor to liquor contractors. We have specially chosen you for this sacred task because of your track record and because we know that you share our government's deep concern for the poor.'

He said this in dramatized Telugu, deploying his extraordinary acting skills, using facial expressions, hand gestures and voice intonation to demonstrate, in that short speech, his abhorrence for drinking, contempt for 'unscrupulous bootleggers', abiding concern for the poor and strong confidence in my ability to implement his programme. I must admit that it felt nice to be so complimented by the CM no matter if you were aware that he did that often and it was nothing special.

NTR added for good measure: 'Brother, do come and see us without hesitation if you have any problem.' This was the most reassuring thing I had heard in the past day. Little did I realize that I was going to put him to the test on this.

I thought of negotiating a longer time frame but decided against it. I didn't even know what the project involved. It would be better to make a preliminary estimate of the costs and time and come armed with proper arguments

---

* NTR always spoke in the royal 'we'.

to substantiate my request should I decide to bargain for more time.

The meeting with NTR lasted barely five minutes. As I was getting up to leave, NTR picked up a sheet of paper from his side table with a flourish, looked at it gleefully and passed it on to the chief secretary. Sravan Kumar looked at it briefly and handed it to me with a faint smile. It was a pencil sketch of clouds of various shapes and sizes and the phrase 'Varuni Vahini' written in Telugu in Gothic script. 'Brother, use this as the design.' He wanted the design to be etched on the bottles.

NTR had evidently come up with this sketch the previous evening, much as he must have sketched background designs for the settings of his movies. Although I knew Telugu well enough, I couldn't decipher what 'Varuni Vahini' meant and realized only after asking around that this was a Sanskritized version of the nectar consumed by angels.

NTR may have expected me to thank him for lightening my burden by taking on one of my tasks. But frankly, I was irritated. There were so many things we had to organize to get this project on stream; an appropriate design for the bottle was nowhere on the horizon at that time.

Given a tough task and then abandoned

I went home after this meeting with the CM, had breakfast and landed up in the Revenue Department at 10 a.m. sharp. The assistant secretary, who sauntered in half an hour later, brushed me off, saying nonchalantly that he needed at least two days to find a room for me as he had to rework his entire space management master plan. Didn't I understand how complex that task was? I was livid, and the uppermost thought in my mind was, 'Okay, if you treat me like this, I am sure to get an opportunity and I will fix you.' I kept my cool though, realizing that this show of anger would be self-destructive.

The joint secretary kindly offered me his car, and I went across to the excise commissioner's office, about fifteen minutes away. I had no prior exposure to the department; both the people and the jobs were new to me. The excise commissioner gave me an overview of the department and its functions and introduced me to his top team. But he got across the message that he and his staff were already overburdened with their regular work and wouldn't be able to offer me much support. In short, I was on my own. Just what I wanted to hear in that moment of despondency!

Not knowing what else to do, I went home and continued to brood. I felt abandoned—given a tough, almost impossible, job, with no office, no support staff and no one to handhold or counsel me.

Subconsciously, I knew that my bitterness over this unexpected transfer was irrational. As an IAS officer, I was duty-bound to work anywhere the government posted me. Besides, why should I feel that I was being singled out for such misfortune? There must have been hundreds of officers before me who had experienced similar rough patches in their careers. Also, was it not hubris on my part to believe that this job was too 'lowly' for me?

I went to sleep that night consciously forcing myself to see things in their proper perspective. After all, this was not the end of the world!

I get cracking

I got up the next morning with a new resolve. If liquor bottling was the job given to me, I would plunge into it and do my best. Why should I start off with the negative thought that this would set back my career? Even if I failed, it's better to have tried and failed rather than not tried at all.

In that positive frame of mind, I went to my old office in APIDC and started consulting some of my colleagues there, especially those who had a technical background, on how to get started. I also persuaded an engineer and an accountant from there to join me on deputation. I was deeply grateful that they were giving up the comfort of well-settled jobs in a well-organized office to join me and rough it out because of sheer regard for me.

By Thursday that week, the assistant secretary had completed the 'gigantic task' of reworking his space management master plan and allotted me a small room with a cubbyhole of a window in the far corners of the department. The three of us sat around one single table and worked sixteen hours a day over the next four days, including the weekend, making phone calls, consulting experts, checking up with companies, civil contractors and suppliers, and prepared the blueprint of a plan with preliminary cost and time estimates along with a listing of government departments and organizations that must be involved in this task.

The following Monday morning, I took the blueprint to Doraiswamy, the principal revenue secretary, and briefed him. Doraiswamy, professional and practical as always, said: 'Subba, I can't guide you very much on project management itself. What I will do is hold a coordination meeting every Thursday afternoon so we can cut through the bureaucratic layers.' This was encouraging and reassuring.

I got cracking on several fronts over the next few weeks. One of the first things we had to do was to identify appropriate land in every district for the bottling plant. We sent a letter to all district collectors to identify suitable government land for setting up the bottling plant. But in about ten districts, no suitable land was available, and we had to explore the option of acquiring private land.

Land acquisition for public purposes under the 'doctrine of eminent domain' is a standard task that governments do all the time. But it's a long-drawn process and can take years even if the 'urgency clause' under the law is invoked. I worried that this delay would be a deal-breaker. The only alternative was to buy private land by negotiation. This was a risky affair as it could trigger allegations of favouritism and corruption.

I was in a dilemma. Should I tell the chief secretary that the project couldn't be implemented in those ten districts because of the land issue? That was tempting as it would reduce my burden enormously. Or should I stick my neck out and suggest that we should buy private land through negotiation no matter that it might expose me to allegations later on? I raised the issue in the coordination committee chaired by the principal revenue secretary, but the committee decided that I should decide! So much for collective responsibility and guidance. Doraiswamy suggested that it would be best to consult the chief minister first before putting anything in writing.

So, I sought an appointment with the CM and went to see him early the following morning. By now, I was a familiar face to the security who ushered me in without fuss. Besides, I now also had an official car to signal my status.

NTR was firm and clear. 'Ask the collectors to buy private land without any hesitation. The government's prestige is riding on this project, and we can't afford any delay.' Possibly sensing my discomfort, he said, 'We have complete confidence in you, brother.' With that clear instruction and vote of confidence in me, I moved a file accordingly and obtained the CM's orders for the purchase of private land by negotiation in those ten districts.

My luck begins to turn

A couple of weeks into my job, the government posted P.V.R.K. Prasad (PVRK), who had acquired a formidable reputation earlier as executive officer of the Tirumala Tirupati Devasthanam (TTD), as excise commissioner. As soon as he got the posting orders, PVRK breezed into my room for a briefing. As he left, he said, 'Subba, I am going to take charge this afternoon. We will meet again tomorrow and decide how to apportion the tasks and responsibilities between the two of us.' What a contrast with the outgoing commissioner!

Meanwhile, the assistant secretary promoted me to a room with a slightly larger window.

My luck was slowly turning!

Over the next two months, I was immersed in project implementation—visiting soft drink bottling factories, talking to engineers, understanding bottling technologies and operational processes; selecting and tendering for bottling machines, bottles, caps, labels, etc. As word spread, several private parties came to see me to market their products. Simultaneously, we laid down the staffing structure for each plant and asked collectors to begin the process of recruitment of core staff following the due process. Because word spread that it was NTR's pet project and possibly because of my reputation too, there were no pressures in procurement or staffing. That was a big relief.

By then my core team had expanded to half a dozen people, all handpicked by me from among those who had worked with me in previous assignments. My office typically resembled a crisis situation room with me and all my team members sitting around two desks from early morning to late evening. We cut through hierarchies and processes to get the job done.

Within weeks, we completed the selection of land in every district, and civil works were underway. Orders were in the pipeline for the machinery, and contracts were being formulated for consumables. We had also begun preparing operation manuals. We incorporated the Andhra Pradesh Beverages Corporation as a public enterprise, which would operate these plants after commissioning. Most things were going as per schedule although every day we had to firefight on several fronts.

PVRK and I began touring the districts by road and by train to inspect the progress. It turned out to be a great opportunity to identify implementation bottlenecks, troubleshoot on the spot and communicate learnings from one district to all districts. Travelling with PVRK was a special delight as he was a consummate storyteller and would tell me of his experiences in TTD, the miracles he saw, the diversity of devotees, the depth of their faith and the many ways in which they expressed devotion, and of all the VIPs he had attended on. I didn't share PVRK's deep faith; listening to his stories, though, was fun and a relaxing way to spend the journey time.

Later on, PVRK put together these stories from his experience in TTD in a book, *When I Saw Tirupati Balaji*, which became a runaway bestseller. Several times in later years until he passed away in 2017, he would tell me that relating those stories to me during our journeys had proved to be the motivation for him to write the book.

The clock was ticking, with just four months to go, and the project seemed to be on stream. I was so immersed in the project that my initial despair, diffidence and frustration had melted away into the background.

NTR orders an inquiry against me

One December morning at around 11 a.m., I was in the office lambasting a contractor for slipping up on the schedule when a middle-aged, neatly dressed, well-groomed man walked into my office and introduced himself as a deputy superintendent of police (DSP) in the state CID. I looked at him questioningly.

'I've come to record your statement, Sir,' he said.

'What about?' I asked firmly if also a bit nonchalantly.

'An MLA from Nellore has filed a complaint that the rate you agreed to pay for the private land in Nellore is far higher than the going rate. The allegation is that the collector and you had colluded to select this particular site even though better sites were available at much cheaper prices.'

I was shocked and sensed anger fast rising in me.

'Who ordered the inquiry?'

'We got a reference from the CM's office, Sir.'

My anger hit the roof. I was at once dispirited, upset and shaken.

Here I was, implementing the CM's pet project, desperately struggling to meet his exacting schedule, compromising on the power and pelf of a regular IAS job without showing any resentment and now this inquiry! The same chief minister who had told me that he had specially chosen me for this task, had told me on every possible occasion that he had complete confidence in my integrity and competence, had told me to go ahead and buy private land without hesitation, had now ordered an inquiry against me! And no one in the CM's office, not even UBR whom I had so respected, had even bothered to check with me informally before launching an inquiry!

I made a valiant effort to regain my composure and politely requested the DSP to come back in the afternoon.

I called up PVRK and related the whole incident to him even as my entire team, equally aghast at this development, looked on. With my anger and frustration boiling over, I took it out on PVRK in haughty, intemperate language, 'I don't want this job. I am applying for leave right away. *You* go and tell *your* chief minister to choose a clean and competent OSD.'

PVRK, ever so mature and balanced, tried to calm me down. 'Subba, just wait. Don't do anything. Don't talk to anyone else about this. I am coming across right away.'

And he arrived, in less than fifteen minutes. 'Come, let's go to the CM right away,' he said as soon as he entered my office.

We walked into UBR's office, and I burst out, 'You know that the CM gave me a near-impossible task. I am firefighting all at once on several fronts. I have no problem with inquiries. But, if I have to spend my time giving police statements and explanations, how can I complete the project on time? You are the secretary to the CM. Please advise *your* CM to defer all inquiries till the project is over, or else move me aside so that I can attend to the inquiry and you can have someone else implement the project.'

UBR didn't know what had hit him. He seemed totally confused. PVRK tried to calm me down and explained to him more coherently what had happened.

UBR's response was cryptic and on message. He said: 'Subba, I will take you to the CM right away. You tell him straight to his face that either he withdraws the inquiry or you will go on leave.'

UBR put the CM's next meeting on hold and ushered us in. We sat in front of the CM.

'What, brother, all three of you together?' NTR said with a beatific smile on his face.

I was livid. Not only had this man ordered an inquiry in clear violation of his assurances to me, but now he was acting so innocent! PVRK was gripping my hand under the table, secretly urging that I should maintain my cool.

I had crossed the line with PVRK and UBR, both senior to me, with my intemperate language. But they were both mature enough to understand my agony and would forgive my ill temper. But being intemperate with a chief minister, that too a larger-than-life personality like NTR, was an altogether different proposition. But with as much courage as I could muster, I said, 'Sir, I can't do this job. I want to go on leave. Please select *someone else in whom you have greater confidence.*' I particularly stressed the last bit, bringing on all the satire I could muster.

'What happened, brother? You are doing a great job. We are close to the finish. We are eager to launch this sacred project as soon as possible. Why do you want to leave now?'

He sounded innocent and honest all right. But wasn't he the one who had set the CID after me? Was he acting? After all, acting was second nature to him!

Signalling that I shouldn't say anything further, UBR explained the developments to him.

'What? We ordered a CID inquiry, that too against you? We are not aware, brother.'

PVRK, not known for mincing words, added, 'Sir, if you start harassing good officers like this, you will forfeit the confidence of the entire bureaucracy. And you will regret that.'

The matter was slowly becoming clear to NTR. He was truly aghast. 'We ordered a CID inquiry? That's just not possible.

'Sorry, brother. I must have signed absentmindedly thinking it was a routine matter. How could I even think of suspecting your integrity? On the contrary, I am impressed

by the way you have been going about your job over the
last several months.'

He sounded genuine and truly apologetic.

Turning to UBR he said, 'Raghavendra Rao *garu*,
please have that inquiry withdrawn immediately. Also,
find out how this mistake happened and make sure we
don't have a repeat in the future.'

NTR then got up abruptly and we got up too. He came
around his desk, put his hands on my shoulders and said
once again, 'Sorry, brother. Please forget about this and get
on with your job.'

We breast the tape in time

The next few months were a blur. Going to the office
before nine every morning, plunging into work headlong,
checking on the progress of civil works, supply contracts,
the recruitment process and training, and troubleshooting
throughout the day without a break, then heading home
well past dinner time. And travelling to the project sites
on an average of three days a week by road, train and air.

What surprised me was that even as work was
hectic and my schedule chaotic, I was enjoying the job.
My earlier misgivings and self-doubt had given way
to optimism and confidence; where earlier I had been
depressed and dejected, I was now upbeat and positive.
The sense that I was pulling off something that I had
initially thought was beyond the realm of possibility was
hugely motivating.

Three days before the deadline, we had twenty-three
bottling plants, one each in every district of the state, all in

place, fully equipped and staffed, all systems and processes tested and ready for the button push.

NTR's arrack bottling project—the Varuni Vahini— went on stream on the first day of the new financial year.

Of course, there were teething problems over the next three months, and we had no respite.

As things started getting on an even keel, I requested the chief secretary for a month's leave and requested that he give me another assignment when I rejoined. He just smiled.

As I look back on my career, I count my one year as OSD for arrack bottling as one of the most challenging and easily the most enjoyable assignment of my IAS career.

Two lifetime lessons learnt

I learnt two lifetime lessons along the way.

In self-help books—*The Alchemist* or *Jonathan Livingston Seagull*, for example—and in leadership seminars, we are told that the secret to success in life is to discover your passion and pursue it.

That advice never appealed to me simply because life doesn't always give you the opportunity to pursue your passion. If you sit around bemoaning your lack of opportunity to pursue your passion, you are sure to be a loser.

The true test of leadership is to play the hand that you've been dealt—to do whatever it is you have to do with passion.

I also learnt that being pushed out of your comfort zone can be a great learning opportunity.

Why me?

Arthur Ashe was the only black man ever to win the US Open, Australian Open and Wimbledon in the 1970s.

Ashe is believed to have contracted HIV from a blood transfusion he received during a heart bypass surgery in 1983. He publicly announced his illness in April 1992 and began working to educate others about HIV and AIDS. He founded the Arthur Ashe Foundation for the Defeat of AIDS and the Arthur Ashe Institute for Urban Health before his death from AIDS-related pneumonia at the age of forty-nine on 6 February 1993.

As Ashe lay dying on a hospital bed, he received enormous fan mail. One fan asked: 'Why does GOD have to select a good man like you for such a bad disease?'

To this, Arthur Ashe replied:

The world over—50 million children start playing tennis,
5 million learn to play tennis,
5,00,000 learn professional tennis,
50,000 come to the circuit, 5000 reach the grand slam,
50 reach Wimbledon,
4 to semi-final, 2 to the finals.
When I was holding a cup, I never asked GOD 'Why me?'
And today in pain, I should not be asking GOD 'Why me?'

9

Capital Heights

Delhi Deputation 1988–93

In early 1988, after much deliberation, Urmila and I opted for deputation to the Government of India.

There were any number of reasons for not going to Delhi.

We both had steady careers in our state cadre of Andhra Pradesh. Urmila was secretary to the AP Public Service Commission and was in the thick of the process of reforming the systems there. Post my stint in arrack bottling, I moved to the AP State Finance Corporation and just about completed one year as managing director, a prestigious and interesting job with many opportunities to support entrepreneurs and enterprises for the development of the state. During the first year, I had invested in learning, and I needed to stay on for a couple of years to put that learning to use and make a difference. On the personal front, our two sons, aged seven and five, were happy going to the Bharatiya Vidya Bhavan School in Hyderabad. Most importantly, my ageing parents lived all by themselves in our hometown of Eluru, just an overnight train journey from Hyderabad. Delhi would be far away.

What tipped the balance was, of course, the resolve to fight the status quo bias, inspired by a *Reader's Digest* article: 'Don't chase stability, embrace change'.

What determines IAS postings?

It's difficult to discern a pattern in IAS postings. There are, of course, broad guidelines about career management, stability of tenure, acknowledgement of seniority and opportunities for specialization. But in practice, expediency trumps the guidelines. Most of the time, it's about matching the available officers with the available jobs. By the time an IAS officer has put in about ten years of service, the authorities have a broad, albeit informal, assessment of her character, personality, work style and performance. It's this assessment that informs postings subject, of course, to lobbying by officers for 'prestigious jobs', interventions by politicians and the priorities and preferences of the chief minister. The process is subjective but by no means random.

The framework for postings in Delhi is less subjective since most mid-career-level officers are not known at a personal level to the decision-makers. They have to be evaluated by their annual confidential reports, which are typically too bland to give a clear assessment of the officer. It's also not always possible to map experience at the state level to the required experience at the Centre. Beyond all this, there is the usual jockeying by officers for specific posts, political interference and the preference of ministers for officers they know from their home states rather than unknown quantities. All this makes postings in Delhi more of a lottery than at the state level. I was quite anxious about whether I would be chosen at all, and if so, where I might land.

By May 1988, Urmila was posted as a director in the Ministry of Defence, and that was a signal that my posting too would come soon. I learnt that there was an opening in the Ministry of Industry, and I was keen on that job. I thought my five years of experience at the state level in industrial promotion would count in my favour notwithstanding the lottery system.

All through my career, I had never lobbied for a job through politicians. But I thought it was fair game to lobby through senior officers known to me, although purists would shun even that. Nevertheless, when I went to Delhi on an official trip, I met Rajamani, a senior officer of the AP cadre who was then additional secretary in the Cabinet Secretariat, and requested him to speak on my behalf to the industries secretary. A couple of weeks later, Rajamani called to say that he did speak to the industries secretary but that she had opted for someone else.

I was disappointed, but not for long. The very next week, I received orders appointing me as a director in the Department of Economic Affairs (DEA) in the Ministry of Finance. This was indeed a pleasant surprise since jobs in the DEA are highly competitive and quite a number of officers are constantly vying for them. I suspected that

Rajamani had pushed my candidature although he was too much of a gentleman to claim any credit for it.

Managing the balance of payments

I was posted as director in charge of foreign exchange budgeting (FEB). In department circles, this was seen as an assignment at the bottom of the pecking order. Desks dealing with the World Bank and the IMF were the most sought after followed by those dealing with bilateral donor agencies. As ambitious as I was, I didn't feel let down by this assignment because the job content seemed interesting and substantive. In hindsight, I realize that this experience did, in fact, prove useful in my future career. But of course, I didn't know this in real time!

The IAS is a generalist service, and a college degree is sufficient qualification for writing the civil services examination. What specific subjects you studied matters less than what you bring to a generalist job from your education. In most IAS jobs, therefore, your specialization in college might be relevant only at a general knowledge level but not at a job-specific level.

This job as director of FEB ran counter to that narrative in the sense that it gave me an opportunity to relate much of what I had learnt in international economics to my job content. For the first time, I was working with actual balance of payments numbers rather than textbook abstractions. As I was moving up the learning curve, I realized that there was a lot of detail and nuance in practical application that you miss in a classroom or a textbook. Take, for example, tourism earnings, which are a standard entry in the balance of payments. When you see that in a textbook, you understand the logic of why tourism earnings form part of the balance of payments, but it doesn't occur to you to drill down further. When you are actually compiling the balance of payments, you have to grapple with questions like: Who is a tourist? What sort of spending by a tourist constitutes tourism earnings?

A similar but even more complex practical question in compiling the balance of payments is: When does an import actually become an import? Is it when the import is contracted? When it's paid for or when it lands at our port of entry? Or is it when it clears customs? I learnt much to my surprise that ships and some aircraft that don't cross the customs border are not counted as imports even though they have been bought. This discrepancy between import data as collected by the customs authorities who track the physical data, and the RBI, which tracks the financial data, is a question that I would encounter in my career several times in the future.

For sure, foreign exchange budgeting would seem heretical today, in the post-reform era, but it was an important and challenging responsibility when we had a pegged exchange rate, limited forex reserves and strict import controls. My job chart included drafting the full year's foreign exchange budget in consultation with the RBI and formulating the guidelines for the allocation of foreign exchange to public and private enterprises, and separately for the Ministry of Defence. The day-to-day work involved dispensing foreign exchange allocations in accordance with the guidelines while keeping track of the overall budget and the liquidity situation.

Allocating scarce resources among competing demands is the quintessence of economics; it's also, as I learnt on this job, an incredibly stressful task because of the pressures that would eat into the best-laid plans.

The Delhi bureaucratic hierarchy

The Delhi bureaucracy is more hierarchical than at the state level. Directors and deputy secretaries seldom get to meet the super boss, the department secretary, unless their joint secretary chooses to take them along for discussions and meetings. My experience, though, was contrarian as both Venkitaramanan and Gopi Arora, as finance secretaries, used to call for me directly if they had a query regarding any detail. If it were a policy issue, of course, they would consult the joint secretary rather than me. This somewhat privileged access to the finance secretary that my peers secretly envied was a great feel-good factor for me.

By the time I started this job, the early signs of the balance of payments crisis that would engulf the economy two years later were already evident. The current account deficit was running high, forex reserves were dwindling, interest rates on our external commercial borrowing were firming up, and unsurprisingly, meetings and discussions on the balance of payments situation became more frequent.

In early 1989, some six months after I started on this job, there was a presentation to be made to Prime Minister Rajiv Gandhi on the balance of payments situation by RBI Governor R.N. Malhotra and Finance Secretary Gopi Arora. I was involved in preparing the material for the presentation. For sure, I was at the bottom of the totem pole in this preparation but being involved in a task like this was a big ego booster.

It is very unusual for director-level officers to attend meetings with the prime minister. I was therefore elated when Gopi Arora asked that I accompany him to the meeting. During the actual presentation, Rajiv Gandhi asked a question relating to some detail although I can't recall what it was. Immediately, Gopi Arora looked around for me, spotted me sitting in the back row and asked, 'Subbarao, can you answer the PM?' It was a heady feeling, and I boasted about it at the dinner table to my sons. Not that they really cared!

Getting inducted into Delhi on the home and office fronts

Settling in Delhi both on the home and work fronts was difficult; the first six months were, in fact, a struggle. At the state level, you could take certain facilities, conveniences and comforts for granted no matter your particular posting. But as a mid-level officer entering the behemoth of the Delhi bureaucracy, you had to struggle even for minimum amenities like an office, phone, computer, etc. The support staff that junior officers were allotted were callous and unhelpful. A colleague told me that when you start off in any department in the Central government, you start at the bottom and get all the castaways. But as you gain in terms of tenure, you will gradually move up. That proved to be true in my case. When I joined the DEA, I was allotted a damp, dark, dingy and windowless room adjacent to the washrooms, and by the time I left five years later, I had graduated to a relatively large room along one of the stately corridors of the North Block with two large windows!

On the home front, we initially stayed in a single room in the Andhra Pradesh Bhavan. The Andhra Pradesh canteen food was famous all over Delhi, but it was difficult to ingest that on a regular basis. Fortunately, within about a month we were allotted a tiny flat in Asia House on Kasturba Gandhi Marg in the woman's quota under Urmila's name. A silver lining in the midst of this disruption was that our sons got admission to the Bharatiya Vidya Bhavan School on a priority basis as they were treated as transfer students from the Bhavan's sister institution in Hyderabad. The school was across the street from Asia House, and either Urmila or I could walk them there in the morning in five minutes. Ironically, a school right across from your house was a convenience we did not enjoy even in district towns like Ongole and Nizamabad back in Andhra Pradesh.

Over the next few months, I saw that several colleagues were approaching Urmila with requests to get their children admission to the Air Force Bal Bharti School on Lodhi Road. Presumably, she had some influence there because she was handling air force matters in the Ministry of Defence. After I witnessed this for about three months, I told Urmila, maybe we are missing something that's available to us on a platter. There must be something special about the Bal Bharti School. Shouldn't we put our children there too? So, eager parents as we were, the following year, we shifted them to the Bal Bharti School even though we, and more importantly our sons, were quite happy in the Bharatiya Vidya Bhavan School.[*]

---

[*] I must note for the record that the boys, in fact, went back to the Bharatiya Vidya Bhavan School in Hyderabad when we returned there five years later and benefited from the value-based education at the Bhavan Schools.

The Asia House flat was small, just a matchbox. The RBI governor's bungalow on M.L. Dahanukar Marg (erstwhile Carmichael Road) in Mumbai where we had the privilege of living twenty years later was at least thirty times as large. It's one of life's ironies—maybe even one of life's charms—that when you have little children running and jumping all around, you live in cramped quarters, and when you become an empty nester, you get all the living space that you don't need.

Aid India Consortium

As director of FEB, the small secretariat for foreign aid policy coordination (FAPC) in DEA was in my charge. India was receiving aid—official development assistance (ODA) in technical terms—from a number of multilateral agencies such as the World Bank and the Asian Development Bank (ADB) as well as bilateral donors such as the UK, Germany and Japan. Each of them had their own aid philosophies, policies, priorities and institutional norms.

The logic for setting up something like the FAPC was that within the government, we should enforce some minimum norms under which we would accept foreign aid. In particular, we resented tied aid—which is when a donor country gave us money but stipulated that the machinery and services required under the project should be procured from their country. This monopoly procurement stipulation not only raised the cost of imports but also made us hostage to firms in the donor country for subsequent maintenance. In the long run, this would prove costlier than receiving no aid at all. Another important prescription we had was that there should be a minimum grant element in the assistance, which was meant to ensure that loans at near commercial terms didn't pass through as official aid.

What sort of aid was acceptable and what was not used to be a contentious issue and defied a satisfactory categorization. Much after I left DEA, India decided, wisely in my view, to not accept aid from small donors where the costs, both tangible and intangible, of receiving aid far exceeded the benefits.

One of my responsibilities as the FAPC coordinator was to provide the secretariat for the Aid India Consortium (AIC) meeting held every June under the aegis of the World Bank. The AIC came into being in 1958 when India requested the World Bank to organize additional financial support to tide over a rapidly deteriorating balance of payments situation. Given India's status as a founding member of the World Bank, and as its largest borrower, the World Bank president at the time, Eugene R. Black, took immediate action and convened a meeting to consult with interested parties and explore solutions to India's emergency.

That meeting was such a success in coordinating aid from multiple donors that the Aid India Consortium became an annual feature. In fact, based on the India experience, the World Bank institutionalized the aid consortium meeting model for several other countries under the nomenclature of 'Paris Club' meetings.

An important part of the preparation for the AIC meeting was the opening statement of the finance secretary, succinctly summarizing India's macroeconomic situation, its external sector position and laying out the demand for external aid. As the director in charge of the FAPC, preparing the first draft of the speech was my task. Building a comprehensive narrative of our macroeconomic situation, weaving into that an assessment of the size and type of external aid we needed was a rewarding learning opportunity, and I thoroughly enjoyed it. The draft would, of course, go through several iterations, but it still felt good to be the author of the initial draft.

I was also part of the small delegation that would go to the AIC meeting in Paris. The meeting in 1989 when Finance Secretary Gopi Arora led the delegation was, in fact, my first international meeting, and I was excited to be part of that. The meeting would start with the World Bank's opening statement followed by the finance secretary's statement and then interventions by the various donors. At a media conference at the end of the two-day meeting, the finance secretary would indicate the broad numbers of aid pledges made by the donors. Our brief for this media conference was to get across to the international media how much higher the pledges were in the current year compared to the previous year.

India has since moved up the ladder on the development aid totem pole. Like Australia, which is the only country in the world to have been a colony as well as a colonizer, today India is not only an aid recipient but also an aid donor.

Japanese aid to India

In July 1990, I was promoted to joint secretary and given charge of currency and coins (C&C) and bilateral assistance

from Japan. I was disappointed that I was not given charge
of the balance of payments given my experience in the area
for two years. But I remembered the lesson I had learnt
earlier when I was posted to set up arrack bottling plants
in Andhra Pradesh: your career—indeed your life—doesn't
always go the way you want. As an IAS officer, your route
to success lies not in bemoaning your fate but in doing
whatever it is you are enjoined to do with passion.

The currency and coins part of the job was quite
routine—handling personnel and procurement issues of
the government mints in Mumbai, Kolkata, Hyderabad
and Noida, and the two currency printing presses in Nasik
and Dewas.

The Japan part of the job was interesting; I was exposed
to a number of policy issues in external aid management.
In the early nineties, the Japanese property bubble had not
yet burst, the Japanese miracle was still an alluring story
and Japan enjoyed enormous clout in international policy
circles. It was not entirely surprising therefore that Japan
was our largest bilateral donor and India was Japan's
largest aid recipient.

The Japanese aid programme around the world was
managed by a separate agency—the Overseas Economic
Cooperation Fund (OECF)*—which was an extended arm
of their Ministry of Finance. The OECF team in Delhi was
quite small, but they made up for it by their characteristic
hard work and diligence. They studied every minute detail
of every project, visited every project site and met with not

---

* The OECF has since been wound up and Japanese bilateral aid is now
  handled through the Japan International Cooperation Agency (JICA).

just the relevant state and local government functionaries but also all the stakeholders.

One of Japan's flagship aid projects in India was the Sardar Sarovar Dam on the Narmada River, which would provide water and electricity to four states: Gujarat, Madhya Pradesh, Maharashtra and Rajasthan. In the early nineties, the Narmada Bachao Andolan (NBA) was at its peak and the agitation found an echo in several Japanese environmental groups. The Japanese government started becoming increasingly uncomfortable about getting caught up in this controversy. The OECF team as well as the Japanese embassy in Delhi closely monitored the situation and sought repeated reassurances from us that the government would address the concerns of the NBA regarding resettlement of the project-affected people and environmental protection.

On one occasion, I was asked to fly to Tokyo along with a senior official of the Madhya Pradesh government to explain the ground situation at the project site and the government's position on the issues raised by the NBA to their finance minister who was being attacked in the Diet (Japanese parliament) for aid to the Narmada project. Eventually though, much to our disappointment, Japan suspended later tranches of the project aid.

Japanese funding for the Bakreshwar project

There was an elaborate screening process for identifying projects for Japanese aid. We would prepare a long list of projects from which the Japanese side would then make a shortlist according to their priorities. There was a lot of behind-the-scenes activity underlying this process though. It was quite common for Central ministries as well as state governments to lobby for their projects with us, and on occasion with the OECF team in Delhi.

I distinctly recall the Bakreshwar fiasco in this regard. During the early 1990s, the West Bengal government was quite upset that the Bakreshwar thermal power plant project, in which they had invested huge political capital, could not secure Central funding or the much-hoped-for Soviet assistance. They set a lot of store, therefore, on getting Japanese aid for the project. Ranjan Chatterjee, the managing director of the West Bengal Power Corporation, met me several times to seek support for the project. Showing uncommon perseverance and dedication, he tirelessly provided all the details that the Ministry of Power, and we in the Ministry of Finance, sought. On top of that, the chief minister Jyoti Basu also canvassed support for the project with the power minister, Kalpanath Rai, and the finance minister, Manmohan Singh. Building Bakreshwar became an emotional issue for the West Bengal government. The Left Front Government under Basu declared that even if no Central support was forthcoming, their government would mobilize public contributions to build Bakreshwar.*

Even with all this background effort, at the final stage, for reasons unknown to us, the Ministry of Power did not include Bakreshwar in their recommended list of power projects for Japanese support. I called up Ranjan Chatterjee and informed him of this omission. He was understandably

---

* 'Controversies that dogged the pragmatic chief minister', Biswajit Roy, 18 January 2010, *The Telegraph,* https://www.telegraphindia.com/india/controversies-that-dogged-the-pragmatic-chief-minister/cid/555483.

upset and cut the call abruptly. As we had to give our recommended list to the Japanese by lunchtime (close of business in Tokyo) that day, I didn't have much wriggle room. We sent the list for the finance minister's approval, pointing out in the note, though, that Bakreshwar didn't figure on it. The finance minister approved the list, and we sent it off to the Japanese embassy in Delhi within the deadline.

After an hour, I called Ranjan to check if he had informed his chief minister of the development. Ranjan said, 'Yes, I told the CM.' 'What was his response?' I asked diffidently. 'He didn't say anything. He heard me and left abruptly saying he was going home for lunch.'

Events unfolded dramatically that afternoon. I remember distinctly because it was just two days after the Babri Masjid demolition and Delhi was still in shock. There was a curfew-like situation on the streets, and the government was functioning only at half capacity. Within an hour of Jyoti Basu going home for lunch in Kolkata, all hell broke loose in the corridors of power in Delhi. Phones were ringing off the hook everywhere as everyone was calling everyone else about the omission of the Bakreshwar project. The prime minister's office was calling the finance minister and the power minister, and the power minister called the finance minister, Montek Singh Ahluwalia, who was finance secretary, summoned me to ask if we had already sent the list to the Japanese embassy and I said 'yes'.

Ten minutes later, Montek called me on the intercom to ask me to withdraw the list. Fortunately, the embassy had not yet sent it off to Tokyo and obliged us. We scrambled for a couple of hours, working along with the Ministry of Power, to rework the list by knocking out a couple of projects to make space for Bakreshwar, got the necessary approvals and sent a revised list to the Japanese by late that evening. The Japanese understood the politics on our side and cooperated fully.

To this day, I am unaware of what triggered that frantic about-turn in Delhi to undo the wrong done to Bakreshwar. It's possible someone high up in the West Bengal government contacted the prime minister's office to let them know that Jyoti Basu felt deeply betrayed, but I can't be sure. I was overawed, however, by the goodwill and political influence that Jyoti Basu commanded, which he always used to good effect. That was probably why he had so much clout in the first place.

The Japanese rescue of our balance of payments

By the time Chandra Shekhar took over as prime minister in November 1990, the balance of payments situation was deteriorating rapidly; the government and the RBI were reduced to managing forex liquidity on a day-to-day basis. It was quite clear that we needed IMF assistance. The IMF was in dialogue with the government but was unwilling to commit assistance until they were assured of political stability. Meanwhile, we needed stopgap funding to tide over the day-to-day squeeze. The Japanese came to our rescue.

Diligent as they are, the Japanese had always closely tracked our balance of payments situation, but now that they had skin in the game, they had a rightful claim to ask for more details and explanations. They would pore over our external sector flows with characteristic diligence and come back to us to seek clarifications. Quite frequently, the Japanese were intrigued that the numbers didn't always add up; on some days, our official tally of forex reserves used to be higher than what the Japanese calculated they should be, and they would quiz us on that quite forcefully, but of course, with their characteristic politeness.

And thereby hangs an interesting tale. At the conclusion of the earlier IMF programme in the 1980s during the Indira Gandhi regime, the government had kept a significant amount of forex reserves in the India Supply Missions in London and Washington, ostensibly to finance defence expenditure but also as insurance for a rainy day. Those reserves proved to be our lifeline in managing this deepening forex crunch. On some days, we would quietly transfer a few hundred million dollars from that account to the RBI's official account, which obviously resulted in a higher level of reserves than the number thrown up by cash flow accounting. This was the discrepancy that the Japanese detected. We would make up an explanation, but I suspect they always knew the inside story but were too polite to push us into embarrassment.

Today, more than thirty years after the 1991 reforms, there is a whole lot of mythology and folklore about the events leading to the blitzkrieg reforms of that year. In my view, the Japanese rescue when we desperately needed it is a much more important part of that story than we tend to acknowledge.

Pledging India's home jewellery

Apart from negotiating Japanese emergency assistance, I also did one other significant thing as part of foreign exchange management during those difficult days. I signed the agreement on behalf of the government authorizing the Reserve Bank to pledge gold to raise a temporary loan from the Bank of England and the Bank of Japan. Quite by happenstance, as governor of the Reserve Bank twenty years later, in 2009, we also bought 200 MT of gold from the IMF to replenish our stocks. The media wrote at that time that having signed away the pledge of gold back in 1991, I was now redeeming the country's honour as the governor of the Reserve Bank by replenishing the gold stocks. As tempting as it was to believe those compliments, it was, of course, sheer coincidence that I had signed the pledging in 1991. And the decision to purchase gold in 2009 as governor was based entirely on objective considerations.

India before and after the 1991 reforms

The younger people of today will find it difficult to imagine the scarcity and lack of choice in pre-reform India. If we travelled abroad, we were allowed a princely sum of twenty dollars of foreign exchange. It took years to get a telephone or LPG connection. We had the luxury of four brands of soap and three brands of shampoo to choose from! It was quite common for people to smuggle in even low-end cameras and tape recorders from abroad. Up until the mid-1980s, only the super-rich had colour TVs because only they had the money and clout to get an import permit. A booking for a Vespa scooter or a Premier Padmini car could be traded like a security receipt. And the government took pride in baking and selling its own brand of bread!

The pre-reform economic system under which a presumably all-knowing government directed virtually every aspect of economic activity was defined by three characteristics. The first was the notoriously famous 'licence-permit Raj'—a web of complex, mindless and vexatious controls that dictated what should be produced, where it should be produced and how much should be produced on the ostensible grounds that absent such controls, scarce resources would be frittered away to produce inessential things—like lipstick, for example, as a bureaucrat of that time put it, as mentioned in a previous chapter.

The second characteristic of the pre-reform regime was a deep conviction that foreign trade and foreign investment are inherently exploitative and that national interest is best secured through self-reliance—producing everything we need ourselves with domestic investment, and to the extent possible, by deploying home-grown technology. And the third defining characteristic was a dogmatic commitment to investment in the public sector in the belief that the private sector, driven by profit motive, would undermine public interest.

The results of this dirigiste philosophy that guided economic management for over four decades were a venal and overlording bureaucracy, high-cost and low-quality goods and services, and an economy that remained locked into backwardness.

It was that deeply entrenched economic system that was dismantled in one fell swoop by the blitzkrieg reforms of 1991. The abrupt change in mindset was all the more remarkable because, as Keynes famously said, 'The difficulty lies not so much in developing new ideas as in escaping from old ones.'

Answering parliament questions

Answering parliament questions is a big part of a Delhi bureaucrat's job chart. The process starts at the very bottom with the undersecretary preparing the first draft of the answer, which moves up at least five stages through the hierarchy before it reaches the finance minister's desk for final approval. When I encountered my first parliament question, I thought the answer drafted by the undersecretary was too cryptic and amplified it to add some clarity. When the file came back to me on the downward journey, I saw that the final approved response resembled more the undersecretary's version than mine. This was a lesson for me—in answering parliament questions, say as little as you can get away with, but make sure that what you are saying is right. I found that ministers, no matter which party or which government they belonged to, were quite comfortable with this minimalist attitude to parliament questions.

Answering starred parliament questions is a bigger burden because, in addition to the draft answer, you also have to prepare a tutorial sheet for the finance minister, called 'note for pad' in officialese, listing probable supplementary questions and suggested answers. There would be a session with the finance minister first thing in the morning every Tuesday and Friday—the designated question days for the Ministry of Finance in the Lok Sabha and Rajya Sabha respectively—with all the senior officers of the ministry present to brief the minister on the answers. This was quite an interesting experience because you got a big picture of issues being handled by other divisions in the ministry.

There is a lot of folklore in Delhi bureaucratic circles about how ministers handle parliament questions. There is a story, possibly apocryphal, that when a particular minister rose to answer a parliament question, he read out not just the answer but the entire note for pad. When, after that, a member got up to ask a supplementary, the speaker chided him saying, 'The minister answered every possible supplementary, how can you still have questions?'

Gender sensitization

There is quite a bit of grunt work in answering parliament questions after the draft is approved. We had to make 800 hard copies, and this was done by cyclostyling since fast printers and copiers were still too expensive at that time. The 800 copies then had to be bundled, bagged, sealed and transported to the Parliament Bhavan during the night to be ready for distribution to the members when the session began. This was typically the responsibility of the undersecretary concerned, and quite often, the whole operation would go on past midnight.

On one occasion, this responsibility fell on Rita Acharya, an undersecretary in my division. At around 9 p.m. when I was leaving the office, I told her: 'Rita, now that the main part of the work is done, why don't you go home? I will ask someone else in the division to handle the leg work.' Rita's face reddened immediately, and I noticed that she was hurt and upset. She said to me, as firmly as an undersecretary can tell a boss two levels her senior, 'Sir, if you don't mind, I will stay and complete my task.'

I was taken aback by this reaction. I thought I was being considerate. Instead, she was telling me, 'Don't you patronize me! I can look after myself.'

Now, many years later, with my gender sensibilities hopefully more refined, I think she was right. It was a powerful lesson to me that a positive gender bias is as reprehensible as a negative gender bias.

The rupee-rouble imbroglio

In 1992–93, the final year of my Central deputation, I moved from the currency and coins division to the foreign trade desk in DEA since Narayan Valluri, who was handling that subject, was deputed as minister (economic) to our embassy in Washington DC. My most important task during this short period was resolving the vexatious rupee-rouble imbalance issue following the collapse of the Soviet Union in 1991.

As per the agreement with the Soviets, we would pay them in rupees for our imports from them, which included oil, fertilizer, newsprint and importantly, defence equipment. They would use the rupees to buy goods from India for import into the Soviet Union. The Soviets largely bought pharmaceuticals, leather goods and tobacco from us. There was an elaborate mechanism in place between the RBI and the Bank of Russia to work through individual transactions and keep accounts.

By the time the Soviet Union fell apart in the latter half of 1991, their side had accumulated huge rupee balances, and the main issue was the exchange rate at which these balances would be liquidated given the massive exchange rate movements not foreseen at the time of the original agreement. After excruciatingly exhausting negotiations, we reached an agreement to settle the balance at the last announced exchange rate under the trade protocol, which was Rs 31.78 to a rouble. The agreement was signed during Boris Yeltsin's visit to India in January 1993.

To celebrate the resolution of the problem, the finance minister, Manmohan Singh, hosted a dinner for the Russian finance minister and his delegation. There were about twenty of us at this sit-down dinner in the Ashok Hotel in Delhi. During the meal, the conversation turned to where one would get the spiciest food in India. The answer—Andhra Pradesh—was a no-brainer. Then someone on the Russian side narrowed the answer down to Guntur in Andhra Pradesh. Then another Russian further narrowed it, saying, 'To eat the spiciest food in India, you have to go to Shankara Vilas on 4th Lane, Brodipet, Guntur.' I was amused to note their intense familiarity with Guntur, which of course, was because of their frequent trips there to buy tobacco. In fact, the Government of India's Tobacco Board is headquartered in Guntur.

As I write this (September 2023), the war in Ukraine is on, and India has entered into an arrangement with Russia to pay them in rupees for the oil we buy from them. The Indo-Soviet accord is a precursor to this. There is an important difference though. The earlier agreement was a pure barter deal, and the Soviets were mandated to use

the rupees they earned to buy stuff from India. Under the
current arrangement though, there is an escape clause,
which gives the Russians an option to ask for repatriation
of their surplus rupees in some hard currency. It is a
different matter that because of the sanctions imposed on
them, Russia does not have too many options.

Learning and unlearning

During my five-year tenure in the Ministry of Finance,
I had seen four finance ministers—S.B. Chavan, Madhu
Dandawate, Yashwant Sinha and Manmohan Singh—
and five finance secretaries—S. Venkitaramanan, Gopi
Arora, Bimal Jalan, S.B. Shukla and finally, Montek
Singh Ahluwalia. They brought their own experience and
world views to the job, and there was much to learn, and
sometimes much to unlearn, watching them work.

Montek, for example, brought a unique sensibility to
the job of the finance secretary. At a weekly coordination
meeting with the senior officers of DEA, N.K. Singh
(NK) who was then joint secretary in charge of World
Bank and IMF affairs, suggested to Montek that he
should take a meeting with all the departments of the
government to formulate a common position on the issues
that would come up during a forthcoming IMF mission.
NK's point was that there should be no dissonance
within the government in what we told the IMF mission.
Montek didn't think it was such a great idea. He replied,
'The IMF knows that there are differences within the
government on many important issues. I don't see any
value in covering them up. On the contrary, it will be

good if the Fund is exposed to the diversity of views within the government.'

Montek's wise response stuck in my mind and guided me when I found myself in similar situations in the future.

Central deputation—pros and cons

My five-year Central deputation ended in July 1993, and it was time to return to my home cadre of Andhra Pradesh. Most IAS officers (and other All India Services officers like IPS and IFoS) find themselves mildly disheartened when their Central deputations end for a variety of reasons, not all of which are easy to explain.

Delhi provides a larger work canvas, the policy and operational issues one deals with are weightier, or at any rate appear to be so, and the diversity of issues, the all-India perspective one gets and the opportunity to work with officers from other cadres and other services is mind-expanding. The work culture in Delhi is more impersonal and work organization and systems are more structured than at the state level.

Central deputation also provides a sense of stability to mid-career officers with schoolgoing children as an officer will work largely in the same ministry, live in the same house, the children will go to the same school and the family will shop in the same grocery and dine out in the same familiar places. Most importantly, deputation to Delhi at the mid-career level provides an opportunity to establish a reputation, which can be quite important in career progression.

I must admit I too was disheartened when my time came to go back. Five years earlier, when I had moved to

Delhi and was struggling with adjusting to work and life there, oftentimes I berated myself quietly for abandoning the comfort and convenience of the home cadre. But Delhi grows on you so much that when it's time to go, you are unhappy.

The five years in DEA gave me an opportunity to work on issues such as the balance of payments, exchange rate management, foreign trade, multilateral and bilateral aid, the production of currency and coins, none of which had any parallel experience stream at the state level. The timing too was serendipitous in some sense. I happened to be in the Ministry of Finance when the historic blitzkrieg reforms of 1991 were afoot. My involvement in the reforms was admittedly peripheral but it was a heady feeling nevertheless to be part of those discussions and conversations. I was going to miss this sense of importance when I returned to my home cadre.

Preserving the all-India nature of the IAS

As an aside, I must add a note about my growing concern that the IAS is losing its all-India character. The organizing principle of the IAS is that officers would switch between the Centre and states. Thereby, the Centre would get the benefit of the front-line experience that IAS officers bring to their jobs in Delhi while the states would get the benefit of their cadre officers being exposed to policies and practices at the all-India level.

The growing tendency of IAS officers to stay put in their home cadres for whatever reason—possibly status quo bias—runs counter to this mutual benefit being realized. In the

1980s and 1990s, during my first deputation to Delhi, there used to be competition among officers to be picked up for Central deputation. These days I gather there are not enough IAS officers willing to break out of their comfort zones and go to the Centre. This is a decidedly disturbing development.

To repair this situation, in 2022, the Central government proposed an amendment to the IAS cadre rules making it mandatory for state governments to offer officers for Central deputation as required under the deputation reserve rules. States baulked at this proposal, saying it ran counter to cooperative federalism. It's unfortunate that this issue has got embroiled in politics. I believe IAS officers themselves must take the initiative in resolving this as it matters for the long-term value of the IAS as a premier All India Service.

Is it okay to be ambitious?

At several places in this book, particularly in this chapter, I have written about being ambitious. That raises two questions in my mind. Is it okay to be ambitious? And should I admit to it?

Whether it's okay to be ambitious depends on what you mean by it. I was brought up to despise ambition. My parents believed that anyone driven by the pursuit of power, position or money was ambitious. In some sense, they thought of ambition the same way as Mark Antony described it in Shakespeare's *Julius Caesar* when he said, 'Ambition should be made of sterner stuff.'

This negative perception of ambition is misleading. Ambition is also the pursuit of success; it drives people to new heights and creates the motivation to improve oneself. The world would be a much poorer place if there were no ambitious people.

My nuanced understanding, shaped by my own life experience, is that ambition driven by outcomes—to achieve results, to improve one's own performance, to help others in a measurable way—is admirable and necessary. Ambition driven by external validation—a high-status position, greater wealth than your neighbour, winning awards—is not desirable; it is also a road to misery.

Given that positive connotation of ambition, I have no qualms in admitting that I was ambitious all through my career.

When I stepped down from RBI in 2013, which in some sense ended my formal career, I told a friend, 'I have no further ambition.' I realized immediately that I had said something that I did not mean. What I really wanted to say was that I was no longer in a hierarchy where success is measured by how high you go. Of course, I continue to be ambitious in my post-RBI life. I set goals for myself and do the best I can to achieve them.

How ambitious should you be? Most people are familiar with the mythological story of Icarus. After his father created wings using candle wax and feathers, Icarus set out on a flight across the Mediterranean Sea.

His father warned Icarus not to fly too high or too low, as heat would melt the wax and the ocean would soak the feathers. After Icarus began his flight, however, he ignored his father's warnings and ambitiously tried to fly higher and higher. As his father had warned, the wax melted, and Icarus plunged to his death.

Hence the moral: it's important not to fly too close to the sun or fly too low near the ocean. Too much ambition or too little of it are both bad. The right level of ambition should be setting difficult but not impossible goals.

Has the IAS Failed the Nation?[*]

Has the IAS failed the nation? I wish the answer were a resounding 'no'. Much to my regret though, that's not the case. The public perception of the IAS today is of an elitist, self-serving, status quo–perpetuating set of bureaucrats who are out of touch with reality, who wallow in their privileges and social status and have lost the courage of conviction to stand up for what's right.

It wasn't always like this. In the mid-1970s when I was a fresh entrant into the service, if the government was being attacked by the opposition on a scam or a scandal, all that the chief minister had to do was to stand up in the Assembly and announce that he would appoint an IAS officer to inquire into the matter. That was enough to shut down the debate. Today if a chief minister were to say that, she is likely to be booed.

It's difficult to put a precise date on when the decline started. When the IAS was instituted soon after Independence as a successor to the colonial-era ICS, it was seen as the home-grown answer to the enormous task of nation-building in a country embarking on an unprecedented experiment of anchoring democracy in a poor, illiterate society. Whether it was agricultural development, land reforms, building irrigation projects, promoting industry, improving health and education delivery, implementing social justice or enforcing the rule of law, the IAS was seen as the delivery arm. IAS officers led this effort from the front, built an impressive development administration network from ground zero and earned for the service a formidable reputation for competence, commitment and integrity.

---

[*] Originally published in the *Times of India* on 25 March 2022.

That reputation began unravelling in subsequent decades. The IAS lost its ethos and its way. Ineptitude, indifference and corruption crept in. Arguably, this negative stereotype view is shaped by a minority of officers who have gone astray, but the worry is that that minority is no longer small. A chief minister once told me that of the IAS officers at his disposal, about 25 per cent were callous, corrupt or incompetent, the middle 50 per cent had happily turned into sinecures and he had to depend on the remaining 25 per cent to get all his work done. The prime minister echoed a similar view when he openly expressed in the parliament last year his disenchantment with the 'babu culture' in the bureaucracy.

What explains this malaise in the IAS? The standard scapegoats are the recruitment examination, the induction training and subsequent in-service training, limited opportunities for self-improvement and indifferent or even callous career management. For sure, these are all areas in need of improvement but to believe that these are the biggest problems ailing the IAS is to miss the forest for the trees.

The biggest problem with the IAS is a deeply flawed system of incentives and penalties. The service still attracts some of the best talent in the country, and young recruits come in with sharp minds and full of enthusiasm to 'change the world'. But soon, they become cogs in the wheels of complacency and acquiescence, turn lazy and cynical, and worse, lose their moral compass.

IAS officers would like the world to believe that this happens because of politicians standing in the way of their delivering results. You can't miss noticing that most IAS memoirs are, at heart, tales of: 'I was going to do great things, but politicians came in the way and stopped me.'

I don't want to trivialize the challenge of political interference; in a democracy, it comes with the territory. But to blame politicians for the intellectual and moral decline of the IAS is self-serving. Politicians will, of course, dangle carrots but why should officers go for them? What happens, though, is that some individual officers with weak moral fabric succumb to the temptation and others follow suit, either attracted by the rewards or simply to save their careers.

The truth is that no political system, no matter how venal, can corrupt a bureaucracy if it stands united and inflexibly committed to collective high standards of ethics and professional integrity. Sadly, that has not been the IAS story.

It strikes me that Prime Minister Boris Johnson of the UK is currently being investigated for alleged 'party-gate' transgressions by the British equivalents of our cabinet secretary and the Delhi Police. And not one member of the UK parliament, not even an opposition MP, has cast any doubt on the integrity of the probes. Such a thing happening in our system is unimaginable, and that is a reflection not of the low esteem in which our politicians are held but of the low esteem in which our bureaucracy is held.

So, what is the problem with incentives and penalties? For a start, when everyone gets promoted by efflux of time, to use a bureaucratic phrase, there is no pressure on officers to perform and deliver results. In a system where the smart, enthusiastic and capable are not assured of rising to the top, and the corrupt, lazy and incompetent don't get weeded out, there is no motivation for officers to upgrade their knowledge and skills. A system that promotes mediocrity and risk aversion rather than innovation and change sinks to a low common denominator as indeed the IAS has.

The IAS has to be reformed into a meritocracy. There will be resistance, of course, but it is doable. How to go about that has to await another opinion piece.

I am deeply conscious that there are hundreds of young IAS officers out there in the field performing near miracles under testing circumstances. Sadly, my generation of civil servants and subsequent cohorts have bequeathed a flawed legacy to these unsung heroes. To them passes the challenge and opportunity of recovering the soul of the IAS.

10

If Something Cannot
Go on Forever, It Will Stop

State Finance Secretary

On my return from Central deputation to my home cadre of Andhra Pradesh in October 1993, I was posted as finance secretary in the state government. This was a surprise because I had no prior experience in finance. Yes, I had worked in the Ministry of Finance in Delhi but my experience there was in handling external finance such as balance of payments, which was far removed from the job chart of a state finance secretary.

Besides, the post of finance secretary is much coveted, and typically, many officers would be vying for the job. It was unlikely that anyone would be posted as finance secretary without at least expressing an interest in the job to the chief minister or the chief secretary. What surprised me more was that our chief minister at the time, K. Vijaya Bhaskar Reddy, a giant of a man in both physical and political stature, did not know me personally. I therefore figured that Jayabharath Reddy, the chief secretary, who regarded me well, must have been responsible for this posting.

All through my career, I had been quite aspirational in the sense that I was never indifferent to the postings I was given. Career trajectory mattered to me. At this particular juncture, though, after spending five years in Delhi, I was uncharacteristically agnostic about what job the state government gave me. Honestly, I was hoping they would give me a relatively stress-free assignment, which would allow me some personal time to regroup. Both my parents had passed away during my Delhi deputation, and I had to emotionally come to terms with this sense of being orphaned. Besides, our two sons were going into senior high school, and I wanted to spend time with them doing both studies and other activities together.

That was not to be. Being finance secretary is anything but stress-free. But I should not complain because it was a very rewarding experience, and looking back, I can say it was a turning point in my career progression.

A caveat here. I was not *the* finance secretary. We had a principal finance secretary (PFS) who had overall charge of coordination, with three secretary-level officers below him with well-defined work allocation. Since my job chart included the quintessential finance functions of budget formulation and treasury management, I was designated as finance secretary while my other two colleagues who looked after mainly expenditure control were designated as secretaries of finance. I remained on the job for five and a half years (1993–99), in the final year becoming the PFS myself. In my entire career, this was the job where I had the longest tenure.

No wriggle room in the budget

I got on to a steep learning curve, picking up both the micro details of budget management as well as understanding the macro picture from a public finance perspective. Very soon I realized, much to my dismay, and even some frustration, that there is very little wriggle room for any discretion or course correction. Much of the budget is pre-programmed both on the resource and expenditure sides.

Take the resource side. A state's resources typically comprise three components. The first is the taxes that states levy themselves—technically called state's own taxes (sales tax—which has since transformed into GST, motor vehicle tax, excise duties on alcohol, etc.) and non-tax revenues (mining cess, interest receipts, etc.). The second component is what states get from the Centre by way of a share in the Centre's taxes and by way of grants. Finally, states borrow substantial amounts from the market; these loans typically comprise a third of their total expenditure.

The first question I explored was the scope for increasing the resources. The answer was disappointing. States had for long given up introducing any new taxes. Even raising the rates of existing taxes had become politically unacceptable. Any increase in tax collection had to come entirely from buoyancy, that is economic growth, and we were resigned to that.

Could we instead plead for more resource transfers from the Centre? Not much chance there either since

Central transfers were made as per the recommendations of the Finance Commission, and there were only incremental variations from one year to the next. Finally, borrowing more was also out of the question since how much a state could borrow was determined by the Centre on the basis of fiscal sustainability.* The net result was that there was virtually no scope for meaningfully increasing the resources, at any rate in the short term.

If the finance secretary could not get much traction on raising resources, could he use his ingenuity to work on expenditure restructuring—reducing unproductive expenditure and raising productive expenditure? Much to my disappointment, I found that the degrees of freedom on this side of the equation were equally limited.

Let me start with the big picture. The two largest components of a state government's expenditure are staff salaries and pensions, which account for about 38 per cent of total expenditure, and interest payments on accumulated debt, which account for another 12 per cent. That meant at least half of a state government's total expenditure was non-discretionary with no scope for any reduction. The other big item of expenditure is subsidies of various kinds. For political reasons, it was difficult to touch them. As someone said, introducing a new subsidy is like joining the mafia: you can get in, but can't ever get out.

Whatever was left after meeting these committed expenditures went into capital spending in sectors such as energy, irrigation, roads and housing. What was allocated

---

* States have since found ingenious ways of circumventing the constraints imposed by the Fiscal Responsibility and Budget Management (FRBM) Act.

for capital expenditure was just the residual. That's a pity since it is actually this capital spending that determines the longer-term growth potential of the state.

In any case, even in capital spending, the scope for any budgetary discretion was limited since allocations across projects were made largely on an incremental basis. If, for example, we allocated Rs 100 crore for the Jurala project last year, the allocation this year would be about the same, or at best just marginally increased.

Not only was our capital spending low, but whatever little we spent, we spent inefficiently. In an ideal world, the government would take on a few projects and complete them quickly so that sunk costs were minimized. In the real world of democratic politics, though, that seldom happens because every MLA has to be satisfied with some project in their constituency. As a result, at any given time, we had a large number of projects under implementation with available funds spread thinly across them. That was one of the reasons why it was typical for projects to take decades to complete and start yielding any returns. It used to be said, only half in jest, that junior engineers who joined service in the Nagarjuna Sagar multipurpose dam superannuated from the project!

I am obviously not clued into the state of state finances today. But from what I see and hear, the situation is much worse both by way of budget sustainability and budget integrity. States are borrowing far beyond their means and spending it on what has popularly come to be called 'freebies'. In a poor country, it's morally right to provide safety nets to the vulnerable, but how much is spent should be constrained by the ability to repay the debts.

Regrettably, the usual checks and balances that should ensure sustainability are not working, with the result that political expediency is trumping economic virtue.

The budget drill

The next budget, due in February 1994, was just four months away when I started my job as finance secretary, and I was quite overawed by the responsibility. It was a steep learning curve.

I realized that some of our systems and processes were actually quite impressive. Take expenditure classification for example. To the uninitiated, classifying expenditure into major and minor heads, sub-heads and sub-detailed heads would likely come across as formidably complex, needlessly confusing and utterly arcane. On the contrary, it is a sophisticated system that reflects years of experience and learning by doing. Designing a uniform budget classification for a large and diverse country like India is no mean task. Our budget classification manages that with extraordinary finesse. It makes it possible, for example, to compare the trend growth in wages of temporary government staff in Meghalaya with that in Andhra Pradesh.

The budget process ran to a well-honed drill. At the heart of this exercise was the long series of meetings we held with all government departments—revenue-earning departments (commercial taxes, state excise, stamps and registration, mining, etc.), spending departments (irrigation, roads, health, education, for example) as well as public sector undertakings (PSUs). As I mentioned earlier, there were only incremental changes from year to year;

nevertheless, these meetings were a wonderful opportunity to get the big picture of the government's working that no other job in the government could possibly give.

A lot of haggling went on in these meetings. As the finance team, we would push for higher collections from revenue-earning departments and lower expenditures from spending departments. Predictably, our counterparties would push back against finance department pressures.

Of course, some subjective judgements did creep in. Here, for example, are some snippets of our post-meeting internal deliberations. 'Spending on irrigation has become more efficient since she has taken over. We must accommodate her request as much as possible.' 'He is useless. Big talk but nothing to show for it. No point giving him more money.' 'Those new schemes he is talking about are too iffy. We must watch before putting more money there.'

Across state governments in the country, more so in finance departments, there are veterans—fonts of accumulated knowledge and experience—who provide continuity and stability. We had ours—Subba Rao (my namesake) and Das. They knew the accounting heads by heart, had the entire budget in their heads and could compute any ratio or trend faster than you could input the numbers into your calculator. Such long-timers added tremendous value, although senior officers seldom acknowledged their contributions.

The flip side of this veteran expertise, though, was that some old hands resisted change. Let me give an example, admittedly trivial, but it illustrates the point. After a particularly tedious session of editing the draft budget speech late one evening, I gave the draft back to Subba

Rao and suggested: 'When you bring the next version, please number the paragraphs and pages.' His impulsive response was to resist. He said, 'Sir, we've never done that before,' as if that was a good enough reason not to break a hoary tradition! As generations of public policy students learn, the power of precedent, no matter how trivial, is overwhelmingly strong in government decision-making. I became testy with his response but just about controlled myself from snapping back at him.

As he was leaving my office, Subba Rao accidentally dropped the sheaf of papers on the floor. As he knelt to gather them, I got the feeling that he was likely thinking of the tedious job of putting the papers back in order. He looked at me sheepishly and said, 'Sir, I will number the paragraphs and pages when I come back with the edited version.'

Getting the chief minister's approval for the budget

We got the first draft of the budget ready about a week before its scheduled presentation in the Assembly.

An important part of the pre-budget exercise was to get the chief minister's approval for the budget. The precise mechanics of going through this step varied from state to state; they were also a function of the personalities of the chief minister and the finance minister and the rapport between them. Chief Minister Vijaya Bhaskar Reddy was quite hands-off and left much of the nitty-gritty to Rosiah, the finance minister. Rosiah, a seasoned politician himself, was a minimalist and did not intervene except to make sure that the political interests of the government were reflected in the budget.

A meeting with the chief minister was arranged, and I prepared for it like I was preparing for an examination because it was my first experience and also because the 'syllabus' was huge and open-ended.

I expected it to be a marathon meeting and thought the chief minister would grill us on the numbers on the resource and expenditure sides. As it turned out, it lasted barely fifteen minutes. The meeting started with my explaining the big picture, but after about three minutes, the CM cut me short and asked how much we were allocating for irrigation. He weighed that in his mind for a few moments, asked for the previous year's allocation and then suggested that the allocation be increased by a quarter. Where we were to cut spending to accommodate his suggestion was not raised; it was just understood that we would do the necessary financial engineering. Then he asked to see the list of irrigation projects and suggested a doubling of the allocation for the projects in his home district of Kurnool.

The meeting was over! I was disappointed that all the preparation that I had done was not put to the test. But in hindsight, I saw some maturity in the way Vijaya Bhaskar Reddy handled the meeting. He knew there was little scope for flexibility, had confidence that the bureaucracy would take care of the nitty-gritty and focused on securing his political interest through the allocations for irrigation.

If something cannot go on forever, it will eventually stop

Budgets are so driven by short-term compulsions that long-term sustainability is seldom discussed. The overriding motivation is to maximize borrowing to maximize spending to satisfy maximum political constituencies.

Borrowing per se is not bad. There is, in fact, a good case for governments to borrow to fund capital projects because that spending would generate growth, which in turn would generate tax revenues and the projects would pay for themselves. But governments borrow not just for capital expenditure but even for current expenditure, which means—in technical jargon—that they run revenue deficits. As the debt stock grows year after year, the interest payments too grow in tandem, eating into an ever-increasing share of the revenues and pushing the state into a debt trap. It's not surprising that interest payments were the single largest item of expenditure of virtually every state budget and their share in total expenditure grew faster than any other expenditure item, showing that the debt noose was tightening.

Yet, politicians largely remain nonchalant. But this is not unique to India. Politicians everywhere have short time horizons. If they can get by today, they go for it; tomorrow, they believe, will take care of itself. Economists describe this as having a high discount rate. If there is a choice between getting Rs 10,000 today and getting Rs 11,000 tomorrow, most people will opt to wait till tomorrow. A politician, on the other hand, will take Rs 10,000 today even if the offer for tomorrow is raised to Rs 12,000.

The obvious way to avoid a debt trap is to reduce current expenditures—what we call revenue expenditures. But much of the current expenditure, as I said earlier, is pre-programmed. Staff salaries and pensions can't be reduced, at any rate in the short term. Interest payments are contractual and there is no scope for pruning them. That explains why much of the discussion around expenditure reduction revolves around restructuring subsidies.

Prime Minister Modi's comment in August 2022 about the *revadi* culture in politics has triggered an interesting, and much-needed, debate on 'freebies'. It's unproductive to try and apportion blame in this regard. Both the Centre and states are guilty, as are all political parties. The only thing I can say is that because state governments are on the frontline, state-level subsidies tend to be more retail in nature with vote bank politics playing an outsized role.

NTR's charismatic populism

NTR first became chief minister of Andhra Pradesh in 1983. His monumental election victory just ten months after starting a greenfield political party is unparalleled in Indian political history. His trademark 'rice at two rupees per kilo' laid the foundations for subsidized rations for the poor, which has now been mainstreamed across the country.

NTR was not just a teetotaller himself, but he had moral indignation for people who drank. He was very keen on imposing a prohibition on alcohol in 1984, soon after he came in as chief minister. But, as I wrote earlier, the bureaucracy pushed back, arguing that the tax we collected on alcohol was a big source of revenue, and if we sacrificed it, we wouldn't be able to finance his flagship schemes such as rice at two rupees per kilo.

How has Gujarat, Mahatma Gandhi's home state, been able to live with prohibition, NTR would counter officials.

The stock response would be that Andhra Pradesh and Gujarat were not comparable. Gujarat was an industrialized state that netted much higher sales tax on a per capita basis than Andhra Pradesh; besides, over the years, Gujarat had been able to adjust to no revenues from liquor.

I don't think NTR bought this story, but he didn't push the point.

NTR, who lived much of his life as a cinema hero in Madras (now Chennai), for long the centre of the south Indian film industry, saw first-hand the industrial progress in Tamil Nadu, and his dream was to make Andhra Pradesh rival Tamil Nadu. The bureaucracy leveraged this ambition of his to scare him away from prohibition. The argument would be that the state would lose out on industrial investments as highly paid executives would find it unattractive to live in a state with prohibition. But here again, NTR came up with the Gujarat counterfactual—the most rapidly industrializing state in the country despite prohibition.

NTR acquiesced in the bureaucratic pushback, but I suspect that from his own moral perspective, he attributed Gujarat's relative prosperity, especially its rapid industrialization, to prohibition.

NTR lost the election in 1989. Fast forward to 1994 and the next election cycle. Being out of office and with no bureaucracy to rein him in, there was no stopping NTR. He ran on a platform of a substantial expansion of his rice subsidy scheme and prohibition in the state. But of course, he had his finger on the pulse of the people. The early 1990s had witnessed a vigorous anti-arrack movement in Andhra Pradesh triggered by a mass awareness campaign

run by the National Literacy Mission (NLC). It started on
a small scale with protests by women in a remote village—
Dubbagunta in the southern district of Nellore—against
alcoholism and domestic violence by the menfolk. The
movement soon gathered pace and galvanized into a mass
and massive ground-level agitation across much of the
state. Unsurprisingly, Rosamma, who was the local leader
of the Dubbagunta agitation, became a folk hero.

Vijaya Bhaskar Reddy, the ruling chief minister whom
NTR was trying to unseat, asked us for a note on the
cost of his rival's poll promises. The note we gave him
said predictably that NTR's numbers didn't add up. State
finances were already overstretched, and we were barely
able to meet even essential expenditure. The budgetary
arithmetic just did not allow what NTR was promising,
a combination of the sacrifice of excise tax, the second
highest source of revenue after sales tax, and a massive
expansion of the rice subsidy scheme.

Reddy used the gist of our note in his own poll
campaign to allege that NTR was making tall promises
that he wouldn't be able to deliver on. Sure enough, at
the next campaign stop, the media asked NTR to react to
Chief Minister Reddy's criticism that he was fooling the
people. NTR gave a cinematic chuckle and a Napoleonic
response, 'Where there is a will, there is a way!' The
accompanying media and the crowd applauded the
dramatic response, and no one bothered to press the
issue further.

End of story? Perish the thought. Within ten days after
that incident, in December 1994, NTR won the election
with a thumping majority. Given to drama as he was, he

decided that a people's chief minister like him could not be sworn in, in a cloister of the Raj Bhavan! Instead, he would take the oath of office in full public view in the Lal Bahadur Shastri Stadium in the heart of the twin cities. The grand finale of that swearing-in ceremony in front of a mammoth gathering was NTR signing the file, right there on the dais, imposing prohibition.

The next day, even as NTR was still revelling in his return to power, we in the finance team sought time from his office to brief the new chief minister on the financial situation. Prohibition was a done deal and, of course, irreversible. Our intent was to convey to him the dire state of state finances and to enjoin him to defer the implementation of his other populist poll promises.

No chief minister likes being told that his big ideas are not workable; NTR had even less tolerance for naysayers. He was clearly unhappy with our party-pooping briefing. In NTR's world view, he was Moses, ordained by God to deliver millions of poor people out of poverty and suffering, and we, the finance people, were heartless bureaucrats, in the style of *filmi* villains who, instead of telling him how to find the magic money tree, were sabotaging his dreams for *his* people.

Predictably, we reached an impasse in that discussion. NTR was not inclined to renege on any of his poll promises, and we continued to plead, with due deference but firmly, our inability to make both ends meet. All of a sudden, he said, 'I will go to Delhi and ask the prime minister for money.'

NTR sincerely believed that he could persuade the prime minister to give a special allocation to Andhra Pradesh to fund his populist schemes. This was not so much arrogance as pure naiveté on his part. I knew in my heart of hearts that this Delhi mission would be a futile exercise but had neither the courage nor the inclination to prevent him from trying his luck.

Sure enough, an appointment with the prime minister was arranged within hours. From my Delhi experience, I knew that chief ministers were seldom denied an appointment with the prime minister. But in the first instance, the Prime Minister's Office (PMO) would ask for the agenda and take a few days to get some background briefing notes for the PM before giving an appointment. On this occasion, that process was short-circuited. P.V. Narasimha Rao was the prime minister, and an unsuspecting PMO gave an appointment thinking that it was just a courtesy call on the prime minister by the newly elected chief minister of the PM's home state.

NTR flew to Delhi the next morning and returned to Hyderabad by the evening flight. The media was present in full force at the Begumpet airport, curious about what could potentially be a dramatic story.* It turned out to be a dramatic story but for exactly the opposite reasons. NTR, ever the actor-politician, told the media in chaste Telugu, frustration and fatigue writ large on his face, 'I am appalled at the prime minister's negative attitude, especially towards his home state. The people of the state gave me a massive mandate to implement prohibition, expand the rice subsidy scheme and implement other welfare schemes. I asked the prime minister for money to implement this

---

* This was, of course, much before the advent of 24/7 news.

sacred mandate. He heartlessly declined any support. This is complete denigration of democracy!'

Not for NTR the nuances of fiscal federalism and formula-driven transfers to states!

Implementing prohibition

The implementation of prohibition was the responsibility of the Excise Department, but I was privy to some ticklish practical issues that came up in the implementation.

What about foreigners? Should prohibition apply to them as well? Wouldn't we lose out on tourism if we denied them the pleasure of drinking? In relative terms, tourism was not big in Andhra Pradesh, but it aspired to move up the ladder. NTR was persuaded to relent in allowing foreigners to drink. A foreign businessman enjoying his tipple in the bar of a five-star hotel while his Indian hosts eyed him with envy must have made an interesting sight!

The armed forces were another exempted category. NTR gave in without much pushback.

He was also persuaded to permit people to drink if they had a doctor's certificate that their condition required them to imbibe alcohol every day. A doctor friend of mine told me that there was no known disease for which drinking alcohol was a cure!

The battle for budget integrity

Andhra Pradesh lifted prohibition in 1996, two years after it was introduced and about a year after Chandrababu Naidu (CBN), NTR's son-in-law and finance minister in his cabinet, ousted him in a palace coup and became chief minister himself.

Although CBN belonged to the same party and the same caste as NTR, he represented a regime change. He lacked NTR's aura, enormous fan base and oratorial flourish, but he made up for that with his energy, enthusiasm, deft political management, pragmatic and modern world view, and hands-on management style.

As chief minister, CBN did not hold the finance portfolio, but he was for all practical purposes the finance minister. The finance minister, Ashok Gajapati Raju, was fiercely loyal to CBN and was quite happy to yield even day-to-day management to the chief minister.

It was under CBN for over four years that I cut my teeth in the nitty-gritty of public finance management. CBN was educated, had been finance minister earlier and ran a private dairy enterprise. He was therefore aware of the importance of maintaining budget integrity. Nevertheless, he had his political compulsions and was given to making off-the-cuff expenditure commitments, leaving it to the finance officials to do the necessary juggling.

Budget processes at the state level are looser than at the Centre. In Delhi, new expenditure commitments proposed in the course of the financial year go through a fairly rigorous vetting process, but state-level processes are more ad hoc. Funding for new expenditure commitments is found through ad hoc adjustments.

Even as the full budget containing detailed expenditure plans, technically called appropriations, is approved by the Assembly, the rules of business provide for finance officials to reappropriate expenditures from one use to another.

There are also enabling provisions to introduce new items of expenditure that were not in the original budget. This flexibility has been built in to allow the executive to meet urgent and unforeseen expenditures without having to wait for legislative approval.

But rules that were meant to be invoked to meet exceptional situations have over time come to be resorted to as a matter of routine. As a result, the ex-post expenditure pattern deviates significantly from the original allocations. The deviations are, of course, sanctified by legislative approval through supplementary demand for grants. Most of the time though, 'the supplementary budget' is passed without any debate, or should there be any debate at all, it focuses on political issues; the issue of budget integrity is never raised.

By the time the numbers come before the Public Accounts Committee (PAC), the budget is history. Besides, even the most effective PAC can at best do only a post-mortem. Moreover, since it is the bureaucracy that faces the PAC, the political executive brazenly gets away with serial transgressions. With checks and balances having eroded in practice, budget integrity becomes hostage to politics.

What I have explained so far is 'how' politicians tamper with the budget, but 'why' do they do it? Because of the compulsions of retail politics—to please a constituency, to maintain the support of an MLA or to win a by-election. The more frontline a politician, the greater the temptation to indulge in pork-barrel politics. Can bureaucrats stop this? They can certainly advise against such decisions, and many often do, but beyond a point, they have to comply with the orders. After all, they are not being asked to do anything illegal or irregular. What can then be the justification for stonewalling? If, in fact, they did that, they would surely be guilty of insubordination.

All in all, preserving the integrity of the budget became a struggle for me as finance secretary. An even bigger struggle was cash management on a day-to-day basis.

State governments maintain their bank accounts with the RBI, and every afternoon at 3 p.m., the RBI office in Nagpur would send a message to the finance department on the balance in the government's account.* If a state's account was in overdraft for longer than ten days at a stretch, the RBI locked the account and the state's cheques were no longer honoured. We used to live in dread of this daily missive from the RBI and had become quite adept at finding 'five minutes to midnight' solutions.

CBN was smart enough to know the tension between short-term pressures and long-term sustainability, but his overriding stance was obviously driven by political compulsions. I remember one occasion when I had a one-on-one meeting with him to decide where to cut budgeted expenditures in order to accommodate post-budget spending commitments. The meeting was relatively brief and when it ended, we were both dissatisfied: he, because he was forced to agree to spending cuts, and I, because I couldn't force him far enough.

Just as I was leaving his office, Rachel Chatterjee, then health secretary, walked in. CBN obviously knew what she was coming for. He stopped me and said, 'Subbarao *garu*,

---

* These days, governments can check their account balance online.

can you please allocate Rs 50 crore to Rachel for repairs to hospital buildings?' This, literally moments after I thought I had made him realize the gravity of our financial situation and the need to be more disciplined about taking on off-the-cuff commitments not included in the budget. By the time I left his office, I was net negative in terms of expenditure commitments!

In the finance department, we were forever looking for an opportunity of a meeting with the chief minister to discuss the state of our public finances and the urgent need for course correction, but getting his undivided attention proved to be ever elusive.

On the few occasions when such a meeting did indeed occur, it didn't get very far. About ten minutes into the meeting, CBN would ask for data, for example, the sales tax we had collected on tamarind, district-wise and month-wise for the last twelve months. In the mid-90s, when we were just about embarking on computerization, getting such data was difficult, although not impossible. But what indeed was the point? As much as it was important to analyse the data on sales tax on tamarind, it had only marginal relevance to the larger issue of public finance sustainability. Around the time we got this far into the discussion, his staff would signal that he was already way behind schedule for a public engagement and that hundreds of people were waiting. 'Why don't you come tomorrow, first thing in the morning with all the data, and we will have an open-ended meeting?' We were forever pushing the issue to tomorrow.

On occasion, CBN would show his exasperation by comparing himself to the chief minister of a neighbouring state known for his epicurean lifestyle. He would remark, 'Look, I am working eighteen hours a day whereas he comes to the office at noon and winds up at 4 p.m. They are getting 18 per cent growth in sales tax while we are stagnating at 10 per cent.' I wanted to tell him that looking for a correlation between the hours put in by the chief minister and the growth in state revenues was a futile exercise. But of course, he knew.

If ever in any meeting we got as far as discussing the deeper issue of the structural gap between our resources and spending commitments, CBN would ask, 'Why don't we get some consultants to advise us on what to do?' This was partly an escapist tactic to avoid doing the politically difficult things and partly a slender hope that maybe with their fresh minds, consultants could lead him to the magic money tree that his bureaucrats were unable to find.

I used to be irritated by this suggestion because the solutions to our fiscal problems were blindingly obvious— raise taxes and cut expenditures. These were politically difficult but inescapable options. For sure, some consultancy could help us, but only after we had plucked the low-hanging fruit; it was premature and counterproductive to spend time, money and effort on consultants before that.

But of course, the chief minister prevailed. We had at one time, almost overlapping with one another, the global consultancy firm McKinsey, two Harvard professors (of whom one was a marketing expert!), a Delhi-based think tank and the World Bank consulting for us on public finance management. I was frustrated by all the homework we had to do to feed the consultants all the data and information they required, only for them to tell us in the end what we already knew—that it is not possible to grow money on trees.

Although my narrative draws from my first-hand experience in Andhra Pradesh, I knew that we were not alone. From informal discussions with finance secretaries in other states, I realized that many of them were worse placed in terms of erosion of checks and balances. And I gather from what I hear and read that financial management at the state level has deteriorated markedly in the thirty years since I left state finances. Political expediency has made ad hoc tampering with budgets, appropriating funds of public enterprises, off-budget borrowing and hiding contingent liabilities commonplace practices. It's possible CBN would look like a saint when measured against today's total disdain, if not contempt, for the sustainability of public finances.

The very first white paper

I recall one of those rare meetings with CBN to discuss structural public finance issues when he said, partly in exasperation and partly as a challenge to us: 'Look, persuading me is only part of your job. I need to get my ministers on board. Why don't you make a presentation to the cabinet and convince them?'

We grabbed this opening he gave us and put a lot of thought into the messages we should drive home in the cabinet note. After much deliberation, we crystallized four points.

Our first point was to say that our public finance situation was unsustainable. If something could not

go on forever, it would eventually stop.[*] Our debt was
growing at a rapid pace and interest payments on the
accumulated debt were eating into the money available
for development expenditure. It was fine for a government
to borrow if the loans were used for investment in social
infrastructure (schools, health services, nutrition) or
physical infrastructure (roads, bridges, power plants,
etc.), which would lay the foundation for future growth
so that the loans paid for themselves. Instead, borrowing
money to spend on current consumption like salaries,
pensions and subsidies amounted to enjoying the pleasure
of spending while passing on the pain of repayment to a
future generation. 'Would any of you contemplate sinning
against your own children?' was the pointed question
we asked.

Our second point emphasized the huge structural
inefficiencies in our spending—allocative inefficiency as it's
called in jargon. We spent far too little on capital projects
because what was allocated for them was the residual after
meeting all other 'committed' expenditures. Even that
small amount was spent inefficiently. Ideally, we should be
focusing on a few projects and completing them in quick
time to avoid sunk costs. Instead, what was happening
was that the available money, already quite limited, was
spread thinly over several projects because of the political
compulsion to satisfy every constituency.

What added to the inefficiency was that there was a bias
for new projects even though spending on the maintenance

---

[*] 'If something cannot go on forever, it will stop.' This famous observation
was made by Herb Stein, senior fellow at the American Enterprise
Institute. It became famous largely because it was just that, obvious.

of existing projects such as dredging irrigation canals, repairing roads and school buildings, etc. yielded higher economic returns (see the tailpiece on 'Edifice complex').

Our third point was on the need to prune subsidies. In a poor country like ours, providing safety nets to the most vulnerable households was not only desirable but even necessary. But we had to do so prudently—first by putting a ceiling on the amount we spent and second by designing subsidies such that they were welfare maximizing. To illustrate the point, we compared our flagship rice subsidy scheme to Tamil Nadu's hot midday meal for school children. Tamil Nadu's scheme was decidedly better as it targeted children who most needed the nutrition; also, the midday meal improved school enrolment and retention rates, especially of girl children. Should we not replace our rice subsidy scheme with one designed on the Tamil Nadu model, which was more efficient?

Our final point was that not only were our budget allocations inefficient, but we also tampered with them, throwing carefully thought-out priorities to the wind.

So, what was the way out? The cabinet note suggested that our structural problems were so deep that band-aid solutions would not help; we needed deep surgery. We needed to prune our subsidies, in particular, raise the price of subsidized rice, lift prohibition and briskly privatize some public enterprises starting with those that were most egregiously eating into budget resources. We also needed to accept some self-imposed discipline on honouring the integrity of the budget.

A reform package as strong as this would be politically difficult for any chief minister, but it was particularly so for CBN because of the political circumstances in which he had risen to the top position.

About a year earlier, in September 1995, CBN had toppled NTR in a palace coup taking advantage of the disenchantment of a growing number of MLAs with NTR because of what they viewed as the undue influence that his wife Lakshmi Parvathi was seen to have over his decisions. The party still swore by NTR's policies, and a majority of the MLAs had, in fact, gravitated to CBN on the understanding that he would be able to implement NTR's policies more efficiently than NTR himself. But now, this cabinet note that we presented was asking him to undo NTR's policies, which could potentially cost him political support! It is to his enormous credit that CBN not only took the risk but even permitted our blunt messaging.

The discussion in the cabinet rolled on for several hours. As would happen in a meeting like this, and on issues as big as these, the discussion was all over the map. After everyone had exhausted themselves, in what would turn out to be a political masterstroke, CBN said, 'Why don't we publish a white paper and generate public discussion on the future course of action?'

These days, it's become quite a common practice for state governments to publish white papers, but in the mid-1990s, ours was a pioneering attempt. Our initiative was also unique in one other way. Most of the time, governments resort to a white paper with a political motive—to show how the previous regime had mismanaged finances. But our white paper was set in a different context—to buy in popular support for what would normally be seen as unpopular initiatives.

The level of public engagement in the white paper was astounding, far beyond what we had imagined possible. We had started out with a modest game plan. We would do a media conference in the hope that the media would then take on the job of dissemination and mobilizing opinion. In the event, the debate caught on like wildfire. There were open discussions by think tanks, seminars in colleges and universities, focus group meetings by NGOs, opinion pieces and editorials in newspapers and panel discussions on TV (which admittedly was a limited medium in those days).

Elated by the response, CBN ordered that the white paper had to be discussed in every zilla parishad at a specially convened district coordination meeting and at party forums at the district and block levels. I recall having done at least twenty-five interactions of various types while my colleagues in the finance department did a similar tour of duty.

While the process was energizing, the outcomes were stunning. There was wide and deep support for the rollback of the populist measures, and surprisingly, even against the backdrop of the anti-arrack agitation a couple of years earlier, the resistance to a partial lifting of prohibition was also quite muted. In fact, support for the reform package recommended in the white paper was so deep that after about two months of the engagement process, people began asking why the government was not acting yet.

I must admit I was quite sceptical about the white paper exercise and even suspected that it was another diversionary tactic by CBN. In the event, the success of the whole exercise is a tribute to CBN's political strategy and administrative acumen.

Within a couple of years of becoming the chief minister, CBN became the poster child of intellectuals and the intelligentsia not just in the country but even internationally. He came to be seen as a new-generation politician who combined grassroots political understanding, a modern outlook, a broad world view and tech-savvy administrative capabilities. The white paper exercise was undoubtedly one of the contributing factors to burnishing that reputation.

As I write this in 2023, CBN is still politically active but out of power. He often boasts that Cyberabad, the burgeoning and sprawling software city adjacent to Hyderabad that these days gives Bengaluru a run for its money, was a result of his foresight and planning. He can be equally proud of the white paper initiative.

Budget discussion in the Assembly

I used to enjoy the budget discussion in the Assembly. It was often lively, and the rich grassroots touch that MLAs brought to bear on budget issues and the clarity and wit in some of their interventions were quite impressive.

The leader of the opposition, Rosiah, who was finance minister himself in an earlier Congress government and would become the chief minister in unexpected circumstances a decade later, was a fiery speaker. During the budget discussion in the Assembly, he once thundered in chaste Telugu: 'Speaker Sir, this government is borrowing like there is no tomorrow. Government debt is exploding, and state finances are on the brink of collapse. Sir, every resident of the state and every household is being pushed into a debt trap. The government has imposed a debt of Rs 1.3 lakh on every man, woman and child in the state. Sir, do you know, your family of six is carrying a debt burden of nearly Rs 8 lakh?' That left the beleaguered Speaker red-faced at how the government was grievously wronging his family without his even knowing, much less consenting!

The finance minister in any state enjoys an enormous amount of clout because of the patronage at his command, and he is often ranked next only to the chief minister. It's not unusual even for opposition MLAs to try to be on the right side of the finance minister.

Within the Assembly though, the finance minister gets pilloried, by the opposition MLAs, of course, but surprisingly also on occasion by their own party members. At the micro level, he gets criticized for not allocating enough for a specific project or neglecting a certain region. At the macro level, he gets flayed for raising taxes or borrowing too much and at the same time for not raising overall expenditure sufficiently. The logical inconsistency of the MLAs' criticism—that spending be increased without increasing resources never deterred them; nor was it ever questioned.

Budget making—The government and the World Bank teach each other

Another pioneering initiative that got on track during my tenure as finance secretary was a World Bank study of state finances. From my experience in Delhi, I knew that the World Bank's operational priorities were dictated by Delhi. It was the Centre that shortlisted the projects that the World Bank should take forward.

Nevertheless, by the late 1990s, the World Bank realized that post reforms, India's states were becoming more important in the country's economic and political landscape. They were keen on getting a better understanding of state-level finances. Possibly with the consent of the Central government, they approached us to ask if they could do a comprehensive study of our fiscal situation. Why Andhra Pradesh of all the states? I suspect it was our white paper exercise and CBN's growing clout as a reformer that pushed them in our direction. They dangled a carrot; that the study could become the platform for an adjustment loan.

The study took a couple of years and there was much learning on both sides during the process. It culminated in the 'Andhra Pradesh Economic Restructuring Programme Loan', which we were told was the first-ever adjustment loan by the World Bank at a sub-national level anywhere in the world. The World Bank's task manager was Fahrettin Yagci, a Turkish national and a sound and competent economist. We were lucky to get him as he worked with energy, enthusiasm and determination to pull this off.

Not surprisingly, Fahrettin and I became good friends. What was surprising though was that Fahrettin became good friends with dozens of our staff as he invested days, even weeks, in talking to each of them and learning the nitty-gritty of our state finances. He would often be seen in animated discussion with finance department staff sitting in the *bazari* canteen in the secretariat compound, sipping hot, milky, syrupy Hyderabadi chai. By the end of the exercise, Fahrettin thoroughly absorbed our work pattern and work culture, became irredeemably fond of Hyderabadi chai, and I suspect even started absorbing the office gossip.

One day shortly after the loan was negotiated and signed off, Fahrettin dropped by my office. Among other things, he told me, 'Subba, the way you people make budgets is wrong and inefficient. You yourself saw all the flaws we reported in our study. There is so much room for improvement. If you approve, I can get the World Bank Institute (WBI) to organize a one-week training programme for your staff on the best practices in budget formulation.'

My immediate reaction was to dispute his suggestion that we didn't know how to make budgets, but I checked myself for fear of sounding arrogant and defensive. Instead, I said, 'Sure Fahrettin, we will go ahead. I will join the programme too.' We even agreed that we should take the staff off-site, maybe to Nagarjuna Sagar Project Guest House, 200 km away from Hyderabad, to avoid distractions. But on one condition, I told Fahrettin. 'Let your staff finish their course in four days and give the last day for my staff to tell your WBI experts why we make the budgets the way we do.'

My point was that as much as we had a lot to learn from the best international practices, there was a lot we could tell the World Bank experts about the political compulsions we operated under. In other words, it was not that we didn't know how to do better; it was that we couldn't do any better.

Although both Fahrettin and I were enthusiastic about this mutual training programme, it didn't take off because both of us moved on from our jobs shortly thereafter.

Paying staff salaries by bank transfer

Notwithstanding all the frustration on the work front, I
had a good personal equation with CBN. He was my age.
I knew he regarded me well and likewise, I had regard for
him. He was educated, intelligent, eager to learn, curious
about a lot of things, and importantly, was never shy about
admitting what he didn't know.

CBN had a well-earned reputation for being computer-
savvy. While I cannot vouch for how good he was
hands-on, I can say that he had the foresight to realize the
transformational impact of information technology on
administration and governance much ahead of most of us.
When Prime Minister Gujral called a national conference
on good governance in 1997, he invited CBN to be the lead
speaker. We worked for a week on his presentation, and
he impressed the Delhi meeting with his substantive and
confident presentation.

One of CBN's pet projects was that we should pay staff
salaries by bank transfer. These days with even illiterate
people making cash transfers on digital platforms using
just their cell phones, what CBN suggested might seem
trivial—and anachronistic. But remember, I am talking
about the mid-1990s when we were in the dark ages in
terms of digital technologies. Most government staff were
paid in cash while the top echelon of senior officers had the
privilege of being paid by cheque, which took several days
to get credited to one's account.

I am ashamed to admit that we pushed back on the
CM's proposal out of sheer pique. We were peeved that
instead of focusing his attention on the big structural

problems in our state finances, this man was forcing us to focus on a relatively low-priority item like paying salaries through bank transfers.

Since it is not possible to defy a CM overtly, I indulged in some guerrilla warfare. I held some token meetings with our treasury staff and with the top brass of the State Bank of Hyderabad (SBH) and Andhra Bank, which were then our treasury banks. After that, the report I gave to the chief minister was that this initiative was not feasible since banks would take three days to make the transfers from the government account to the individual accounts of the employees. This would mean we would be cash out at the end of the month for three days, which we couldn't countenance given our liquidity constraints on a day-to-day basis. Besides, the banks were quoting a huge service fee, which was avoidable given our poor finances.

CBN probably saw through my half-hearted attempt and called the bank's top brass for a meeting with him. He drove a tough bargain, and the banks yielded some ground. And we became the first state in the country to do cashless payment of salaries.

I learnt a lesson from this episode—to be open-minded to suggestions and not let personal prejudices come in the way of dealing with the political masters.

On one occasion, I sought a short meeting with CBN to discuss an urgent issue. I made an appointment, but he remained busy and was running way behind schedule. And then he had to go out for half an hour. Sensing my disappointment at missing another appointment with him, his staff suggested that I sit in his car and do business on the way.

As we set off, I realized that he was going to pay his last respects to a retired IAS officer who had passed away that morning. Thinking it inappropriate to do business at such a time, I didn't raise the issue, and our brief conversation was focused on the retired officer. But on the way back, I couldn't hold back. The ride was going to be short, indeed very short since the chief minister's convoy faces no traffic. I was anxious to get my business done. Barely had we exited the house, I started on my spiel. He looked at me with a wry smile, patted me on the shoulder and said, in some sense urging me to hold back without at the same time being seen as reprimanding me: 'Look Subbarao *garu*, when we see death with our eyes, we are reminded of the futility of our daily anxieties, pursuits and frustrations. But within moments, we succumb to the pressures and frailties of the world.' That was an uncharacteristically philosophical moment, I suspect, for both of us.

Capacity constraints in government

Many years after my tenure as finance secretary of Andhra Pradesh, in fact, when I was governor of the Reserve Bank, Bob Zoellick, the president of the World Bank, invited me to a one-on-one lunch when he was visiting Delhi. We were reasonably well acquainted with each other through the biannual Fund-Bank meetings and periodic G20 meetings.

Bob was keen to get my views on the economic and political situation in the country. At some point, our conversation moved on to capacity constraints in state governments in India. His staff had advised Bob that in its operations in India, the World Bank should give top priority to capacity-building in state governments.

I was not surprised at the brief he had got. That dearth of capacity is among the causes of India's poor governance standards is a familiar refrain heard in virtually every seminar, panel discussion or think tank report.

I have a slightly different perspective on this issue though. Admittedly our governance standards are poor, our processes are inefficient and the stereotypical view that government staff are callous and indifferent has some truth. But is capacity the main problem here? Or is it more a lack of accountability?

I draw this inference from my own experience. When I was working at the World Bank in the late 1990s, one of the bank's priorities was to implement value-added tax (VAT) in African countries. So, in every mission to African countries, we used to evangelize to their governments about the merits of moving from single-point sales and excise taxes to an integrated VAT. Our counterparts, the staff of African governments, would ask some questions and raise a few queries and then they would request us also to raise the proposal with their finance minister, or on occasion, even their prime minister. They would ask eagerly if the bank would help them implement the new tax system, train their staff and hold their hands until the new system was on track. In just about three missions, the World Bank would seal an agreement on implementing VAT.

Contrast that with my experience in India when I was finance secretary of Andhra Pradesh a few years before my World Bank stint. That was the time we were implementing VAT. The IMF and World Bank missions would visit us at intervals to guide us on the implementation. At one such meeting, I told the IMF mission that instead of interacting only with us at the state level, they should also interact with our field-level staff since they would have operational questions that we could not think of. So, we went with the Bank-Fund mission to Rajahmundry so our staff would have the benefit of learning from these experts.

What transpired in Rajahmundry was a pleasant surprise. The mission members asked questions, which our staff answered. And there were questions from our staff to the mission members, which they answered. But there were also quite a few questions from our staff for which the mission members did not have ready answers. Here were some of the world's leading experts on VAT who had no ready answers to some of the operational-level questions of our commercial tax staff operating at the ground level, some at four levels below the top.

That is a telling example of the depth of capacity in India compared to say, Africa. And that was the gist of my response to Bob Zoellick's question on capacity levels in India.

The unhappy task of saying 'no'

An occupational hazard of a finance secretary's job is having to say 'no' most of the time. Ministers and colleagues approach you with projects and initiatives to seek funding. Charged with the responsibility of balancing the government's books, having to say 'no' becomes unavoidable no matter how inclined you are to be positive. But how you say 'no' makes a difference. Colleague secretaries in the government were given to dividing finance secretaries into two categories. The first category of finance secretaries were those who, even if they said 'yes', you came out of their office with a glum face. The second category were those who, even if they said 'no', you came out with a happy face. I hope I was classified in the latter category, but no one has said that to me yet!

NTR on a one-rupee salary

Let me end this chapter with another favourite NTR story of mine. One morning, soon after he returned as chief minister in 1994, NTR summoned me. The appointment was fixed for 5 a.m. Not knowing what the summons were about, I went to the meeting with some trepidation. My apprehension was that he had thought of another populist scheme and was going to task me with finding the money for it.

In the event it turned out to be for an entirely different although equally ticklish issue. With a wide grin on his face, he told me once again using the royal 'we', 'Brother, you know we didn't come into politics to make money. We came to serve my people. Every paisa available to the government should be spent for the welfare of people. We feel bad therefore taking a salary. Please take me off the salary roster.'

I was not prepared for this request, but some instinct told me that implementing his request wouldn't be straightforward. I nodded politely and told him in some vaguely nuanced way that I would check on it. The impression I wanted to give was that I could not give a clear indication yet of how to go forward.

I then checked with my staff as well as the law department. It turned out that no minister could work for free. As people who had taken an oath of office, ministers were governed by conduct rules, but those conduct rules could only be applied to 'employees'. The law department told us that a person who was not drawing a salary could not be deemed to be an 'employee'.

I went back the next morning to request NTR that he should take at least a token salary of Re 1. NTR was clearly not happy with being denied even this simple request. What he was actually unhappy about was that I was denying him bragging rights about toiling for the poor people of his state without a salary!

Whatever may be history's judgement of NTR's legacy, three things, I believe, stand out. During her long regime as prime minister, Indira Gandhi centralized power, tilting the Centre-state balance in favour of the former. NTR's first signal contribution was to militate against that assault on state sovereignty. In fact, it was this strident anti-Centre stance at the heart of his political platform that catapulted him to a massive electoral victory. He famously said, 'The Centre is a myth.'

The second legacy of NTR would be to assert the distinct and separate identity of the south Indian states. He was aggrieved that north Indians viewed everyone south of the Vindhyas as a Madrasi, glossing over the diversity of cultures, languages and traditions in peninsular India.

Third, NTR implemented far-reaching reforms that a more 'politically calculating' chief minister would not have ventured into. He abolished the colonial-era village officer system, ended capitation fees in private colleges and enacted a law to give daughters an equal share in inheritance more than twenty years before the Centre amended the Hindu Succession Act.

The defining posting of my career

It is the lot of IAS officers to flit from one job to another, and from one organization to another. In a typical thirty-five-year career span, an officer does about fifteen different postings on average; some do as many as thirty-five either because they are crusaders who are shunned by politicians or because of their personality or work style angularities. On the other side of the spectrum, there are those who have exceptionally stable careers with no more than ten postings, either because they are too good to be sent elsewhere or because they manage to plod on without rocking the boat.

No matter where one falls on this broad spectrum, every IAS career is defined by one single posting; a job with which an officer is identified. By that yardstick, I would think being finance secretary of Andhra Pradesh for over five and a half years was my defining posting. I learnt a lot, enjoyed the job, made many friends because of the privileges of the job and hopefully no enemies despite the compulsions of having to say 'no'.

Edifice complex

Rulers everywhere are prone to what development economists call an 'edifice complex'. They love to build physical structures that people will associate with them long into the future. But there is a difference between building a Taj Mahal and a Nagarjuna Sagar Dam or a sports stadium or a parliament building. They are all edifices, but the motivation for building them is different. The Taj is an epitome of beauty and splendour while Nagarjuna Sagar, which Pandit Nehru ranked among the temples of modern India, is the largest stone masonry dam in the world and has provided livelihoods to millions of farmers. A sports stadium and a parliament building have a functional use.

In Hyderabad, my home base, we have a brand-new building—the Ambedkar Bhavan—for the state secretariat, a marvellous piece of architecture and a showcase for a twenty-first-century public office. It will forever be associated with former Chief Minister K. Chandrashekar Rao.

The edifice complex, although a term originally coined pejoratively to describe the tendency of politicians to build physical structures for electoral gains, is not necessarily bad if it rallies people behind a collective cause or unites people with a common sense of pride and purpose. The almost universal acclaim for the Ambedkar Bhavan in Hyderabad suggests that the new secretariat building has galvanized the people of the nascent state of Telangana with a renewed sense of unity.

But it's possible to take the edifice complex too far as I narrated through my travails in public finance management.

Jyoti Basu to the Rescue of Our Federalism

Deve Gowda became prime minister in June 1996 with the support of chief ministers, which made him politically hostage to them. Soon, chief ministers demanded their pound of flesh—asking for larger financial flows from the Centre. The Tenth Finance Commission had just given its report covering tax devolutions and non-plan grants, and tampering with that arrangement was not an option. The only way to meet the chief ministers' demands was to increase plan grants to states.

You will be excused for not knowing, but there is an obscure body called 'Inter State Council' (ISC) in the Home Ministry, which occupies two dingy, cobweb-infested rooms in the Vigyan Bhawan Annexe. Gowda entrusted the task of finding a solution to the chief ministers' demands to a subcommittee of the ISC, comprising twelve chief ministers under the chairmanship of Indrajit Gupta, then home minister. Chidambaram, who was the finance minister, and Pranab Mukherjee, then deputy chairman of the Planning Commission, were also enlisted into the subcommittee.

The chief ministers had a ball making strident demands both in their state capitals and in Delhi for larger financial flows from the Centre to the states. The aim was to maximize media attention so as to be heard in Delhi, of course, but more importantly, to be heard also in their home constituencies. Why does the Centre need so much money? After all, we are on the frontlines, and we know what the people want. Why should the Centre spend on education and health, which are state subjects? Give us that money, and we will spend it more efficiently. You are imposing surcharges rather than taxes to avoid sharing the proceeds with states. That is unfair. Give us a share in the surcharge collections also.

I was finance secretary in the Andhra Pradesh government at that time and Chandrababu Naidu (CBN) was our chief minister. It might be recalled that during the parleys of the United Front coalition for leadership a year earlier, CBN was offered the throne, which he 'did thrice refuse', and instead wisely chose to be the kingmaker.

As the Indrajit Gupta Committee got to work, it went through the rite of passage for any government committee—subcommittees, sub-subcommittees, etc. The apex committee of the chief ministers met about three to four times. The states pitched high. They started with the demand that 90 per cent of the Central tax pool should be given away to the states and gradually brought down their demand to 75 per cent but would not budge any further even in the full knowledge that 75 per cent was an absurdly high share.

Indrajit Gupta was exasperated. I recall the final meeting we had in Vigyan Bhawan on a Saturday afternoon in April 1997. With a dozen chief ministers, three Central ministers and their entourages, we were about 150 people in the jam-packed room. The chief ministers were seated along a large horseshoe table with one official next to each chief minister. I was there on the frontline alongside CBN.

Expectedly, the meeting was noisy and acrimonious and went on for about two hours with no compromise in sight even as fatigue was setting in. And then a vexed Indrajit Gupta appealed to the chief ministers to be reasonable and flexible given the Centre's fiscal constraints. Chidambaram put in his bit too. Over the next fifteen minutes, a consensus emerged that the total Central transfers to states (plan and non-plan) would be a minimum of 50 per cent of the Central tax pool. One by one, the chief ministers fell in line.

The only one holding out was CBN. A hundred and fifty pairs of eyes were boring into him, willing him to nod his agreement so that we could wind up this vexatious business and adjourn for a sumptuous tea (Vigyan Bhawan catering was reputed for its taste and elegance). But our man was impassive. He turned to me and asked if he should agree. I told him, 'You've made your point, Sir. Everyone else has agreed. We could also go along with that. Fifty per cent is much more than we expected.' Even though our conversation was brief, private and in Telugu, all eyes were on us, trying to make out what was transpiring from our body language. CBN continued to stare at the roof even as everyone was staring at us. I was mortified, struck by self-consciousness and fear that everyone would think I was playing spoilsport.

As Andhra Pradesh—alphabetically first—we were seated at one end of the horseshoe. West Bengal was at the other end. There was pin-drop silence in the room, which was pregnant with tension. Then Jyoti Basu got up. At first, everyone thought he was taking a bathroom break. But, instead of heading to the exit, he started walking around the table, tripping over dozens of toes along the way. It took him nearly a minute to come from his end to where we were sitting. As he approached us, I half rose to offer my chair to him. He firmly held me down with one hand, put his other hand on CBN's shoulder and said to him, 'Look, Babu, we all made our case. The home minister and the finance minister are saying that the Centre is in financial difficulty and can't give away so much. Let's defer to them. This is the time to look at the big picture and take a nationalistic view.' Even as he was speaking to CBN, person-to-person, what he said could be heard across the hall, as it perhaps was intended to be.

Quietly, without even waiting for CBN's reply, Basu gracefully started walking back to West Bengal.

Ten seconds perhaps. CBN half nodded, everyone smiled—more out of relief than a sense of accomplishment—and we all promptly adjourned for our well-earned tea.

Within two weeks of that, the Deve Gowda government fell. I don't believe anyone even bothered to record the minutes of this meeting!

11

Shun Beauty Contests

My World Bank Assignment

By mid-1997, I had completed four years as finance secretary of Andhra Pradesh. I was getting restless with both the familiarity and the pressure of the job and was keen on a change.

At around that time, the Government of India liberalized the rules governing civil servants applying for international jobs. Prior permission was no longer required at the application stage; it was enough to seek clearance if and when you got a job offer. Taking advantage of this relaxation, I applied for a couple of jobs at the World Bank and the Asian Development Bank (ADB) in response to their job postings.

Meanwhile, towards the end of 1997, when the state government, as per standard procedure, asked for IAS officers who were willing to be offered to the Government of India for deputation, I put in my name. I was eligible for

Central deputation since I had completed the mandatory three-year 'cooling-off' period between two deputations. Many of my batchmates from other cadres were already in Delhi, and I thought it was important for career reasons for me too to go to the Centre.

When I checked a couple of weeks later, I learnt to my dismay and disappointment that Chief Minister Naidu had not approved my name for inclusion in the offer list for Central deputation. I checked with S.V. Prasad (SV), the secretary to the chief minister; he told me that the chief minister had just cryptically asked for my name to be deleted but hadn't said anything beyond that. SV helpfully offered that he would set up an opportunity for me to speak to the chief minister directly if I so wished. So, a couple of days later, at the end of a meeting when everyone had left, I tried to raise the issue with the chief minister. Even before I could utter a full sentence, Naidu cut me short and said politely but firmly, 'Don't even talk about going anywhere till after the elections.'

Naidu's response was, as they say in the game of bridge, a shutout bid—no further negotiation on the issue. The elections were still two years away. I was forlorn, but any effort to press my request would likely be seen as insubordination. It felt nice to be wanted; an ego trip, certainly. But at the same time, there was always that lingering concern about career progression.

A few months later, in early 1998, in response to my applications, I got interview calls from both the World Bank and the ADB. These were preliminary phone interviews, and I decided to go through with them despite Naidu's clear message that he would not release me till after the elections. Within a month, I got a regret letter from the World Bank. The ADB invited me to Manila for a subsequent interview. Lacking the courage to go back to Naidu to request that he allow me to go, it was my turn to regret the ADB offer.

Entry into the World Bank

As those disappointments were fading into the background, in February 1999, I got a cold call from Peter Miovic, division chief in the Africa Region of the World Bank in Washington DC, asking if I'd be interested in joining his team as a senior economist in the Ethiopia office of the bank. This was a surprise since I hadn't applied for this job, and it had been nearly a year since my earlier interview for another position in the World Bank where I did not make the grade.

I asked Miovic how he had narrowed his choice down to me. He said that he wasn't happy with any of the formal applications he had received for this job posting, so he had gone to the bank's database of applicants for previous jobs and had shortlisted me. He said that he was particularly keen on me because the World Bank had a difficult agenda in Ethiopia and only a person who held a senior position in the government with hands-on experience would inspire the confidence of the Ethiopian government. That was certainly ego-boosting. He offered that if I were positively inclined, he would trigger the formal interview process.

I wavered, in part because I had never been to Africa, and lacking in 'frontier spirit', I harboured all the standard stereotypical misgivings about living and working in Africa. Besides, there was Chief Minister

Naidu's stipulation that I should not reopen the issue of leaving till after the elections.

Over the next couple of weeks, Miovic called three times to market the job to me. By now, we were on first-name terms even though we had not met. He said he would offer me a 25 per cent higher salary than that of the senior-most economist in his group, which would be in addition to the substantial benefits that go with a field job in the bank.

I levelled with him on my apprehensions about working in Africa, especially going there as a fresher, without any prior experience in the bank. I added that my interest was in a headquarters job in Washington DC. Peter said, 'Subba, you work in Ethiopia for two years and I will bring you to the headquarters in my group. To reassure you, I will put that guarantee in the contract.' I told him about the difficulty of getting a leave of absence and asked if he could wait till the end of the year. He said that wouldn't be possible because of the urgency of getting work started in Ethiopia. He, in turn, asked if I could resign from the IAS since what he was offering me was an open-ended job. But of course, I was not prepared to resign from the IAS.

As this conversation over the phone was going back and forth, Peter offered to organize a short visit to Ethiopia for me so I could check the job and the place for myself. So, off I went to Addis Ababa for a week in March 1999. Nigel Roberts, the World Bank's country manager in Ethiopia, arranged for me to meet senior government officials, including some cabinet ministers. I gave a talk in the bank, another talk to the donor group in Addis Ababa and interacted with several bank staff in Washington via video, which, I later learnt, actually doubled as a job interview. I had a brief tour of Addis Ababa and a few places nearby. By the end of the week, I was attracted by the challenge of the job, the work atmosphere and surprisingly, even by the charm of Addis Ababa.

As expected, Peter called soon after I returned to Hyderabad to ask if I had any further questions. I told him about my misgivings about what I'd do outside of work in Addis Ababa. In relative terms, I am quite a self-contained person, but I was concerned that time might weigh heavily on me. Note that the Internet was still in its infancy then, and I was unsure of what Addis offered by way of relaxation and entertainment. Peter's response was, 'Subba, I am sure there must be many books that you've always wanted to read but didn't have the time. You can plough through them now. Your compensation includes a generous book grant; moreover, you can borrow books from the World Bank library in Washington and the books will be couriered to you in the bank's weekly pouch.'

In part because of Peter's persuasion, I had become quite keen on the World Bank job. I told him I was on board, subject, of course, to getting government clearance.

This was in March 1999, nearly a year and a half after my previous conversation with Chief Minister Naidu on moving on. I remembered his stipulation that I stay till after the election, but my hope was that he would relent since the election was now close—only about six months away. Although I had a fairly comfortable relationship with him, I felt diffident about requesting him directly. I thought it best to go through SV since he could plead my case better than I could myself. SV told me the next day that the CM had agreed to let me go but had added that he was miffed with me for not honouring our implicit understanding. It was an uneasy feeling, but I had to make choices.

It took about two months to get all the paperwork done on both sides. I went to take leave of Naidu before leaving. He was polite but surly, and understandably so.

In Ethiopia

I joined the World Bank in Addis Ababa in May 1999. I was going alone since Urmila had a job in Hyderabad, and she was enjoying her posting in the MCR HRD Training Institute of the state government, and our two sons were away in the IITs.

Settling in Addis Ababa turned out to be easier than I had imagined thanks to the help of the bank staff who went out of their way to assist me. The house I rented on Bole Road was way more comfortable than any house I had lived in in India, and the bank provided a generous grant for furnishing it. Because there were quite a few Indians in international organizations in Addis, it was quite easy to get household help who knew Indian cooking. In fact, the maid I hired—Mulu—turned out to be a treasure. She was a versatile cook and competent in managing the household. She spoke only broken English but did so with surprising confidence and charm. Ethiopians are a proud people, and Mulu represented the quintessence of that pride.

Within weeks I bought a used car—a Mercedes at that—from a Food and Agriculture Organization (FAO) staff member who was leaving after completing his tenure in Ethiopia. It was easy to drive around in Addis not only because the traffic was light and the roads broad, but also because for a developing country city, Addis met developed country road discipline standards, which I found unbelievable given my perceptions shaped by the indiscipline, noise and chaos on Indian roads.

* * *

My job involved advising the government on public finance management. Very early on, I realized that in terms of budget integrity, Ethiopia was far more disciplined than India; where they were weak was in the budget systems and processes. As I got familiar with my job content, I understood why Peter had been so keen to get me into this job; I found that senior government officials felt comfortable with me since they saw me more as a colleague from another government rather than as a standard issue World Bank professional. I earned their respect too because they realized that I was speaking with personal hands-on experience.

At the time I joined the bank in Ethiopia, public expenditure reviews (PERs) were becoming popular in the World Bank since experience showed that an understanding of the public finance situation of a country enabled the bank to tailor its loan conditionalities on a more country-specific basis.

A PER for Ethiopia was my first task. This turned out to be a crash course in understanding Ethiopia. I got to meet all the senior officials and ministers across the government, held several meetings and discussions with think tanks and other donors and held several seminars and focus group discussions. When Nick Stern, then chief economist of the bank, visited Ethiopia, we had a two-day offsite meeting at a resort outside Addis attended by senior officials from the bank and the government. Surprisingly, the prime minister spent a day and a half at the event. I was impressed by how informal the meeting was without the hustle and bustle surrounding prime ministers and chief ministers that I was accustomed to in India.

In November 1999, about six months after I got to Addis, a shooting war broke out between Ethiopia and its northern neighbour Eritrea. Eritrea, which had earlier been part of Ethiopia and was about a tenth of its size, had seceded from the united country in 1993 because of ethnic tensions. A disputed border at the time of division resulted in continuous tension, which occasionally burst into open military conflict. The parallel with the India-Pakistan border tension was inescapable.

In Addis Ababa, far in the interior, there was no threat to our security. However, the sudden burst of defence expenditure threatened the fiscal stability of the country, and it became the central issue of the PER. I felt quite sheepish commenting on this given how sensitive we in India would have been if an international agency had commented on the size of our defence expenditure and its implications for financial stability especially when we were fighting a war.

Both in Delhi as also at the state level in Hyderabad, I had several times sat across the table from IMF and World Bank staff when they presented their draft reports to us in the government before finalizing them. It was quite common for us to ask the bank and fund staff to edit some content or bring some nuance into the discussion.

It felt strange now to be on the other side of the table as a bank staff member discussing a draft report with the Ethiopian government. My several meetings with the government on the draft public expenditure review turned out to be quite tense since I was more forthright in my messaging than the government had been previously used to. Finance Minister Sufian in particular felt that there was far too much emphasis on the size of the defence expenditure. He thought the report was overstepping its brief by questioning the justification for the war whereas I thought we were only commenting on the implications of the sudden spurt in defence expenditure for fiscal sustainability. He was also irked that the PER hadn't given sufficient credit to the government for other reforms it had implemented. The government's objections to the nuances of the messaging were, of course, familiar fare, only I was getting to see the exchange from the other side. Overall, I thought the Ethiopians were more reasonable than we in India would have been under similar circumstances.

Ethiopia—the country and the people

The IAS pays you enough to live a comfortable life, and I had never craved the luxuries that my salary couldn't buy. But living in Addis Ababa on a World Bank salary was a strange experience. You couldn't help feeling guilty when you compared your big salary to the average earnings of a person on the street.

As I settled in Addis, I began enjoying living there. I made friends, both Ethiopian and from the expat community. Since I was living alone, there were no pressures of day-today family life, and I had more leisure than at any time in my career, which gave me time to catch up on reading as Peter had suggested. Besides, I was travelling to the bank headquarters in Washington DC about once a quarter on average, which provided relief from the monotony.

At an altitude of 2600 metres (for comparison, Mussoorie is 2100 metres) above sea level, Addis is among the highest capitals in the world. But because of its proximity to the equator, the weather is cool and pleasant throughout the year. The altitude also protects it from mosquitos and malaria, which were rampant in the plains.

Two things about Addis Ababa impressed me, especially given the stereotypical views people have about crime and civic discipline in cities of the developing world, particularly in Africa. First, the city was safe. On occasion, I would walk back home from the office, a distance of about 3 km, well past 7 p.m. through dark, quiet alleys. In the beginning, I would get nervous if I heard footsteps behind me. But over time, I gained courage and confidence and even became nonchalant because there was little street crime.

I also discovered that Ethiopians were a law-abiding community, and they respected authority. For example, I was once standing in a check-in line at Addis Airport. We were probably about five people in the line, and I was second. The person ahead of me had accidentally crossed the yellow boundary line that's drawn about five feet away from the check-in counter. A female guard instantly appeared on the scene and ordered him to go to the end of the line as a penalty for trespassing. The man moved silently to the back of the line without any protest! I was surprised at this obedience. Back in India, we routinely crowd around check-in counters, and accepting a penalty for breaching a rule would have been unthinkable, And if any guard attempted disciplining of this sort, an argument and possibly a scuffle was sure to ensue.

Ethiopians are a proud, dignified and handsome people. According to their national epic, *Kebra Negast*, Ethiopia's first emperor Menelik I was born of a union between King Solomon and the Egyptian Queen Sheba, and they believe this lineage sets them apart as distinct from other black people in sub-Saharan Africa.

Ethiopia is only one of two countries in Africa, the other being Liberia in the west, never to have been colonized. However, the country did come under Italian occupation when Mussolini invaded Ethiopia in 1936 and remained as such until the British released it in 1941. Although the Italian occupation was relatively brief, Italian influence remained strong even sixty years later. Small, boutique coffee shops serving freshly baked focaccia bread and aromatic macchiatos with elegance and pride still dot the major streets of Addis Ababa.

Unlike the rest of East Africa—Kenya, Tanzania and Uganda—where large numbers of Indians, mostly Gujaratis, had gone for business and settled there, the Indian community in Ethiopia was relatively small. A large number of teachers, mainly from Kerala, had gone to Ethiopia in the 1960s and 1970s under Pandit Nehru's larger plan of cooperation with Africa. In Ethiopia, like in India, teachers commanded respect bordering on reverence, and I became a beneficiary of that goodwill. I was asked several times by people on the street, especially elderly Ethiopians who had been taught by Indians, if I was a teacher.

In the 2000 Sydney Olympics, Ethiopia won eight medals, including four gold, one silver and three bronze. The most celebrated victory was of Haile Gebrselassie who won the Olympic gold in the 10,000-metre race for the second time in a row. There was a jubilant victory parade along the main streets of Addis Ababa when the athletes returned home, which I watched from the window of my office. As much as I rejoiced in their success, the contrast with India, which for a population ten times that of Ethiopia had bagged just a lone bronze medal, did not escape me.

Work in East Africa

Disappointingly for me, Peter took voluntary retirement from the bank within months of my taking up the job in Ethiopia. Fred Kilby, who came in his place, thought that I should not remain confined to Ethiopia and gradually got me involved in the bank's economic work in Kenya and Tanzania too. This required extended missions to those countries, which I enjoyed both because of the change of scene and the diversity of experience.

What surprised me in Africa, although I didn't see it so much in Ethiopia, was that one or more experts funded by donor agencies actually sat in the finance ministry and worked alongside the domestic staff. The donors meant well, expecting that this handholding would help build domestic capacity through a process of osmosis. What happened in practice, though, was the opposite since the expert did all the work by herself giving the domestic staff no opportunity of learning by doing.

The warlords of Somalia

The World Bank had no operations in Somalia as the government there had fallen apart; the vacuum was filled by warlords who carved out their own territories. The bank, however, launched a 'watch' mission with the task of keeping track of developments in the country. The idea was that if and when a regular government was established, the bank could hit the ground running in providing assistance. I was part of this mission, and since bank rules disallowed travel to Somalia because of safety concerns, we operated out of Nairobi. Our task was to regularly meet with staff from other donor agencies, NGOs and think tanks who continued to operate in Somalia, gain some understanding of the ground situation with regard to law and order as well as financial conditions and report them to our division chief.

During these 'watch Somalia' missions to Nairobi, I would seek out a wide array of stakeholders to check on the humanitarian crisis in Somalia. Invariably, the discussion would meander to the widespread addiction of Somalis to chewing *khat* (*qat*) a flowering plant native to East Africa. Classified as a stimulant, khat-chewing is said to cause excitement and euphoria. I gathered that most adults imbibed khat soon after lunch, which meant they were no longer alert enough to work after that. This indulgence meant huge economic loss and social strife. Khat had to be chewed fresh. Although the warlords fought among themselves, often quite fiercely, they cooperated in running a fairly sophisticated supply chain so that fresh khat reached every nook and corner of the country by early afternoon.

Surprisingly, the warlords performed all the sovereign functions of the government—collecting taxes, maintaining law and order, providing security, issuing currency and even defending their strongholds from encroachment by rival warlords. But there was one thing they could not do, which was to issue passports that would be internationally acceptable. It struck me that as much as we crib about government rules and regulations that come in the way of living our everyday lives and doing our businesses, we still need a government because there are some services that only a government can provide.

We do need governments, no matter that we often despise them.

Moving to World Bank headquarters

By mid-2001, I had completed two years in Ethiopia and was good for a transfer to the World Bank headquarters in Washington DC. Thanks to Peter, my contract guaranteed me a position in the Africa Division at the bank headquarters; nevertheless, I wanted to explore options in other parts of the bank. In the World Bank, every job opening is technically open to international recruitment although insiders have an edge because of their experience and contacts. I applied for two jobs—one each in the East Asia Division and the Europe and Central Asia Division. I was duly interviewed for both and was offered both jobs.

I opted for the East Asia Division job because I was enticed by the main task there, which was to do a flagship

study of decentralization across countries of East Asia—
from continental-size China to tiny Laos. I had first-hand
exposure to decentralization in India in all its dimensions—
administrative, political and fiscal. As finance secretary
of Andhra Pradesh, I had the opportunity to study fiscal
federalism and had also written extensively on the topic
in journals and newspapers. Most importantly, my PhD
dissertation was on this topic.

Layered over that experience, studying decentralization
across East Asia turned out to be an interesting as also a
rewarding learning opportunity. Although the motivation
for decentralization was common across the region—
better service delivery and local accountability—it evolved
differently in different countries, reflecting both a shared
culture and varying histories.

Chinese political centralization (in the imperial
authority in the past and in the Communist Party in recent
decades) has historically been tempered by a unique blend
of political centralization with economic and administrative
decentralization—another distinctive feature of the
Chinese governance system. No matter the dominance of
the Communist Party, I found, much to my surprise, that
Chinese provinces, in practice, are more independent than
subnational units in other federations, including states in
India. *Shan gao, huangdi yuan*—'The mountains are high,
and the emperor is far away.' This traditional Chinese
saying alludes to the relative nonchalance with which local
officials deep in the hinterland disregard the wishes of the
central authorities in distant Beijing.

The reforms initiated by Deng when he opened up
China to the world in 1979 are best known for introducing

the market economy into an authoritarian regime. What is less well known though, is that those reforms also involved deepening decentralization, which encouraged local innovation and competition among provinces. Chinese decentralization is most notable for its emphasis on results over rules.

Indonesia, one of the most centralized countries in the world under Suharto, embarked on a radical and vigorous decentralization in the post-Suharto period. Even as it was struggling to design decentralization suited to an archipelago of over 17,000 islands, Indonesia had to cede independence to East Timor because of grievances over resource sharing. Vietnam embarked on an ambitious decentralization programme in 1975, but the country is still struggling to prevent unhealthy competition among provinces for foreign investment.

As much as studying decentralization across East Asia was a fascinating experience, managing the task proved to be daunting. Although I had colleagues from within the division on my task team, I nevertheless had to source and employ both domestic and international consultants. It involved extensive travel to the region, each trip typically lasting over a month. Travel plans were also interrupted by the outbreak of SARS in the region in 2002–03.

Even as I was struggling with deadlines on the decentralization study, Homi Kharas, a smart, intelligent and anglicized Pakistani, the sector director for the East Asia division in the bank and my boss, asked that I also take on economic work in Papua New Guinea (PNG) and the Solomon Islands. This meant additional work and additional travel, but in hindsight, it turned out to be a rich experience as it exposed me to the Pacific Islands' culture and their very unique economic and governance challenges.

The World Bank's internal processes for vetting and reviewing their reports and documents are quite extensive and impressive. Every study has to start with a concept paper, which is presented and reviewed in an open meeting of the entire division. The draft report has to be peer-reviewed by staff from outside the division with relevant expertise in the field. The report also has to be presented to the entire division for comments and criticism. While this system ensures quality and consistency, it also has some flipsides. The collective review process has a bias towards conservatism, and the bar for introducing innovative ideas gets set quite high. (See the tailpiece: 'Shun Beauty Contests'.)

Also, reports can sometimes become hostage to special interest groups within the bank. For example, when I was presenting a report on the reform of public audit systems in PNG, the gender specialists pointed out that I did not explicitly reckon with the gender dimensions of public audits. Similarly, the HIV/AIDS and climate change constituencies wanted to push their narrow agendas. While these are undoubtedly important concerns that should inform every study, trying to reflect every concern in every reform can arguably dilute the focus on the main objective.

Working in the bank turned out to be a valuable experience in improving oral and written communication. There was an emphasis on focused messaging and writing in clear and crisp English. I also learnt some of the best practices in presentations by seeing how some colleagues structured their presentations, the manner in which they delivered them and the techniques they used to enhance effectiveness. I recall an instance when Miria Pigato, a colleague of mine, and I were both assigned to read a draft report of another team member and comment on it. Miria came into my office late one evening to show her irritation with the report. 'There is just too much English here, Subba', she said, meaning the main messages were getting lost in verbose writing.

Extension of deputation

In mid-2002, my three-year leave of absence from the government had come to an end. Since the rules allowed for a total of seven years of deputation, I applied for an extension. A couple of months later, forget about an extension, I got a missive from the Government of India asking me to explain how I had accepted a World Bank job. For good measure, the letter added that if the government did not receive my explanation within two weeks of that letter, I would be deemed to have resigned from the IAS.

I panicked about the deemed resignation. I was, of course, having a fairly successful run in the bank and was well regarded by both managers and colleagues. But I had no intention of quitting the IAS to make a career in the bank. I was also confused about the government charge against me since I had with me a letter from the government in black and white permitting me to accept the bank job.

I called up Suvrathan, my batchmate, who was then a joint secretary in the cabinet secretariat, to check on what was happening behind the scenes. Suvi was not dealing with the subject, but he inquired with the relevant division. What he gathered was that the government had taken umbrage at my accepting an open-ended job with the World Bank, which was akin to accepting another 'permanent' job. How can you have two permanent jobs at the same time, was their question. As per their interpretation, only fixed-term contracts or consultancy assignments were permitted under the rules.

I was both annoyed and frustrated by the government's stance. It wasn't as if I had acted in stealth or covered up facts. I had attached the bank's job offer with my request when I sought initial permission three years earlier. If anything, they should have raised their objection then. Moreover, they were applying a rule without trying to understand whether an open-ended job in the bank was a 'permanent job' in the sense it is interpreted in our government. What galled me most of all was that several other colleagues were in international organizations with contracts similar to mine and they had secured extensions without any questions asked. In my view, the principle of 'show me the man and I will show you the rule' was playing out.

As it happened, I was going to Indonesia the following week. I broke my journey in Delhi for a couple of days to sort this out. Fortunately, I got an appointment with the cabinet secretary quite easily. I explained to him that an open-ended job in the bank was not similar to a permanent job in our government. The bank could terminate my services at any time without giving me notice or showing cause why they were doing it. In contrast, in a permanent job in the government, in the IAS, for example, there has to be due process. After hearing me out, the cabinet secretary asked if I could get the bank to clarify on those lines.

I sought an extension of time to give my explanation. Soon after I returned from my travels, I explained the problem to the HR division in the bank and requested them to issue a clarification on an open-ended job on the lines I had explained to the cabinet secretary. From my bureaucratic experience, I expected them to push back and say that they would not be able to do so unless the government wrote to them directly. That would have squeezed me between two intransigent bureaucracies. Much to my surprise though, they readily issued the clarification that I had requested without a fuss. And my extension came through a month after that.

Apart from the agony I went through, this experience also illustrated to me the difference between a callous and indifferent bureaucracy like ours and a sympathetic and caring bureaucracy like that of the bank.

Quit or stay on in the World Bank?

By the second half of 2004, I had to make a big career decision about whether to stay on at the World Bank or return to the IAS in India. I was comfortably settled in Washington, I was enjoying my job and most importantly, I was well regarded in the peer group. On the other hand, the IAS beckoned. Several of my well-wishers in the service advised me that if I wanted to make a career in the IAS, I couldn't afford to be away for too long. After all, no one has a right to be remembered!

In the bank, no matter how well I did, I would be stuck in middle management, whereas back in the IAS, I would potentially have the opportunity to be part of the senior management in the government. I was conscious, of course, that there was no guarantee that my career would pan out as I planned or wished. The remaining five years of my service could end unspectacularly in some inconsequential postings! But then I reprimanded myself for the temptation to stay in my comfort zone rather than chase uncertainty and take my chances.

So, at the end of October 2004, I resigned from the bank job, some six months before my extended leave had expired.

The IAS rules required that I return to my home cadre and cool off there until I earned at least one ACR (Annual Confidential Report) to become eligible for Central deputation. I thought it best to start the clock sooner rather than later.

Looking back, working in the bank was a rewarding learning experience. There was, of course, job stress, but much less so than in the regular IAS postings back home. There were fewer surprises at work, and it was possible to organize your schedule with a fair amount of certainty. The systems and processes were transparent and fair, and it was the closest to an ideal meritocracy that I had seen, no matter that some staff still quibbled.

What I valued most of all from my World Bank experience was the international exposure it gave me. Travel was only a part of it; even more enriching was the opportunity to work with colleagues drawn from different and distant parts of the world. When in Hanoi once on mission travel, when about eight of us went out for dinner, I realized that within the eight of us, we represented every continent, every major race, every major language and every major religion in the world. Within that enormous diversity, what unified us was not just that we were all employed by the same institution, but more importantly that at a fundamental level, we were all human, sharing the same frailties, concerns and anxieties.

Shun beauty contests

Imagine you are in a contest to choose the three most beautiful actors ever to have graced the Indian screen from a panel of a hundred names. You win not if your choice matches that of the judges but if your choice most closely matches that of the majority of contestants.

A naïve strategy would be to pick three—say, Madhubala, Meena Kumari and Nargis—who you think are the most beautiful. A sophisticated strategy would be to base your choice on what you think the majority choice will be—Madhubala, Suraiya and Waheeda Rehman, for example. An even more sophisticated strategy would be to take this iteration one step deeper and consider what other contestants, all of whom are looking at the problem from the same point of view, think the majority choice would be.

This beauty contest is the brainchild of John Maynard Keynes, arguably the most influential economist of the twentieth century, who used this thought experiment to explain how bubbles form in financial markets because market players spend their time anticipating 'what average opinion expects average opinion to be'.

Although Keynes' motivation was to explain irrational behaviour in markets, the beauty contest analogy can also help to explain 'groupthink'—a phenomenon that occurs when a group of individuals reaches a consensus without critical reasoning or evaluation of the consequences or alternatives. Groupthink manifests when individuals in a group fall in line with the majority view without speaking up even if they have a contrary view for fear of being considered outliers or spoilsports. It's obvious that when there is strong pressure to conform, groups can make bad or even disastrous decisions.

Virtually every institution and every bureaucracy is susceptible to groupthink. I often wondered if the World Bank, where the bar for revising a ruling economic orthodoxy is set quite high, is more susceptible to groupthink than most bureaucracies, the IAS, for example.

Take the case of capital controls. The old orthodoxy was that capital flows are good always and everywhere because they provide much-needed resources to developing countries for investment. That belief gave rise to the Washington Consensus that capital controls are suboptimal and full capital account liberalization is the holy grail that developing countries must have.

Guided by the Washington Consensus, the World Bank and the IMF had for long been evangelizing full capital account liberalization to developing countries even though evidence was piling up that premature capital account opening was seriously impairing financial and macroeconomic stability in developing countries.

Many World Bank and IMF staff saw these negative consequences first-hand but never spoke up against the institutional view.

The result of this groupthink was a series of financial crises in developing countries stretching from Latin America to Eastern Europe to East Asia.

The reality is that every institution is susceptible to groupthink, some more than others. And every institution would do well to internalize what the Mexican artist Frida Kahlo reportedly said, 'I don't want you to think like me. I want you to think.'

Should We Be Sinning against Our Children?*

How things change! In just one decade, fiscal austerity has gone from being a virtue to a vice. The IMF, which used to hold fiscal austerity as gospel, has since buried that faith. It now urges countries, at any rate the rich ones, to borrow and spend generously, not just for their own good but also for the good of the rest of the world.

Here in India, the turnaround in the world view has been even swifter. We routinely berated our finance ministers for being spendthrifts and blamed fiscal irresponsibility for all our macroeconomic problems. But when Nirmala Sitharaman announced a big borrow and spend programme in the budget for 2021, she was widely acclaimed for her boldness and sense of responsibility. The finance minister didn't say anything about debt sustainability, budgeted a higher-than-expected deficit of 6.8 per cent of GDP for the coming year and opted for a slower-than-expected medium-term fiscal consolidation path. Yet, even staunch fiscal hawks thought that was par for the course.

What explains this astonishing shift in economic orthodoxy? Why has the fear that mounting debt is a sure-fire route to disaster given way to such nonchalance? No, it's not economics that has changed; what has changed is the real world to which economics applies. And that change predates the coronavirus.

In rich countries, the fundamental real-world change goes under the name of secular stagnation, a condition caused by structural factors such as ageing populations, rising inequality and slowing productivity. Older people who expect to live longer spend less per capita as do low-income households who don't

---

* Originally published in the *Times of India* on 20 February 2021 as 'Don't Sin Against Our Children'.

see their economic prospects improving. As people consume less and save more, investment opportunities decline and the economy goes into a low-growth, low-inflation syndrome of secular stagnation.

Central banks respond to this downturn by cutting interest rates to zero or even making them negative. When people's confidence about their economic prospects is low, even that doesn't help. As they say, it's like 'pushing on a loose string'. The solution then, it is argued, lies in governments taking advantage of the low interest rates to borrow and spend. In a low-interest-rate scenario, the multiplier effect of spending will be so high that public debt, far from exploding, will actually pay for itself.

Does this logic apply to emerging markets, India in particular? Certainly not. Our structural factors are totally different. With a median age of twenty-nine, our population is young, and our economy is consumption-driven and inflation-prone. Far from secular stagnation, any increase in incomes here quickly translates to consumption. And if production falls short of demand as it often does, we get inflation.

We differ from rich countries in terms of public finance dynamics too. In rich countries, interest payments are just a small proportion of total government spending, and that fraction is declining. On the contrary, in India, because of accumulated debt, interest payments are the single biggest item of government expenditure and eat up more than 40 per cent of total revenues, leaving that much less for spending on growth-enhancing sectors like education, health and infrastructure.

So, how much debt is too much? If one works through the algebra, it will turn out that two conditions have to be met for debt not to explode. The economy's growth rate has to be higher than the interest rate on the debt; and second, the government must be collecting enough in taxes such that it is borrowing, if at all, only to pay the interest on the debt. In India, we meet the first condition but are far from meeting the second. It is this vulnerability that pegs our sustainable debt at a low level.

After working through the feedback loops, the Fiscal Responsibility and Budget Management (FRBM) Committee determined that the sustainable level of debt for us is 60 per cent of GDP. As against that, it is estimated that our debt will rise to 90 per cent of GDP by the time we exit the coronavirus crisis. It is this high level of debt and the low probability of tax revenues rising sufficiently to bring the debt ratio down that will weigh on rating agencies as they evaluate our medium–term prospects.

Can we be nonchalant about the judgement of rating agencies? Unfortunately not. Ratings matter in shaping market perceptions, and adverse perceptions feed on themselves and spiral into self-fulfilling prophecies. History is evidence of this. In his influential books on depression economics, Nobel Laureate Paul Krugman says that leading into the Asian financial crisis in the 1990s, Australia, a rich country, and the Asian economies, all of them emerging markets, had a similar risk build-up. However, the markets allowed Australia to make a smooth adjustment and avert a crisis, even as they denied a similar privilege to the Asian economies and pushed them into a devastating crisis. The short point is that markets are much less forgiving of policy excesses by emerging markets. It's unfair but true.

For sure, going into the budget, the finance minister was locked into an 'impossible trinity' of sorts. She had to spend more, not raise taxes and keep borrowing under check. Something had to give, and she chose to breach the borrowing limit on the calculation that the additional debt-financed expenditure would generate rapid growth such that the debt would pay for itself.

That outcome is plausible but not inevitable. Our growth prospects and hence our debt sustainability depend critically on private investment pouring in. For that to happen, we need a lot more things to fall in place than just a well-crafted and well-intentioned budget.

If today's debt-financed spending does not generate rapid growth, the burden of debt repayment will pass on to our children through higher taxes. We don't want to sin against our children!

12

'Subbarao Is Too Quiet'

Secretary to the PM's
Economic Advisory Council

In November 2004, I returned from the World Bank and reported to my home cadre of Andhra Pradesh. Mohan Kanda, the chief secretary, advised that I meet the chief minister, Y.S. Rajasekhara Reddy (YSR), before he decided on a posting for me. Although I had run into YSR on a couple of occasions over the years, we didn't know each other well. When I called on him, he was very welcoming and suggested that I wait a while till he could think of a suitable post for me where my 'enormous international experience' would be useful.

When this 'compulsory wait' extended to a month, I began getting anxious. The whole idea behind my quitting the World Bank and returning to the IAS had been to pursue a career in Delhi, and I wouldn't be eligible for Central deputation until I earned an Annual Confidential Report

(ACR), and I couldn't earn an ACR until I had a job. After all, there are limits to being an 'outstanding officer' while on compulsory wait!

I met the chief secretary again and requested him to make a quick decision so that my clock would start ticking. It was thus that I came to be posted as the chairman of the Andhra Pradesh Industrial Infrastructure Corporation (APIIC), which Mohan told me was a stopgap posting. This was not an executive job; there was a full-time managing director who was the chief executive.

Chief ministers typically use posts of chairman of public enterprises to accommodate political supporters, and sacrificing one of those slots for an IAS officer entails a huge opportunity cost for them. In fact, within a week of my joining there, a couple of MLAs came calling to tell me that I shouldn't be wasting my time in a job like this. For good measure, they added that the government should have better sense than wasting an 'outstanding officer' like me in such an inconsequential job! I assuaged their concern by saying that this was a stopgap posting and that the government might soon move me out.

Delhi beckons again

While on a visit to Delhi a few weeks later, I called on Dr Rangarajan, who was then chairman of the Twelfth Finance Commission. I had known Rangarajan well both from my days in the Ministry of Finance in Delhi when he was deputy governor of the RBI (he subsequently became governor too), and when he was later governor of Andhra Pradesh. He told me that the Finance Commission would be submitting its report within that month and after that, he would be going as chairman of the revived Economic Advisory Council (EAC) to the prime minister. During the conversation, he asked if I would join him as secretary to the commission. I was enthusiastic, but I told him that I had to cool off in my home cadre and wasn't eligible for a Delhi posting.

The following week I got a call from T.K.A. Nair, principal secretary to the prime minister, asking if I would join the EAC as its secretary. Apparently, Rangarajan had asked for me. Nair said that if I was willing, he would, as a special case, get the ACR requirement waived.

This was a post at the joint secretary level. My batchmates in Delhi were already empanelled for the next higher grade of additional secretaries. My empanelment was deferred as I had been away on deputation to the World Bank. I asked Nair if this out-of-turn posting would also mean an out-of-turn empanelment so that I would be at level with my batchmates. He said, 'Subbarao, you come and join here, and we will take up your empanelment as soon as you get an ACR.'

So it was that in March 2005, I returned to the Government of India for the second Central deputation of my career.

Bringing the EAC back to life

The EAC had been defunct for some years; restarting it therefore turned out to be a greenfield project. Setting up a new office in the government is a tortuous and frustrating process as I had learnt the hard way over my long career.

Once the order is issued, virtually everyone washes their hands of it, and you are expected to fend for yourself. It's your job to do all the running around, starting from identifying office premises, getting them furnished, getting computers and telephones installed and getting some minimal staff in place.

That 'exciting opportunity' of re-establishing the office of the EAC came my way. Here I was, thirty years into the IAS, returning from the World Bank in the hope of doing some exciting policy work, and I found myself shopping for window curtains and bathroom supplies. But I surprised myself by how involved I got in these 'mundane' tasks. I liberally exploited our connection to the prime minister's office to get things moving, which meant they moved slightly faster than the snail's pace they were accustomed to. So, within a month, we had the semblance of an office going in the Vigyan Bhawan Annexe in central New Delhi.

Ticklish issues on our plate

The EAC runs on the prestige and influence of the chairman. In that sense, we were fortunate because Dr Manmohan Singh had great regard for Rangarajan. Very soon, we were loaded with enough work to be more than fully occupied.

I remember the very first issue assigned to us was the redesign of the Exim scrips to limit the uses to which they could be put. In subsequent months and years, we were assigned a variety of tasks: the levy of royalty on coal, the formula for pricing of petroleum products and for determining oil subsidies, determining the viability gap funding for infrastructure projects under public-private partnerships (PPP), the design of the National Employment Guarantee Scheme, the position India must take on service exports in the World Trade Organization (WTO) negotiations, the incentives to be given to special economic zones, the special fiscal support to be given to the north-east states—just to name a few.

Soon enough, it became clear to me that the issues being referred to us were those on which a consensus couldn't be reached within the government because of intractable differences among ministries and departments. Whenever there was an impasse, the prime minister asked that the issue be referred to Dr Rangarajan for advice.

The variety and complexity of issues referred to us was therefore huge. On every new task, we had to do a lot of preparatory work to learn and understand so we knew enough to 'advise'. In short, we were behaving like consultants who take on a project with not much exposure to the issue but add value by bringing fresh thinking unsullied by all the guff and the turf battles.

Very soon, Rangarajan and I fell into a comfortable work pattern. On any new task, I did the preliminary running around to meet the relevant officials in the departments and obtained material from them to study and understand the issue at hand based on which I would prepare a position paper. After that, meetings were arranged between the chairman and the relevant officials. When those consultations were over, Rangarajan and I would discuss and determine the broad contours of the view we must take, based on which I prepared our advice note. We referred the draft to the EAC members—Saumitra Chowdhury, M. Govinda Rao and G.K. Chadha—reflected their feedback in the draft and thereafter sent it to the PMO.

The brighter side of the job

There were many positives to my job in the EAC. First, there was the sheer variety of tasks and the huge learning opportunity it provided. I was also able to establish contact with senior officials across the government. Second, we ran a bare-bones office, and there wasn't much administrative work unlike in a regular ministry where every officer, no matter at what level, is burdened with routine tasks and meetings. There was no travel unless we chose to, no routine meetings and no vexing staff issues.

Third, working with Rangarajan was a delightful experience. He was learned, of course, but also quite pragmatic. And I learnt a lot from his insights and his ability to think through complex issues. In his public career, Rangarajan had chaired so many committees and commissions that, for an academic, he had a surprisingly keen understanding of how the government functioned. A friend of mine who occasionally tutored MA economics students once confided in me that his standard advice to the students before any examination was: 'If you know the answer to a question, write it. If you're not sure, preface your answer by saying, "As the Rangarajan Committee said in its report" and then do some intelligent guesswork. No examiner in the country would have the guts to challenge that.'

A seat at the high table by proxy

By far the most important attraction of the EAC job for me was the regular opportunity to attend high-level policy meetings at the prime minister's level. Dr Rangarajan was a regular invitee to these meetings, and I would tag along with him as an invitee too. Before every meeting, we both would brainstorm on the issues and the interventions that Rangarajan could make at the meeting.

What used to strike me about these high-level policy meetings was how intractable issues were. No solution was totally benign; every solution had a downside and oftentimes it was a question of choosing the least bad option. Let me illustrate by giving two examples.

Solving fiscal deficits through an accounting fix

One of the issues that came up frequently in the PM's meetings those days was the urgency of cutting the fiscal deficit. Year-on-year high fiscal deficits are bad for a number of reasons. They raise aggregate demand and stoke inflationary pressures. By pre-empting the available savings in the economy, they crowd out private investment. By raising the interest burden of the government over time, they pre-empt productive expenditure. And importantly, fiscal deficits spill over into the external sector and manifest as current account deficits. Our balance of payments crisis in 1991 and the near crisis in 2013 were at heart a consequence of extended fiscal profligacy.

To cut the fiscal deficit—its net borrowing requirement—the government has to increase its revenue or reduce expenditure, or both. Raising revenues by raising the tax rates or introducing new taxes was politically infeasible. Whatever increase there was had to come from faster growth. Reducing expenditure—contrary to public perception—is not easy either because the bulk of the government's expenditure is non-discretionary. Salaries, pensions and interest payments are formula-driven and cannot be cut, at any rate in the short run. Defence expenditure is a 'holy cow'. Incidentally, the austerity measures that the government introduces from time to time such as ministers and civil servants travelling by economy class are all mere optics. They don't make a dent in the overall government expenditure.

One area where there is some discretion is subsidies. But the straightforward option of pruning subsidies wasn't politically feasible especially as the UPA-I was being supported from the outside by the left parties. As Milton Friedman famously said, there is nothing more permanent than a temporary government programme.

Fiscal deficits can be justified, albeit with some caveats, if the borrowed money is used for capital spending on the argument that the assets so built would generate revenue for the government in the future, and the debt would pay for itself. But our governments, both at the Centre and in states, use borrowed money not just for capital expenditure but also for current consumption. That is to say that we have a fiscal deficit and a revenue deficit.

As an analogy, consider a family that borrows money to put a girl through college. This can be justified on the grounds that the girl will earn enough in the future to repay the debt. On the other hand, if the household borrows money to perform an expensive wedding, that would be equivalent to a revenue deficit. Revenue deficits are fundamentally unsustainable, and we needed to trim the revenue deficit in order to trim the fiscal deficit.

At one of the meetings where this came up for discussion, Montek Singh Ahluwalia, the deputy chairman of the Planning Commission, suggested that the Centre's effective revenue deficit was, in fact, lower than what we were showing in the budget books and that the government should take credit for the lower number by changing the accounting method. His argument was that a portion of the grants from the Centre to the states was being used by the states to build capital assets, and therefore this part of the grants should be shown in the Centre's accounts as capital expenditure rather than revenue expenditure. The 'lower revenue expenditure' would translate to lower revenue deficit.

I thought it wasn't as straightforward as that. For sure, the change in accounting that he suggested would reduce the Centre's revenue deficit. But we have to extend the same logic to the states as well. States that were showing these funds as revenue grants would now have to show them as capital grants, which meant a higher revenue deficit. Consequently, the combined revenue deficit of states as a whole would go up by exactly the same amount that the Centre's revenue deficit had declined. What matters for macroeconomics management is the combined fiscal deficit of the Centre and states and this modification in accounting would not change that.

After all, you can't solve a macroeconomic problem through a mere accounting fix.

RBI's capital flow management—a zero-sum game?

Another illustration of the absence of completely benign options was the Reserve Bank's capital flow management. 2005–06 was the period of the 'Great Moderation' in advanced economies when their interest rates were low, and as a consequence, capital was flowing into emerging markets in search of higher yields. The rupee, quite uncharacteristically, was under upward pressure and the Reserve Bank was buying foreign exchange in the market to stem the appreciation of the rupee.

But this operation had an unintended side effect. In the process of absorbing the dollars, the Reserve Bank was printing rupees and injecting them into the system. This forced increase in money supply would stoke inflationary pressures. To ward off this threat, the government and the RBI came up with the ingenious Market Stabilization Scheme (MSS) bonds. These bonds would be sold to banks for which they would pay with their reserves, which would effectively suck out the liquidity injected through dollar purchases.

But here was the trick. The bonds were issued on behalf of the government in the sense that the interest burden on them was to be borne by the government. However, the proceeds of the bond sale would not be given to the government for spending as that would raise the fiscal deficit. Instead, the funds would be sequestered by the RBI. In other words, the government was paying interest on a loan it was not permitted to utilize. That was the cost to be paid by the government for preventing an undue appreciation of the rupee.

All in all, this looked like an ingenious sterilization scheme and that the government had all flanks covered. When this came up for discussion in one of the meetings with the prime minister, I pointed out that this would not be as completely benign as we thought. The financial tightening that we intended to achieve through the MSS bonds would put upward pressure on the interest rate and that would encourage further capital inflows. In other words, we would end up exacerbating the very problem that we were trying to solve. This would be a curious variant of the 'Dutch Disease'.

It took some effort on my part to articulate my point, but eventually, I believe I got the message across. Sanjaya Baru, who was media adviser to Prime Minister Manmohan Singh, told me later that the prime minister remarked to him after the meeting: 'Your friend Subbarao is smart. Why doesn't he speak up more often?'

Fiscal federalism—loaded against states?

One of the topics I pursued quite energetically while in the EAC was fiscal federalism. Rangarajan, who was earlier chairman of the Twelfth Finance Commission, had a masterly overview of the perspectives of the Centre and states on fiscal federalism. While I did not have his breadth of exposure, I had hands-on experience in dealing with fiscal decentralization issues as finance secretary of Andhra Pradesh. Also, while in the World Bank, I had task-managed a flagship study on decentralization across East Asia. While the architecture of fiscal federalism varied across these countries, the core concerns were similar.

The stereotypical view among economists and commentators is that our arrangements of fiscal federalism in India are loaded against the states. Abstracting from all the details, in specific terms, states' grievances are twofold. First, they have a structural deficit problem because their expenditure responsibilities are higher than their revenues and therefore the Centre must give them more resources. Second, their autonomy in raising resources and spending money is restrained by the Centre.

I don't believe the issues are as black and white as that. Some of the state's concerns are genuine, but the Centre is not as guilty as it is made out to be either. There is a need for greater efforts at cooperative fiscal federalism by the Centre and states.

The Centre must realize that starting with the economic reforms in 1991, the fiscal centre of gravity has slowly but decisively shifted in the states' favour. Ballpark estimates suggest that the Centre collects about 60 per cent of the combined revenue (Centre and states) but gets to spend only about 40 per cent of the combined expenditure. This asymmetry is mirrored on the states' side. Together, they collect 40 per cent of the combined revenue, but have the pleasure of spending as much as 60 per cent of the combined expenditure.

What this implies at a big-picture level is that our macroeconomic stability, and hence our ability to generate investment and growth, will depend on the collective fiscal responsibility of the Centre and states.

The states on their part must acknowledge that our arrangements of fiscal federalism—even if not yet the best practice—are not necessarily skewed against them as is commonly believed.

In September 2021, when the DMK government came into office in Tamil Nadu, they released a white paper on the financial position of the state. Following this chapter, there is an op-ed I wrote in the *Times of India* at that time which summarizes my views on Centre-state fiscal arrangements.

A fifth wheel without traction

By mid-2006 when I had completed nearly a year and a half in the EAC, I began to get concerned about my career prospects. As much as I enjoyed the job content, the EAC was effectively a fifth wheel that was strictly not necessary for traction. I was yearning for a more hands-on assignment. After all, I had given up the World Bank job and returned to an IAS career in the hope that I would be involved more directly in policy formulation and implementation. If all I had to do was 'advising', I might as well have stayed on in the World Bank where I was also advising but getting paid much more for it.

Meanwhile, Rakesh Mohan, who was deputy governor at the RBI, had moved to the government as secretary, economic affairs, in early 2005. Y.V. Reddy, who was governor, asked me if I would be interested in coming in as deputy governor in Rakesh's vacancy, but the big proviso was that I had to resign from the IAS. I wasn't prepared to take that plunge as I was still hopeful that the IAS route would provide better career prospects.

By mid-2006, I was still a joint secretary while my batchmates had been additional secretaries for over a year by then. What worried me even more was that our batch was being considered for empanelment as secretaries and that I may not figure in the zone of consideration because I had not even become an additional secretary. The promise made to me when I joined the EAC that my case would be taken up for empanelment was forgotten. When I checked with the joint secretary in the cabinet secretariat, he told me that I had to earn at least two ACRs to be eligible for empanelment, never mind the oral assurance given to me that it would be taken up as soon as I got one ACR.

I requested Rangarajan to intercede on my behalf. He was kind enough to speak to the cabinet secretary and the principal secretary to the prime minister to take up my case for empanelment as was promised. At last, in October 2006, I was empanelled as additional secretary, and in quick succession thereafter as secretary in December 2006 along with the rest of my batch.

I was aware that I would get posted as a regular secretary within the next few months. Ever since I had been a mid-level joint secretary in the Ministry of Finance in the early 1990s, I had hoped to someday hold the post of secretary of the Department of Economic Affairs both because of the job content and the prestige it enjoyed in the peer group. I also believed I had the credentials for the job given my prior experience in the ministry, my experience as state finance secretary and my international experience in the World Bank. Ashok Jha, who was then secretary, economic affairs, was due to retire in two months, and I was hoping that the government might consider me for that job.

Once again, I requested Rangarajan, who spoke to the prime minister. The PM evidently told him that he had known me from the time he was finance minister and I was a joint secretary in the Ministry of Finance in the early 1990s. Nevertheless, he was non-committal but advised Rangarajan to also speak to the finance minister. Chidambaram did not know me although he had seen me in the meetings at the PM level. When Rangarajan approached Chidambaram, the latter told him that he already had someone in mind. My hopes were dashed.

It was therefore a delightful surprise when towards the end of April 2007, I was posted as secretary of the Department of Economic Affairs. I learnt later that even as Chidambaram did not warm up to me, the prime minister nudged him saying something along the lines of, 'Subbarao is quiet, but he is smart.'

A question for which economists had no answer

In November 2008, at the height of the global financial crisis, the late Queen Elizabeth II visited the London School of Economics (LSE) to inaugurate a new building there. The LSE authorities were apprehensive that the Queen might reprimand them for the modernist architecture of the new building. She did reprimand them, although for a different reason. She asked the world-renowned economists of the LSE lined up to greet her, 'Why didn't any of you see the crash coming?'

That was a question a lot of people around the world were asking at that time. The assembled economists fidgeted and mumbled some answers to get through the situation.

It is not considered in good taste to keep the Queen waiting, but she had to wait a full eight months before a group of eminent economists wrote her a well-considered reply on what caused the crisis while also apologizing to her for failing to predict it.

As per a web post of the Imperial College, London, the letter ended with: 'In summary, Your Majesty, the failure to foresee the timing, extent and severity of the crisis and to head it off, while it had many causes, was principally a failure of the collective imagination of many bright people, both in this country and internationally, to understand the risks to the system as a whole.'*

---

* Complete text of letter available at: https://www.ma.imperial. ac.uk/~bin06/M3A22/queen-lse.pdf.

States' Grievances against the Centre on Resource Transfers*

In relative terms, Tamil Nadu is a well-governed state. With a per capita income of Rs 2.25 lakh in 2020–21 against the national average of Rs 1.29 lakh, Tamil Nadu is also, in relative terms, a prosperous state. Against this backdrop, the recently released white paper by the Tamil Nadu government saying that its fiscal position is precarious and that the state is deeply mired in debt makes for distressing reading.

The white paper predictably blames, albeit mildly, the previous state government and the central government for many of its ills. My intent here is not to join issues with the specific contentions of the white paper but to use that as the context to make a broader point—that even if our arrangements of fiscal federalism are not the best practice, they are not necessarily skewed against states as is commonly believed.

The big picture first. Fiscal federalism is a politically contentious issue in all federations. East Timor separated from Indonesia entirely because of a deep-seated grievance about resource apportionment. The current troubles in Ethiopia are only superficially ethnic; at their core are tensions over resource sharing. Given our vigorous democracy, it's not surprising therefore that the debate over central transfers to states hits high decibels.

It is certainly true that states are structurally disadvantaged in raising revenues commensurate with their expenditure needs. The entire scheme of central transfers to states is

---

* Originally published in the *Times of India* on 7 February 2021 as 'Grow Up, States'.

premised on correcting that imbalance. Importantly, the bias in the scheme of resource transfers to states, and in the matter of autonomy over their use, has over time shifted substantially in favour of states.

Consider the following evidence.

As per the original Constitutional mandate, states were getting a share in just two central taxes—personal income tax and union excise duties. That arrangement was changed in favour of states through a Constitutional amendment in 2000 by giving them a share in the total taxes collected by the Centre on the grounds, among other things, that states should enjoy the buoyancy of the entire pool of central taxes rather than just a couple of them.

The abolition of the Planning Commission too has increased the autonomy of states vis-à-vis the Centre. Under the Planning arrangement, the Centre decided how much grant to give each state and for what use. Now states get that money as part of statutory transfers with full discretion over where and how to spend it.

Centrally Sponsored Schemes (CSS) are another perennial sore point. States chafe at the straitjacketed nature of CSS funding and see it as an assault on their autonomy. Give us the money and we will decide how to spend it. Being closer to the frontline, we know the local priorities better, is their standard refrain. A neat argument in theory, but far from credible in practice given how several states have often diverted CSS funds for other purposes including, at times, for meeting their salary bills.

The argument that the Centre is using the CSS as a mechanism to wade into subjects assigned to states under the Constitution is also misinformed. CSS monies are given to states invoking the provisions of Article 282 of the Constitution. The very intent of Article 282 is to enable both the Centre and states to spend on any public purpose no matter that the purpose is beyond its normal legislative responsibilities. The Centre uses CSS to signal national priorities, and that is entirely consistent with not just the letter but also the spirit of the Constitution. I must add though that there is much room for reform of CSS, for example, by having a basket of schemes and allowing states to choose those that match their needs and priorities.

The introduction of GST has opened another battlefront. It is short-sighted to see the GST as a central initiative in aid of which states have been forced to make compromises. For sure, states have surrendered some of their autonomy in raising taxes but so has the Centre. Since the GST rates are decided by the GST Council, every state cannot get its way on every rate; some give and take is inevitable in a national project like this. Eventually though, as the GST expands the tax base and arrests tax leakage, both the Centre and states stand to benefit. It is that promise of a positive sum game that must inform states' stance on GST.

My big-picture assessment of fiscal federalism will not be complete if I do not point out the egregious practice by the Centre of increasingly resorting to the levy of cesses and surcharges rather than raising taxes. The Tamil Nadu white paper points out that the proportion of cesses and surcharges in the Centre's total tax revenue has nearly doubled from 10.4 per cent in 2011–12 to 20.2 per cent in 2019–20.

There is a perverse incentive in operation here. If the Centre raises an additional rupee by way of tax, it has to part with 41 paise to states whereas it gets to keep the full rupee if it is raised by way of a surcharge. When the Constitution was amended in 2000 giving states a share in the Centre's total tax pool, the implicit understanding was that the Centre would resort to cesses and surcharges only sparingly, and not as a matter of routine as has become the practice. States are right to feel aggrieved.

The bottom line. No matter how vociferous their demand, states are unlikely to get substantial additional support from the Centre given the latter's own fiscal compulsions stretching into the medium term. It is therefore imperative for states to restore the health of their finances through their own efforts if they want to get on to a virtuous cycle of growth and development.

13

North Block Ruminations

Finance Secretary to the
Government of India

When I took over as secretary of the Department of Economic Affairs (DEA) on 30 April 2007, it marked my return to the Ministry of Finance after a gap of fourteen years. As a mid-level officer in DEA during my earlier stint in the early 1990s, every time I entered the finance secretary's corner office in the North Block for a meeting or a discussion, I would be overcome by awe and apprehension about whether I would have answers to the questions that the finance secretary would raise. And here I was occupying the same office that had housed some of the iconic names in India's financial history. It was a heady feeling.

I had to hit the ground running. Within hours of taking charge, I was told that I would have to head out to Kyoto in two days for the annual meetings of the Asian Development

Bank (ADB). Finance Minister Chidambaram, who would normally have been the head of the Indian delegation, had opted out as he was politically busy. I was therefore to be the head of the delegation as well. So, in the midst of frantically settling down in the job, I also had to work on our formal intervention statement and get briefed on the issues on the annual meeting agenda. Besides, I was scheduled to be on two panel discussions on the sidelines of the meetings, and I had to get tutored on those topics. It was a far cry from the steady, unhurried job I had been doing for over two years as secretary to the Prime Minister's EAC in a quiet corner of the government.

The DEA before and after reforms

In the fourteen years between my two stints, there had been a sea change in DEA's job chart and policy orientation. Gone were the controller of capital issues, exchange rate management and foreign exchange budgeting. New regulatory bodies had come into being and established themselves—the Securities and Exchange Board of India (SEBI) for capital markets, the Insurance Regulatory and Development Authority of India (IRDAI) for insurance, and the Pension Fund Regulatory Development Authority (PFRDA) for pensions—taking away, and quite appropriately, regulatory work from the ministry. With ad-hoc treasury bills ended and the Fiscal Responsibility and Budget Management (FRBM) Act on the statute book, the Reserve Bank had become more autonomous. Much of the responsibility for external sector management, especially on the capital account side, stood transferred to the RBI with the government being consulted only if the RBI was effecting any major policy changes.

Earlier, the joint secretary for foreign trade used to focus almost exclusively on commercial relations with the Soviet Bloc countries; now, we had global ambitions. With the Doha Round of multilateral trade agreements all but abandoned, we were negotiating and signing bilateral trade arrangements (BTA) at a frantic pace. Alexander the Great, it is said, worried that he had no more lands to conquer. I started wondering whether sometime soon we would worry that there were no more countries to sign BTAs with.

During the Vajpayee government, India decided, quite wisely in my view, to stop accepting bilateral aid because that was subjecting us to interlocution on our policies by the donors even as their assistance in relative terms was small. Only Japan, which had always been a large donor, continued to be a valued partner. The World Bank and the ADB were still important in the overall scheme of things, not so much for the quantum of loans they gave us but as dialogue partners on policy issues, which arguably was helpful to both sides. We became more assertive in discussions with the IMF on our external sector and overall macroeconomic management.

In my earlier stint in the DEA as a mid-level official, I was the nodal officer for the annual Aid Consortium Meeting held in Paris every June. Our mission then was to get the donors to pledge the maximum possible aid, and we used to take pride in how much higher the total aid pledges were compared to the previous year. By the time I returned to the DEA in 2007, the Aid India Consortium had become a relic. This shift away from foreign aid (official development assistance—ODA—in official terms) to private capital flows as the main buffer for our balance of payments was by far the biggest change between the old DEA and the one I had returned to.

Our policy focus now was on liberalizing capital markets, instituting policies for public-private partnerships for infrastructure-building and encouraging trade and foreign investment. We were campaigning for a higher shareholding in the World Bank and a higher quota in the IMF commensurate with our growing status as a large and growing economy. We had established protocols for annual bilateral economic dialogue with the US, EU, UK, China and Japan as equals.

'The finance secretary'

The convention is to designate the senior-most secretary in the Ministry of Finance as the finance secretary. K.M. Chandrasekhar, who was revenue secretary and finance secretary, had moved as cabinet secretary in June 2007, and so, within a month of going into the finance ministry, I was also given the much-coveted designation of 'finance secretary'.

It is difficult to define the job chart or to describe the typical workday of the finance secretary. The canvas is very wide since the finance ministry's opinion is mandatory for virtually every policy decision in the government. The practice in the Central government is for policy issues to be vetted by a committee of secretaries (COS) in the cabinet secretariat before they go to the cabinet or the relevant cabinet committee. The finance secretary is a default invitee to most of these COS meetings. Besides, the finance secretary is required to be in attendance for cabinet meetings, which are held every week with only occasional exceptions. There are meetings in the planning commission and in the prime minister's office. There are committees such as the Foreign Investment Promotion Board (FIPB) and Viability Gap Funding (VGF) that the finance secretary chairs. And there is a regular stream of visitors—MPs, representatives from corporates and financial markets, potential investors, international officials, officials from other ministries, etc. Most importantly, there is the core business of meetings and discussions with the finance minister and with your own staff.

It was by far the busiest job of my career. My son Raghav, when he was a school kid, used to ridicule me saying, 'The IAS job is so easy; all you have to do is sign files.' If he had seen me as finance secretary, he probably would have changed his view to: 'The IAS job is so easy; all you have to do is flit from one meeting to another.' I didn't mind the frantic pace; in fact, I enjoyed it. What used to upset me was the constant juggling you had to do with your own schedule. You slog over the weekend to clear your table and plan the week ahead but within ten minutes of the start of business on Monday morning, your whole schedule and work plan go haywire.

The subtle art of listening one step down

As I moved up the civil service ladder over thirty-five years, I had seen many bosses, each of whom had their distinct personality and work style. I saw their positives and negatives. Now as finance secretary, I was at the top of the hierarchy myself and was deeply conscious that I must reflect the lessons of experience in designing my own leadership style in order to improve my productivity and performance.

I don't want to turn this into a discourse on leadership in government, but I do want to mention just one facet of that leadership style that I carefully practised, which was the subtle art of listening one step down. If I had an issue to discuss, I made it a practice to call not just the joint secretary concerned but also the deputy secretary below him and hear her view as well. This would give me a different nuance and give her a sense of involvement, which can be highly motivational.

This art of listening one step down is not as simple as it sounds. You have to listen not just to what's being said but also to what's not being said. Is the one-step-down officer hesitant to express her view because it runs counter to yours? Is she afraid to speak up in front of her immediate boss? How do you ensure that the joint secretary does not see this one step down as your distrust of him?

I wasn't a perfect leader. Far from it. But I can say this for myself that I made a conscious effort to reach the best practice.

Drama and excitement of the budget

Much of the outside world associates the finance ministry with budget-making. Even if the top officials in charge of the budget change from time to time, there is significant institutional expertise in the system, which ensures that the budget process runs to a well-honed drill. The bulk of the work on calling for estimates on non-discretionary expenditure, new expenditure proposals and revenue inflows is standardized. The budget staff handle that as per a well-established calendar and with exemplary efficiency.

The visible, and in some sense the discretionary, part of the budget process kicks off with the finance minister's consultations with stakeholders such as banks and non-banks, financial markets, economists, corporates, medium and small industries, trade bodies and farmers groups. Since 2014, the government has rectified a critical lacuna in this consultation process by including a consultation session with state finance ministers.

These 'consultations' are typically one-sided conversations, with the government side in a listening mode save for seeking clarifications. I have heard some cynical comments that this whole process is an eyewash and that what is said in these meetings seldom influences the budget. That is uncharitable. Most of the time, what is said in these meetings has already been said and discussed before; so, it has possibly already been considered. Besides, the stakeholders typically roll out a charter of demands, but budget constraints do not permit accepting all these suggestions. However, if there is an original idea or some lateral thinking in any of the views, it certainly influences the budget in an important, even if non-discernible, way.

Over the years, the budget has become quite a media event with the print and electronic media running series such as 'Ask the finance minister' or 'Tell the finance minister' about what the public expects from the budget and with economists and commentators advising the finance minister on what she should do. Just as with stakeholder consultations, these views and suggestions do influence the budget more by a process of osmosis than through any explicit and exhaustive consideration of every issue and idea.

In making budgets, finance ministers are confronted with an impossible trinity of sorts—they are enjoined to raise expenditure without raising taxes and without increasing borrowing. That, of course, is mathematically impossible. Something has to give way, and the finance minister's wisdom and discretion lie in deciding where to take some leeway. All I can say is that given all the political compulsions and the fiscal arithmetic, the latitude available to the finance minister is much smaller than is commonly believed.

The policy component of the budget comprises tax proposals, which are within the realm of the Department of Revenue, new expenditure proposals within the ambit of the Department of Expenditure and the overall macroeconomic stance such as fiscal and revenue deficits and debt sustainability, which is the mandate of the DEA. Typically, 'the Budget Group', comprising secretaries of revenue, expenditure and economic affairs along with the chief economic adviser (CEA), discusses these proposals, which are then further discussed with the finance minister and finalized. However, since Chidambaram was a hands-on minister who was on top of virtually every issue, this standard process was short-circuited to a single stage of discussion at the level of the finance minister.

The awe and secrecy surrounding the budget are part of the drama. Budget files are hand-carried or moved in double-sealed covers. In the weeks before the budget, the Ministry of Finance goes into a 'shut period' and the finance minister stops speaking in public for fear of giving away signals on what's coming. Only three people in the entire hierarchy are privy to the full budget—the finance minister, the finance secretary and the joint secretary in charge of the budget.

But I always felt that we make too much of a fetish about secrecy. Taxation proposals, of course, need to be secret and there needs to be confidentiality about some other budget numbers. Beyond that, the budget will perhaps be better served if some of the broad policy options and expenditure proposals are discussed in the public domain. After all, there is something to be said for the wisdom of crowds.

In a welcome move, starting in 2021, the finance minister, Nirmala Sitharaman, has made the budget a paperless exercise, which I expect has put an end to the tedious practice of about a hundred-odd staff of the finance ministry being locked in the budget press in the basement of the North Block to manage the printing of the budget documents. And I also hope the finance ministry has instituted some ERP systems for moving budget proposals online across the hierarchy, putting an end to the vexatious and wasteful practice of moving files in double-sealed covers.

The 'one-time' farm loan waiver

I was finance secretary for just over a year, and it is therefore one of my disappointments that I got to work on only one budget—the one for 2008–09. The centrepiece of this budget was the 'one-time' farm loan waiver for small and marginal farmers amounting to over Rs 70,000 crore. In fact, Sharad Pawar, as agriculture minister, had been canvassing for relief for farmers for over a year, but the Ministry of Finance had pushed back with the standard plea of fiscal constraints. That impasse was broken by the impending general election in 2009, which helped coalesce a consensus on the issue. In fact, pollsters attributed the UPA victory with an improved margin in 2009 to the relief provided to farmers.

There are, of course, many well-known arguments against loan waivers. First, there is the moral hazard that in the future farmers will deliberately default on repayments in the expectation of a loan waiver. Second, because there is an interest rate subvention on farm loans, even farmers who don't need a loan take it anyway and then on-lend it, making money on the interest rate differential. An expectation of a waiver raises the incentive for such free-riding.

Third, even though farm loans are supposed to be collateral-free, it is standard practice for banks to insist on collateral—mostly gold. This generates an 'adverse selection' in the sense that only the relatively better-off farmers who can provide collateral get loans and hence become beneficiaries of a future loan waiver while the really small ones get left behind. Fourth, loan waivers make banks more cautious about farm loans. They cannot, of course, forsake farm loans altogether since they are mandated to meet the minimum laid down under the priority sector lending quota, but they manage to meet their quota by lending to larger farmers, and that too by insisting on collateral. Finally, farm loan waivers are discriminatory. Millions of small and marginal farmers and landless labour fall back on informal moneylenders because they are not 'creditworthy' for the formal sector. They don't get any relief on their debt.

Advocates of farm loan waivers chafe at these arguments. Their typical retort is that industrialists routinely have their loans written off by banks when their ventures fail or when they deliberately run them into sickness by siphoning off money. Why should we then grudge loan waivers to farmers who are so obviously more genuinely distressed?

The 2009 mega farm loan waiver was touted as a loan waiver to end all loan waivers. It turned out to be the exact opposite by setting off a series of loan waivers. Although hard numbers are difficult to come by, a research study by NABARD estimates that state governments had written off farm loans amounting to over Rs 2.6 trillion during 2012–21.[*] That the farm sector continues to be distressed despite repeated loan waivers is clear evidence that loan waivers are not a solution but, in fact, a problem. But in a democracy, short-term compulsions trump long-term sustainability, and farm loan waivers have become a staple of political manifestos. The NABARD study also says that only four out of twenty-one parties have lost an election after promising a loan waiver since Haryana's Devi Lal government pioneered it in 1987.

---

[*] Farm Loan Waivers in India: Assessing the Impact and Looking Ahead. NABARD 2021. Available at: https://www.nabard.org/auth/writereaddata/tender/2304223730farm-loan-waivers-in-india-assessing-impact-and-looking-ahead_compressed.pdf.

Farm loan waiver is an example of a larger problem of asymmetric incentives that drive public policy choices. Loan waivers, whether for farmers or for industrialists, are not free; there is an opportunity cost to the money spent on them. That money could, for example, be spent on education or health, which would benefit the larger public. But the larger public does not see the cost-benefit calculus in such explicit terms. They behave as if the farm loan waiver is a bilateral issue between the government and the farmers with no implications for them. An important consequence of this indifference, what economists call 'the collective action problem', is that a lobby or a voting bloc organized around a single issue gets its way while those who lose out by the decision don't even realize that they are paying the price.

Following this chapter is an op-ed I wrote in the *Times of India* in December 2021 on the lessons to be learnt from the aborted farm reforms, which expands on this issue of the logic of collective action.

Aid for Sainik Schools

One of the perks of being a finance minister is the opportunity to play Santa Claus with the budget—offering goodies to specific interest groups or regions with an eye on the vote bank or occasionally to earn goodwill. The amounts involved are large for the recipient interest group but relatively small in proportion to the size of the budget. This has become such a hoary tradition across democracies that it's likely the public would be disappointed if there were no Santa Claus drama.

I played my own bit role in this drama. I encouraged the joint secretary in charge of Sainik Schools in the Ministry of Defence to send a proposal for a one-time grant to each of the schools for capital improvement. Chidambaram acceded to my request and approved the proposal, allowing me to pay a debt of gratitude to my alma mater—Sainik School, Korukonda.

Demystifying the budget

One thing that has always troubled me in all my years in public finance at the state level, in Delhi as well as the RBI is that we don't do enough to demystify our work and disseminate our policies to the larger public. Our public documents are written in complex language that is beyond the reach of the common people. To some extent, the media bridges this 'understanding gap' by translating complex officialese into more comprehensible language, but that can hardly be a substitute for an outreach by the government itself.

On the budget, for example, such an outreach could start with a short document explaining in plain, non-technical language the budget decisions and their rationale and implications for the people. Imagine, for example, that the government withdraws the railway concession for senior citizens, which will obviously upset the senior citizen bloc. But if the finance minister is able to say that the Rs 3000 crore thus saved was being spent to improve the infrastructure in rural schools, the public would be able to appreciate the 'opportunity benefit' of the withdrawal of the railway concession to senior citizens.

In fact, a dissemination document like that can become the basis for a broad engagement with the public. The finance minister and senior officials of the ministry can then hold a few town hall meetings across tier II or even lower-level towns across the country, which could be nationally televised. This would be an opportunity for the government to promote its policies and for the public to seek accountability.

India in Fund-Bank meetings

Among the many positives of the job of secretary, DEA, is the opportunity to attend the IMF-World Bank meetings—Fund-Bank meetings for short—held twice a year—the spring meetings in April and the annual meetings in October. The finance minister is the governor for India on the governing boards of both the IMF and the World Bank while the RBI governor is the alternate governor for the IMF and the finance secretary is the alternate for the World Bank. I was involved in these meetings in my earlier stint in the DEA, mostly by way of preparing notes for the bosses who attended the meetings. Now, it was my turn to be the 'boss' myself.

These meetings provide an opportunity to get exposure to the frontier issues in the global economy and to put forward our position on those issues. Since China has to a large extent pulled away from the pack with its own idiosyncratic problems and concerns, India is often looked upon to serve as the voice of the emerging economies and developing countries* in these meetings, an informal

---

* This grouping has since acquired a shorter moniker—the Global South.

obligation that India takes seriously but does not always perform very satisfactorily. These meetings are also an opportunity to network with counterparts from other countries and discuss common concerns and experiences. Besides, the events on the sidelines of these meetings such as panel discussions and seminars, which bring together academics, practitioners and public intellectuals on a single platform, are valuable learning opportunities.

Subbarao's law on capital flows

One of the topical issues then, one that continues to be so even today, is the challenge for emerging markets of managing volatile capital flows. Financial globalization has made it possible for global investors to move capital across borders with enormous ease and little expense. As a result, capital floods into emerging markets when they offer higher returns and flees equally swiftly at the slightest hint of any problem.

Emerging markets do, of course, need foreign capital to aid their growth, but they want the stable, long-term type, not the fickle, short-term type that flees at the first hint of trouble. In fact, I have formulated a law about it: 'No emerging market gets capital of the right type at the right time in the right quantity. It's always of the wrong type, wrong size and wrong timing.' The net result is that emerging markets are condemned to volatile capital flows, which puts pressure on their exchange rates and impairs their financial stability.

In practice, emerging markets have employed a host of capital controls to protect themselves from the vagaries of volatile capital flows, such as prescribing a lock-in period for capital inflows or taxing capital at entry or exit. Experience has shown that these measures are not foolproof and often entail costs that exceed the perceived benefits. Besides, the IMF, obedient as it had been to the Washington Consensus, frowned on capital controls, evangelizing to emerging markets that their best interest lay in providing unfettered freedom to capital to enter and exit.

Emerging economies have consistently agitated on two issues at the IMF meetings. First, that the IMF dictum that emerging markets should not impose any capital controls is not only impractical but even detrimental because there are circumstances in which capital controls become unavoidable. Second, that advanced economies should be sensitive to the spillover impact of their macroeconomic policies that ignite volatile capital flows rather than abandoning emerging markets to fend for themselves.

Emerging markets have had some success on the first issue. Based on the lessons of experience, the IMF has moved from its rigid orthodoxy to a more nuanced position. It now accepts that in the face of large and volatile flows, capital controls are not only inevitable but even desirable to defend the economy against financial instability. The IMF change of heart comes with many caveats, but it is nevertheless a step forward. On the second issue of spillovers, advanced economies have consistently argued that their macroeconomic policies are tailored to their domestic circumstances, and they can't subordinate their domestic mandate to an international obligation. It's an issue that continues to defy resolution.

Management of capital flows is an issue that travelled with me from the finance ministry to the RBI. When I was finance secretary, the problem was capital inflows triggered by the easy money policies in advanced economies, which were putting upward pressure on the exchange rate. We had to intervene in the market to buy foreign exchange to stem rupee appreciation. When I was in the RBI, the problem was the opposite. Both in the aftermath of the global financial crisis in 2008–09 and during the 'taper tantrums' in 2013, the problem was of sudden exit of capital triggering a sharp drop in the exchange rate. In this case, we had to intervene in the market to sell foreign exchange to fend off rupee depreciation.

Defending the rupee both against appreciation and depreciation was a big part of my job chart both in the finance ministry and the RBI. Capital flow management was such a big elephant in the room all through those years that I used to be regularly featured as a speaker in conferences and panel discussions in the IMF, G20, BIS and other international fora.

A more humble and responsive IMF

The IMF has historically been criticized for its obduracy and 'know it all' attitude. Emerging markets were particularly bitter about the harsh conditionalities it imposed on them when they sought support from the fund in times of crisis. This despite ample evidence from across Latin America through the 1980s and 1990s, and even more so from the Asian Crisis of the late 1990s, that these 'one size fits all' conditionalities did more harm than good. The grievance of emerging markets was that the IMF was hostage to the diktats of rich countries, especially the US. But over the last decade, there have been reasons to believe that the IMF is changing—becoming more responsive, more sensitive to emerging market concerns, and most of all, becoming more humble.

The first evidence of this change in the IMF came in the aftermath of the global financial crisis in 2008–09, which was triggered by excessive leverage in the US banking sector. Under its Articles of Association, the IMF subjects every member country to an annual Article IV consultation to assess the country's economic health so as to forestall future financial problems. Had an emerging economy built up excessive leverage in its financial sector like the US had, the IMF would have frowned on that in the annual Article IV consultation. But such signalling about pressure building up did not happen in the case of the US because the US was not subjecting itself to Article IV consultation.

In the IMF and G20 meetings following the outbreak of the crisis, all countries, including European countries, blamed the US for inflicting a devastating crisis on the world and blamed the IMF for tacitly yielding to US exceptionalism. Both the US authorities and the IMF admitted that not subjecting the US economy to the same level of scrutiny as all other member countries was, in fact, a mistake; an Article IV scrutiny of the US has since become a regular annual exercise at par with all other member countries.

Another instance where the IMF admitted its mistake relates to the impact of fiscal austerity, a standard condition it imposes while extending support to countries in trouble, on growth and welfare in the recipient country. This came about via the eurozone sovereign debt crisis of 2010–11. In the bailout programmes of the PIGS (Portugal, Ireland, Greece and Spain), which were at the centre of this crisis, the IMF asked for a drastic reduction in their public spending in order to bring their loan books into balance. There was recognition that this might hurt growth, but the understanding was that the negative impact on growth would only be in the short term. In the medium term, the argument went, growth would pick up since the austerity programme would enable more efficient private investment to replace the less efficient government spending.

Then, in 2012, the IMF came out with a study of its own showing that the fiscal multipliers in the eurozone countries were indeed higher than originally projected, implying that the negative growth impact of the fiscal austerity imposed by the IMF on PIGS would be larger than the figures built into the bailout programmes. In plain English, this was an admission by the IMF of an error of judgement as also a case for softening the fiscal austerity conditionality so as to reduce the hardship on the public of the crisis countries.

Interestingly, this IMF study played out in India too. By 2012, I was nearly four years into my tenure as RBI governor and had been frequently and publicly asking the government to prune its fiscal deficit as excessive spending by the government was eroding our fight against inflation. The finance ministry was miffed by these suggestions and showed it. When the new IMF research came on the scene, some senior officials in the ministry cottoned on to it and argued that as in the eurozone, in India too, the adverse consequences of fiscal deficits were being exaggerated and that the Reserve Bank was being misguided in taking a negative view on the government's fiscal adjustment path.

I was dismayed by this effort to extend the eurozone arguments to India without reckoning with India's altogether different macro parameters. Our fiscal adjustment road map was by no means aggressive; besides, the IMF research applied to countries with a demand recession and a negative output gap, certainly not to a country like India where a cocktail of sizzling demand and strained capacity was stoking inflation pressures. My standard response to the government was that whereas the debate in Europe was fiscal austerity *versus* growth, for us in India, it has been, and will continue to be, fiscal austerity *for* growth.

India's soft power in Guyana

I had an interesting experience when I visited Georgetown, Guyana, in April 2008 for the Commonwealth finance ministers meeting. I was deputing for the finance minister who could not travel because of other commitments. During the plenary session in the morning, I got a message from the Indian High Commission official who was attending on me that the Guyanese prime minister, Sam Hinds, had invited me to tea that afternoon. My immediate thought was whether there was any ticklish issue relating to the finance ministry in the bilateral relations between our two countries. I checked with the high commissioner, but he was equally clueless about the agenda for this meeting. I emailed my colleagues in Delhi but wasn't hopeful that they would revert in time for the rendezvous since it was night-time back in India.

I was surprised and pleased that the PM received me, not in his office, but in the living room of his house and hosted me to a grand tea. We talked about India, Guyana, the Caribbean and the world. And of course, we talked about cricket. After about half an hour, when the PM still hadn't gotten into anything substantive, I asked him if there was anything specific he wanted to discuss with me. He said, 'No, I heard you were in town, I just wanted to thank you for all the support India has been giving us.'

As I was leaving, the PM asked me if I had seen the Providence cricket stadium just outside Georgetown, which had been built for the 2007 World Cup with financial support from the Indian government and was executed by Shapoorji Pallonji. When I said I hadn't, he insisted that I see it, and to make sure that I did, he sent me there along with a senior member of his staff.

I was, of course, deeply touched by the PM's courtesy and basked in the reflected glory of the high esteem in which India is held in this far-off country in the West Indies. Another instance of the power of 'soft power'.

The 2G scam—hero or villain?

As finance secretary during 2007–08, I was involved in decisions relating to the pricing of the 2G spectrum, an issue that embroiled the UPA-2 government in charges of mammoth corruption. Unfortunately, two issues—first, procedural irregularities in the selection of licensees, and second, the price at which the spectrum was to be given—got conflated in the public discourse. The government lost control of the narrative while a frenzied media painted a picture of a massive scam, which obscured a reasoned debate on the underlying issues.

As I recall, the story unfolded as follows. In 2007, the Department of Telecom (DoT) under the ministerial charge of A. Raja of the DMK, a partner in the UPA coalition, determined that there was a case for licensing more 2G operators in each of the twenty-three telecom circles in the country in order to encourage competition in the sector. The department consulted TRAI (Telecom Regulatory Authority of India), and TRAI, in turn, endorsed the need to increase the number of operators and recommended that fresh licensees should be given spectrum at the same price at which incumbent operators had gotten it, which was the price set in an auction in 2001. The absence of a level playing field, TRAI argued, would disadvantage fresh entrants and defeat the goal of deepening telecom services.

The 2001 cabinet decision stipulated that all future pricing of spectrum would be decided jointly by DoT and the Ministry of Finance. When the issue came to the finance ministry for opinion, I took the view that it would be inappropriate to sell spectrum in 2007–08 at a price set in 2001 and that we must rediscover the price through a fresh auction. My opinion was informed by the experience in India and around the world during the intervening years that spectrum was a scarcer commodity than originally believed. It was only appropriate that the government should garner a part of that scarcity premium by rediscovering the price through a fresh auction.

The DoT wrote back to say that they saw no reason to revisit the pricing issue and that they preferred to go along with the TRAI recommendation. For sure, there was some logic to the DoT position. If the objective was to deepen telecom penetration, it made sense to keep the price of spectrum low; competition among operators would then ensure that the lower price was passed on to customers.

Even as this disagreement on pricing remained unresolved, the DoT went ahead and invited applications for licences in September 2007 and awarded 120 licences to forty-six companies on 10 January 2008. Although these licences were given away at the 2001 price, the licence agreement contained a clause that the price could be increased later to accommodate the possibility of the finance ministry's view prevailing.

The whole licencing process turned out to be controversial and contentious. There were allegations of arbitrarily advancing the cut-off date for receipt of applications, abrupt announcement of the successful applicants, tampering with the first come, first served principle and allowing a very narrow window for payment of the licence fee to favour some parties. This licensing part was an issue in which I was neither involved nor had any locus standi.

In July 2008, some six months after the licences were issued, the two ministers, Finance Minister Chidambaram and Telecom Minister Raja, reached an agreement that this round of 2G spectrum would be given at the 2001 price while all future spectrum, including 3G, which was then on the anvil, would be auctioned. Both ministers presented this agreed package to the prime minister at a meeting where I was present. I recorded that decision in the file.

In the months after the issue of licences, stray reports began appearing that spectrum had been given away at a throwaway price. These reports gained momentum when two of the licensees were able to sell equity to foreign investors at a huge premium, suggesting that the true value of spectrum was much higher than what was reflected in the 2001 price.

Very soon the trickle of allegations of corruption turned into a flood. That the government had ignored the advice of its own finance secretary added fuel to the fire. There was a furore in the parliament. The decision was attacked in the Public Accounts Committee (PAC), the Central Vigilance Commission (CVC) ordered a CBI investigation, the Comptroller and Auditor General (CAG) decided to take up a special performance audit and a public interest litigation was filed in the Supreme Court. This meant that the 2G issue was simultaneously the subject of a CBI investigation, a PAC inquiry, a CAG special audit and a Supreme Court probe. And subsequently, it would be the subject matter of a Joint Parliamentary Committee (JPC) inquiry as well.

The CAG report, signed off by Vinod Rai, incidentally my IAS batchmate, was tabled in the parliament in November 2010. Its most important conclusion was that the government had incurred a 'presumptive loss' of Rs 1.76 trillion by selling spectrum at below market price. This huge number, as much as 3.6 per cent of GDP, was explosive and turned the 2G issue into a full-blown scam.

The locus standi of the CAG to take up a special audit is unquestionable. However, the CAG's decision to go into the question of a 'presumptive loss' to the government and its methodology of quantifying that loss are questionable on several grounds.

The CAG estimated the 'presumptive loss' by calculating the difference between the revenue actually generated and the revenue that would have been generated under four different hypothetical prices for spectrum. The assumptions underlying the estimates of these hypothetical prices are contestable. Moreover, in burrowing deeply into just the pricing issue, the CAG did not reckon with the significant recurring revenue the government would earn via larger spectrum charges consequent on the expansion of telecom. Finally, the CAG did not take into account the substantial equity and efficiency gains that would accrue to the economy via deeper telecom penetration.

The reality is that it's difficult to quantify the costs and benefits of decisions like this without making heroic assumptions. Arguably, it's possible to come out with a study that would, in fact, show 'presumptive gains' to the government—that the overall benefits to the government far exceed the costs it incurred—by making assumptions that would be no less robust than those underlying the CAG findings.

More important than the estimate of presumptive loss, questionable as it was, was the CAG's locus standi in questioning the right of the government to decide to sell spectrum at below market price. If a democratically elected government decided to forgo revenue in order to serve a larger public good of deepening telecom penetration, was it open to the CAG to substitute his own judgement for the government's? If the CAG was allowed to enter into this issue, then what would stop him from going on logically to question every tax concession in the budget as a presumptive loss? Surely that would diminish, not enhance, our democracy.

The 2G issue continued to haunt me even after I moved, in September 2008, from the Ministry of Finance to the RBI. In the midst of fighting inflation and exchange rate tantrums, I had to appear before the PAC, subsequently before the JPC, and also depose as a prosecution witness before the CBI court that was trying former minister Raja and a host of officials on charges of corruption.

My experience with parliamentary committees has been that the interaction is almost always adversarial. It's interesting that members who are cordial and friendly towards you while having tea in the lounge outside the meeting room immediately assume a hostile demeanour as soon as the meeting begins. Both in the PAC, and subsequently in the JPC, I was grilled on why I did not persist with my initial suggestion of a fresh auction. I tried to explain that my suggestion was overruled by the agreement between the finance minister and the telecom minister, and that as a bureaucrat, I had no locus standi to press my view beyond a point. But the members refused to be persuaded. I went into these meetings expecting to be lauded as a hero for taking a proactive stand on the pricing issue in the best interests of the government. Instead, by the time the meetings ended, I was made to feel like a villain who had failed to further the best interests of the government.

In the CBI court, I was called in as a prosecution witness. The main question to me was the same as in the PAC and JPC probes—why did I not press the suggestion for a fresh auction? My explanation too was the same—that as a civil servant, my responsibility was to offer advice, but then to defer to a minister's decision as long as there was nothing irregular in that decision, as indeed there wasn't in this case.

In the course of my evidence in the CBI court, the judge asked me if I believed it was right for the government to incur such a huge loss of revenue. I replied that it was misleading to call it 'a loss of revenue' when it was actually 'a sacrifice of revenue' and added that it was very much open to a democratically elected government to sacrifice revenue if it believed that the resultant gains, both tangible and intangible, exceeded the forgone revenue. I was gratified by what the CBI court judgment said about me: 'Sh D. Subbarao displayed the quality of a sterling witness by remaining reasonable and objective in his deposition and in the end deposed that there was no loss to exchequer but only some sacrifice of revenue was there.' *

Much after both of us had retired, K.M. Chandrashekhar, former cabinet secretary, and I happened to meet, and we compared notes. Shekhar, wisdom personified, said to me: 'Subba, as bureaucrats, we sign off on hundreds of files every day. Potentially, any file could snowball into a scam, and that happens usually after we've left the scene. It's only with the benefit of hindsight that you realize where you should have been more careful and diligent, but in real-time it's difficult to see which file would blow up into a scam.'

---

* Para 1793 at page 1529 of the CBI Court judgment dated 21 December 2017. Available at: https://www.hindustantimes.com/static/ht2017/12/CBI%20Vs.%20A.%20Raja%20and%20others.pdf.

My experience with the 2G scam perfectly fits that surmise!

Arbiter between North Block and Mint Street

As finance secretary, I inadvertently turned into an arbiter between Finance Minister Chidambaram and RBI Governor Reddy on their policy face-offs. Their differences were not so much on the direction of travel but on the speed. Chidambaram was typically for more aggressive liberalization whereas Reddy was more studied. This was par for the course as they looked at issues from different perspectives, and wisdom, as experience shows, arises from arguing out differences. Both were strong personalities and had the intellectual gravitas to argue their case. Often their discussions ended in an impasse.

When that happened, both Chidambaram and Reddy would vent their annoyance to me separately. After a clash like that, Reddy would storm into my office, which was adjacent to the finance minister's, red-faced and visibly upset and complain in a mix of English and Telugu about how the finance minister was pushing him into actions that would erode our carefully built buffers. Chidambaram, on his part, would tell me how the governor was being much too cautious without seeing the big picture. In a couple of months, I realized two things. First, they both respected each other; second, both wanted me to argue their case with the other. It was an unenviable role, but I enjoyed it all the same.

One such ticklish issue was the use of forex reserves for financing infrastructure. Remember, those were the heady days of public-private partnerships (PPP) in infrastructure building. Montek Singh Ahluwalia, deputy chairman of the Planning Commission, had suggested that a part of the RBI's forex reserves could be lent out to infrastructure builders. His argument was that the RBI was getting meagre returns on its reserves; on the other hand, infrastructure developers were raising foreign loans at high rates of interest. If the RBI lent to the developers, the RBI would get higher returns and developers would get cheaper finance—a win-win option. The Deepak Parekh Committee on infrastructure finance had made a similar recommendation.

Chidambaram embraced the suggestion enthusiastically while Reddy was characteristically circumspect. Reddy's argument was that the strength of our reserves as a buffer against external sector pressures would erode if they were encumbered. Chidambaram thought that it was a manageable risk when seen against the benefits that would accrue via infrastructure building. We were at a familiar place—another impasse between the two.

As per the set pattern by now, both Chidambaram and Reddy argued their case with me, separately of course. On this issue, I veered more towards the governor. I told the finance minister that he was right to argue that the amount sought to be earmarked was too small to make a dent in the reserves, but the amount was also too small to make a dent in the huge amounts required for infrastructure finance. I also feared that this might become the thin end of a wedge; it would henceforth become a standard practice to dip into the reserves for every forex need of the government. Chidambaram was not persuaded by my argument and asked me to talk to Reddy and bring him around. Reddy told me that he would have to take the issue to the RBI board.

As finance secretary, I was on the board of the RBI. I assured Chidambaram that regardless of my personal view, I would argue the government's case in the board as best as I could. Chidambaram thought we should do some groundwork before the board meeting. He said, 'Why don't you call each of the board members beforehand and explain the government's position to them?' This was absolutely par for the course, but I worried about doing that for fear of offending Reddy; he might think that I was operating behind his back. So, I called up the governor and informed him of the task given to me by my minister. He was miffed, but I proceeded to perform my duty.

The proceedings after that went as per plan. I canvassed the government's position with the board members individually on the phone beforehand. At the board meeting itself, the governor was generous enough to allow me to lead the proposal and manage the discussion. In the end, the board approved the proposal although I suspect at least a couple of members fell in line in deference to the government's view in spite of their reservations.

Although the whole affair wasn't exactly pleasant, I had the satisfaction of performing the dharma of a civil servant—to pursue the government's decision regardless of my personal inclination and importantly, to do that in a straightforward, professional manner.

Swachh North Block

When we were together in a car once, Chidambaram remarked to me that we at senior levels must pay some attention to the upkeep and cleanliness of the toilets and washrooms in the North Block. Many people, including foreigners, visit the North Block every day and the state of our toilets is an embarrassment. We work so hard to woo foreign investors, organize roadshows to attract them to India, host meals and entertainment for them, but don't realize that all that effort can be undone by the perceptions they form about our work and work culture through the many things we neglect.

Chidambaram's suggestion resonated with me. Soon after returning to the office, I summoned the joint secretary in charge of housekeeping and accompanied by him and his team, we inspected all the toilets and washrooms in the North Block. After the inspection, I tasked them with preparing a plan for renovation and upgrading, which they got ready in a week. We showed it to Chidambaram who offered to go on an inspection himself, made some suggestions and we had an agreed plan ready within ten days.

That was the easy part. What followed was an exasperating experience. We wanted to entrust the job to a private contractor even if it cost more money so that we could get to 'international standards'. The CPWD, which had a monopoly over the maintenance of government buildings, was obviously miffed and went into a non-cooperation mode. They claimed they alone had the expertise to repair and refurbish plumbing systems dating back to colonial times. They resisted giving us the design drawings under one pretext or another. It took three months before we could actually break ground and another three months for the job to get done.

We even had Chidambaram cut a ribbon to inaugurate the refurbished toilets and washrooms of the North Block.

Working with Chidambaram

Working with Chidambaram was an interesting experience. He is universally acknowledged as being brilliant and is almost universally acknowledged as having an abrasive streak. I think the second part is an unfair assessment; at any rate, I never experienced that side of his personality. He always treated me with courtesy and respect. Sure, he would on occasion show some irritation, but certainly no more irritation than I did with my own colleagues in the office. Chidambaram's behaviour towards me after I became governor was even more meticulous. For example, if he was running late for an appointment with me, his office would invariably call my office to let us know so as 'not to keep the governor waiting'.

Chidambaram is also a man of grit and determination, an aspect of his personality that I saw in the aftermath of the terrorist attacks in Mumbai on 26 November 2008, about two months after I became governor. The financial sector was already reeling under the impact of the global financial crisis, and the terrorist attacks came as a double whammy. Mumbai shut down and there was fear and anxiety all around.

We were anxious that there should be no contagion from the terrorist attack to the financial markets. Our top priority was that the payment and settlement system, which is the nerve centre of our financial sector infrastructure, continue to function. That there indeed was no disruption is a tribute to the commitment of the RBI staff and a testimonial to the robustness of our technology systems.

Chidambaram was on the phone several times a day during those tense and anxious days, asking when we could reopen the markets. He was determined that we demonstrate to the world that India would not be cowed by terrorists and that our financial markets were too resilient to be hit by anyone. We in the RBI coordinated with SEBI, and in the event were able to reopen all our financial markets and clearing houses by 28 November, just two days after the attack. It was undoubtedly Chidambaram's grit and determination that pushed us into acting with such urgency and alacrity.

I also saw in Chidambaram an impressive stamina for work. He unfailingly visited his constituency every weekend unless work commitments beyond his control stopped him. He would fly to Chennai on Friday evening and take an overnight train to Shivaganga, his constituency, to be there by Saturday morning. He would retrace the path Sunday overnight and be in the office on Monday by 9 a.m. even as staff of the North Block were still shuffling in.

When we were in Washington for the Fund-Bank meetings in April 2008, he asked me to contact the prime minister's office and schedule a meeting of a cabinet subcommittee the day after we returned since an urgent issue had to be resolved. When I contacted the PMO, I was told that the PM was going to be away for three days following our return and that a meeting could only be scheduled later in the week. When I reported that to Chidambaram, he asked me, 'What time are we returning to Delhi on Monday evening?' When I replied, '5 p.m.', he looked at me with some irritation and said, 'Then, why can't we have the meeting at 6.30 p.m. on Monday?' as if it was the most obvious thing that should have occurred to me. So, of course, after a fatiguing return journey of nearly twenty hours, we drove straight from the airport to 7 Race Course Road for the cabinet subcommittee meeting.

There were many instances when I saw Chidambaram's wit and presence of mind. Here's one.

In April 2008, Gopal Nair, a director in the DEA, came to my house around 10 p.m. to get my approval on an urgent matter. The issue was that a private member's bill proposing a slot for a part-time director on the board of SEBI was listed for discussion in the Lok Sabha the following morning. We in the finance ministry were opposed to this proposal as it ran counter to our policy of preventing conflict of interest in capital market regulation.

Rule 68 of the 'Rules of Procedure and Conduct of Business in Lok Sabha' says: 'The order of the President granting or withholding the sanction or recommendation to the introduction or consideration of a Bill shall be communicated to the Secretary-General by the Minister concerned in writing.'

In compliance with this rule, we had to get the President's approval for withholding sanction for the private member's bill. After signing off on the file, I called up Chidambaram to explain the matter to him and told him that Gopal would go over to him right away to get his approval. Chidambaram said: 'Sure, Gopal may come to my house. But can he go and wake up the President in the middle of the night especially when she is flying over the Atlantic?'

As it happened, President Pratibha Patil was returning that night from a South American tour, which neither Gopal nor I knew but Chidambaram did.

It was a different matter that there was bedlam in the parliament the following morning and no business was conducted.

From North Block to Mint Street

My tenure as finance secretary ended almost abruptly when I was appointed governor of the RBI in September 2008, just about sixteen months after I had taken over. Breathtaking as the rush and volume of work was, it was a job that gave me a tremendous sense of importance and self-esteem, and a job that I thoroughly enjoyed.

I was touched by the farewell given to me by my colleagues and staff in the DEA. The DEA attracts some of the best civil service talent in the country, and over the previous year and a half, I had built valuable professional relationships and personal friendships. Together, we had accomplished many tasks even as several initiatives that we launched were still works in progress. My DEA colleagues were proud that one of their own was going as governor, while on my part, I was sad to break these bonds, and apprehensive about jumping from the comfort and familiarity of the known to the fear and uncertainty of the unknown.

A case for plain English

In early 2009, in the midst of the global financial crisis, seventy-one-year-old Chrissie Maher of Liverpool, England, received a letter from her bank with the subject line: 'Personal and Private Banking—Keeping you Informed'. Annoyed by the letter's pompous and jargon-filled language, Maher wrote a missive to the bank saying that they should change the subject line of their letter to 'Keeping You Confused'. To show that it's possible to do better, she sent the bank her translation of their letter into plain English, changing phrases such as 'maximum debit balance' to 'the most that can be owed'.

Chrissie Maher was not just another customer of the Royal Bank of Scotland. She was by then a forty-year veteran of a grassroots movement to urge and pressure the government and public agencies to use plain and simple language in their communication.

The movement had a dramatic start when Maher went to Parliament Square in London in 1979 and began shredding thousands of official forms. When a constable apprehended her and read the Riot Act, she asked: 'Does that gobbledygook mean we have to go?' Her point was made, and the Plain English Campaign was born.

The campaign that Maher started by asking a simple question, 'Why isn't the public given a chance to understand public information?' has spread to other countries. Across the world, especially in Western democracies, people are demanding government communication in simple, plain language as a democratic right. Success has been slow but significant. There have been several improvements in communication and more importantly, in the language used in drafting legislation. Some countries, notably New Zealand, have enacted laws that mandate the use of plain language.

One of the many initiatives launched under the 'Reinventing the Government' campaign headed by Vice President Al Gore during the Clinton Administration was to mandate the use of plain language by government and public agencies. The general guide to plain language enunciated by Gore was: short is better than long; active is better than passive; everyday terms are better than technical terms, and—you can use pronouns like 'we' and 'you'; in fact, you should. As many government departments and agencies are already finding out: when you apply these rules, a seventy-two-word regulation can shrink to six words; the title of a regulation can change from 'means of egress' to 'exit routes'. And letters to customers can create understanding instead of confusion and frustration.

I've written earlier about my hope that the Ministry of Finance would launch an initiative to disseminate the budget to the larger public in plain, understandable language. The ministry should look upon this not as a favour but as a measure of redeeming accountability.

Going beyond just the budget, there is, in fact, a strong case for the government to communicate in plain English. The language that the government uses for its communication, including the language for the laws and regulations that we are expected to obey, is so unintelligible that it's not just annoying; it can be despairing. Such gobbledygook reflects not just inadequate writing skills but indifference and callousness.

It's necessary to do better if we wish to be a meaningful democracy. And it's possible.

Why Farmers Won, People Lost*

What lesson can we learn from the farm laws episode (2021) for navigating reforms in the future? The prime minister himself alluded to one big lesson when he admitted in his concession speech that his government failed to disseminate the benefits of the proposed reforms. He was spot on.

Economic reforms produce winners and losers. In the case of the farm laws, the losers were the relatively large farmers with a marketable surplus who feared losing the protection of the minimum support price (MSP). On the other side, the potential winners were the larger public who would have benefitted by way of a cleaner environment and lower agricultural prices as market forces gradually engineered a shift in production from cereals to cash crops. The public would also have benefitted, albeit less obviously, via the alternative use of the money saved on MSP—better schools and health facilities, for example.

In theory, any reform measure where the winners gain more than the losers lose should sail through. In practice, things hardly ever work out that neatly. Many real-world factors—interest group dynamics, biases and even misinformation—come in the way of the best policies getting through.

Consider for example the unequal incentives of the winners and losers to mobilize and agitate for their cause. In the case of the farm laws, the farmers were a relatively small group, united by a single cause, each of them losing heavily if the reform went through. On the other side, the benefits of the reform would have spread thinly across the vast public; for any single individual, the reward was small, the cost of getting organized

* Originally published in the *Times of India* on 14 December 2021, as 'Why Farmers Won, People Lost'.

high and the incentive to agitate quite low. In the absence of any effort to mobilize the larger, amorphous group behind its interest, the smaller group held sway.

The play-off between winners and losers is also complicated by the time dimension. For the farmers, the cost if the reform went through would be immediate, which therefore galvanized them into action. For the public on the other side, the benefits of reform, although cumulatively substantial, would accrue over time. How much weight will they attach to a benefit that comes not today but later? Overburdened as they are with today's problems, from their point of view, it's not worth their while to invest time and effort into agitating today for a benefit tomorrow—yet another reason a small interest group gets its way.

Beyond asymmetric incentives to agitate, collective action is also hampered by ignorance. Oftentimes, the winners don't even realize what they might gain by a specific reform. Take procurement under MSP for example. Although the MSP scheme covers twenty-three crops, the bulk of the expenditure is on buying rice and wheat from a small segment of farmers in relatively prosperous states. Procurement then becomes in effect a silent fiscal transfer from the Centre to those states.

Juxtapose that with the acrimony that surrounds Central fiscal transfers to states via the Finance Commission awards and Centrally sponsored schemes. Chief ministers cry foul over their state getting less than its due. Economists hold forth on whether the transfers are efficient and equitable. Analysts pore over which states got more or less compared to prior years. And all of them fail to reckon with under-the-radar transfers such as those under the MSP.

As the Nobel Prize-winning economist Gary Becker argued, there are many factors that make small, well-organized groups benefit in the political process at the cost of the vast majority. To promote the larger public good, therefore, governments need to invest effort in communication and consultation to prevent the debate from getting hijacked by a narrow interest group.

This is not to say that the farmers who felt threatened by the farm laws would not have come out on the streets had the government explained the case for the reform. But such a proactive effort would have helped build a constituency for the reform.

On the usefulness of prior consultation in navigating contentious reforms, I speak with some personal experience. Back in the mid-1990s, in the Andhra Pradesh government, we were confronted with a serious resource crunch, which called for politically painful expenditure restructuring. We had to chop many subsidies including raising the price of subsidized rice— the government's flagship scheme. Chandrababu Naidu, the chief minister at the time, agonized over it for quite a while and then, instead of deciding on the issue right away, suggested that we put out a white paper explaining the financial situation and the difficult choices the government had to make.

Frankly, I thought it was all a waste of time since common people would not understand public finances, and in any case, they would not support a measure that would directly hurt them. How wrong I was! Naidu, politically savvy as he had always been, organized extensive dissemination of the white paper both through the government machinery and his party structure. In several focus group meetings, I heard ordinary people, whose understanding I had underestimated, ask if they would get better roads or drinking water in their village from the money saved on the subsidy. After weeks of this, I can't say there was total support for the subsidy cuts, but the opposition to them was substantially attenuated.

We have always taken pride in our reforms being robust because they are vetted by a democratic process. But we should not risk reforms becoming hostage to the distortions of that democratic process.

Jean Claude Juncker, the former President of the European Union, famously said, 'We all know what to do, we just don't know how to get re-elected after we've done it.'

Modi, with arguably the strongest political capital of any Indian leader in decades, has the challenge and opportunity of proving Juncker wrong.

14

Baptism by Fire

North Block to Mint Street

When I signed on as governor of the Reserve Bank of India on the afternoon of 5 September 2008 in the midst of one of those heavy Mumbai downpours, the dominant concern of the RBI was persistently high inflation. In fact, the only thing I could think of saying when I was ushered in front of the media for a soundbite minutes after the paperwork was done was that reining in inflation and anchoring inflation expectations would be my top priority. Little did I know that in less than a fortnight, my priority as governor would so dramatically turn topsy-turvy.

Two days after I took office, on 7 September, the US government took over the two giant home mortgage firms, Fannie Mae and Freddie Mac, amidst signs that they were crumbling. On 9 September, Countrywide Financial, another massive home mortgage firm, went down. On 10 September, investment banking behemoth

Merrill Lynch vanished. On 12 September, AIG, the giant insurance company, came to the brink of a meltdown. On 13 September, the crisis spread to retail banks; Washington Mutual, America's largest savings and loans association, was liquidated, and Wachovia, one of America's largest bank-holding companies, began sinking. On 16 September—the Big Bang. The colossal Lehman Brothers crashed into bankruptcy, making it the biggest corporate failure in history.

Big-name financial institutions in the US were collapsing like a house of cards. Those seismic tremors sent the world's financial system reeling into a near-death experience. The global economy was heading into the deepest downturn since the Great Depression of 1929. Markets were seized with fear and panic. Governments and central banks all around the world were bewildered and anxious. And ordinary households everywhere were scared and worried.

The governor brings on the crisis

The crisis that originated in the US spread like wildfire— first to Europe and then to the rest of the world. Virtually every country in the world was affected, and so was India. All our financial markets—equity markets, bond markets, money markets and currency markets—came under intense pressure. Red-hot demand, which had been fuelling inflation until the previous week, cooled, growth plunged and the rupee headed into a steep decline.

But there was dismay, denial and disbelief in India about why we should be affected by the crisis. After all, our banks did not indulge in any subprime mortgages and our financial markets did not have any toxic assets. Our financial firms across the board were all well-behaved. For sure, there was a demand collapse around the world, but that should affect huge exporting countries like Germany and China, not a country like India with only a tiny share in global trade. Most of all, had we not 'decoupled' from the rest of the world because of our improved macroeconomic management, robust foreign exchange reserves and a well-regulated financial sector? Then why should anything that happens in the rich world impact us?

After stepping down from the RBI in 2013, I have spoken about my challenges in leading the RBI during those turbulent times on various platforms within and outside the country. As a result of repeating that story several times, I've been able to weave a nice, somewhat embellished, tale about why India was impacted by the crisis, which goes as follows.

The public in India believed that by rights, we should not have been hit by the crisis at all since there were no excesses in our financial sector like in the West; but we were hit all the same because this new governor came and brought the crisis with him! Not having an option, I took that in my stride. Wherever I went in the country, the media and people would ask me, 'Sir, when will the crisis end?' No one on the planet had an answer to that question, least of all I. But I used to play along and say, 'You people think I brought on the crisis. So, logically, the crisis will end when my term ends.' For good measure, I would also tell them when my term would end.

But here's the thing. The crisis ended the week after I left the RBI. Growth started trending up, inflation started trending down, the rupee stabilized and the economy was back on its glorious path of growth and stability!

If there is one prophecy I wish I had been wrong on, it is this. But that was not my lot. As a greenhorn governor, I was plunged into leading the RBI through an extraordinary crisis.

It was baptism by fire.

But I am getting ahead of myself. Let me first tell you how I came to be appointed as governor of that iconic institution, the Reserve Bank of India, before resuming this story.

Cabinet secretary, not governor

As a career civil servant, my ambition had always been to become the cabinet secretary to the Government of India, the highest civil service position in the country. That was within the realm of possibility too since both age and seniority at the top of my batch in the IAS were on my side. I was also confident that my ratings in the annual confidential reports, for whatever they were worth, would be above average. But you can never be sure of your career trajectory in the civil service as appointments are based on a number of factors, not all of them transparent or contestable.

When I became finance secretary in April 2007, I was within striking range of the cabinet secretary's job as the position was expected to open up well before my scheduled superannuation in August 2009. The reason for this long preface is only to say that the job of the governor of the Reserve Bank was not on my career radar.

Y.V. Reddy's term as governor of the RBI was ending in early September 2008. By the summer of that year, the media started speculating on a potential successor. My name too figured on some journalists' lists, which meant nothing more than friends and colleagues asking me if the prime minister or the finance minister had sounded me out on the job.

I found this kite-flying by the media irritating, or amusing, depending on my mood. To be honest, the question of whether I had the profile and experience to be the governor would occasionally cross my mind. True, compared to many of my civil service colleagues, I had long experience in public finance management, both at the state and Central government levels, if only because of accident and luck in postings. My CV was also burnished by my international experience in the World Bank for over five years. But all this was mostly on the fiscal side—not the bread-and-butter business of central banking. Besides, like almost everyone else, I thought Rakesh Mohan, who was the incumbent deputy governor, would get the job.

Interview for the governor's job

Finance Minister Chidambaram was in the habit of coming to the office shortly before nine every workday morning even as the cleaners were finishing up their work and most staff were still shuffling in. After a few months of working with him, I realized that this early morning slot was the best time to touch base with him if I had to discuss any urgent issue before the day's schedule engulfed both of us. So it was that on Tuesday, 26 August 2008, I had gone to catch Chidambaram during this short morning window mainly to tell him that I would be leaving that night for Brazil to attend the G20 deputies meeting. As my boss, Chidambaram had approved my foreign travel, but that was some time ago, and the exact dates of my absence from office may not have stayed in his mind. In particular, I needed to check if he wanted me to attend to anything before I left.

My hunch was right as he went into some silent calculation when I told him about my trip. He asked when I would be back, and when that date registered in his mind, he paused briefly and asked me if I would be interested in being considered for the governor's job. Frankly, I was surprised. Notwithstanding all the media speculation, I thought that the prime minister and Chidambaram had already decided on Rakesh Mohan as the next governor. Even before I replied, he suggested that I could think about it and give him my answer by lunchtime.

Being the governor of the Reserve Bank would, of course, be a great honour and privilege, an exciting opportunity to steer the country's economy. There was hardly any need to think through the offer further; the decision seemed straightforward. I immediately thanked Chidambaram for putting my name on the shortlist and requested him to take my candidature forward. I don't think he was surprised by my enthusiastic response but added for good measure that the prime minister had wanted him to check with me since I was in line to be the next cabinet secretary.

With the big issue settled, we quickly moved on to deciding the logistics. He asked me what time my flight was, which, unsurprisingly for a westbound international flight out of India, was in the middle of the night. 'Could you then,' he asked, 'come to my house at 8 p.m. for a chat with Dr Rangarajan and me?' 'Rakesh is coming in at 7 p.m.', he added, possibly guessing a question on my mind. Dr Rangarajan is a former RBI governor and at that time, was chairman of the prime minister's Economic Advisory Council.

I had a heavy schedule for the day stretching late into the evening, including a briefing session with my staff on the agenda of the G20 meeting that I was going to attend. On top of that, I now had to make space for this interview. I called up Urmila and told her. Her reaction was typically nonchalant. 'If that's what you want, I wish you all the best.'

By the time I showed up for the 'interview' at Chidambaram's house, I was exhausted, but neither anxious nor tense. It struck me that the interviewers were Rangarajan, my former boss in the prime minister's Economic Advisory Council, and Chidambaram, my current boss—two people who could evaluate my professional competence and personality even without an interview. In the event, the interview turned out to be a relaxed, informal discussion on a few professional topics such as bank branch licensing, shifting to an inflation-targeting framework and the division of responsibilities between the government and the RBI on exchange rate management.

It was well past 9 p.m. by the time the conversation ended. Chidambaram walked me to my car, which was parked in the driveway of his house, and wished me a safe flight. I was touched by this gesture as few ministers would extend such courtesy when their staff came to see them at home, but then I had always known that Chidambaram was far more courteous than he is given credit for. Of course, he can't suffer fools, but that is a different matter.

At any other time, I would have rehashed the interview in my mind, thinking through where I could have put across my views better or argued more coherently. But just then, I was too preoccupied with more immediate concerns like getting ready for the journey in a few hours and all the preparation I still needed to do for the G20 meeting. I got home, scurrying to pack, shower and eat, and set off for the airport. My mind automatically switched off from all that had happened that day as I boarded the plane for Frankfurt on my way to Rio de Janeiro.

Fast forward five days. As my flight landed in Delhi on the early morning of 2 September, my phone started beeping incessantly with an unusual flood of messages. I was confused about the congratulations since not one of them contained any clue as to what they were for. I called Urmila, who gave me the news of my appointment as governor and did not miss the opportunity to complain that since the previous evening she had done nothing but field phone calls from literally hundreds of people, many of them not even known to us.

Transition from North Block to Mint Street

I had barely two days to prepare—physically, mentally and emotionally—for this most unexpected turn in my career. I met Chidambaram and thanked him for selecting me for this responsible and prestigious position. I called on the prime minister, and the conversation went along predictable lines about how he reposed confidence in me and of all the challenges that the government and the Reserve Bank had to jointly address. The prime minister also encouraged me to brief him on the macroeconomic situation regularly, and added for good measure, 'I will always make time for you.' As I look back, I can say that the prime minister stood by his word. Not only did he always give me time no matter how pressing his schedule or the preoccupations on his mind, but he also seemed to enjoy those meetings.

There was also a strange irony in my appointment as governor. I say this more from hearsay and my own inferences rather than any hard evidence. A year and a half earlier when I was being considered for the position of finance secretary, Chidambaram did not know me and was understandably circumspect about taking me into his team. I gathered that Prime Minister Manmohan Singh, who knew me from my earlier posting in the Ministry of Finance in the early 1990s, had to nudge him into it. And now when it came to my appointment as governor, I understand it was Chidambaram who was more actively sponsoring my candidature and it was the prime minister who had to be nudged.

On 5 September 2008, I took an early morning Air India flight from Delhi to Mumbai, a two-hour journey that would mark by far the most significant transition of my career. Even as I was drained—physically, mentally and emotionally—I couldn't help but think about the potential challenges of the job and concerns about how I might perform as the governor of the Reserve Bank of India.

I was put to the test almost immediately.

Midnight huddle in the office

When Lehman Brothers filed for bankruptcy in New York on the morning of 15 September 2008, it was around 9 p.m. in Mumbai. Deputy Governor Shyamala Gopinath, who was in charge of financial markets, got to know of it before the news broke on the wire. She called me immediately to inform me of this development and to ask if I could come to the office right away since we had to take some immediate action. I could sense Shyamala's hesitation in asking her freshly minted boss to come to the office late in the night, but like a karma yogi, she was doing her duty. Honestly, I didn't see why we couldn't wait until the morning but deferred to Shyamala's suggestion and reached the office shortly after 10 p.m.

Some senior management and support staff were already there. As I wrote earlier, there had been tremors in the US financial system over the previous two weeks, and we were tracking them on a daily basis. My first question was why the Lehman collapse was different and a potentially bigger danger than the crumbling of several storied institutions over the previous fortnight. Shyamala said that in all previous instances, the US authorities had rescued the institutions that were faltering, but in this case, they had left Lehman to die. The markets would see this abandonment as a shift in policy and would likely panic.

The discussion rolled on for about an hour. We then decided on our first step—ringfencing the two Lehman Brothers subsidiaries in India—a primary dealer and a non-banking financial company (NBFC). There was a suggestion that we should issue a short press statement saying that the RBI was watching the situation and was prepared to take whatever action was necessary to maintain financial stability. I wondered about the need for such a banal statement that said nothing beyond reiterating that we would be doing what we were, in fact, expected to be doing. Nevertheless, I had the good sense to defer to their advice, and we released the statement by 1 a.m. to catch the morning print and electronic media.

The markets opened the following day with distinct unease and uncertainty. Within minutes, it became clear to me that there would have been mayhem but for the RBI's 'banal statement'. The whole midnight action was a tribute to the RBI's institutional wisdom, and I silently complimented myself for deferring to that wisdom.

The bloodbath in the Western markets continued for days and weeks following the Lehman bankruptcy. Virtually every big-name financial institution was engulfed in rumours of imminent collapse. Markets were seized with fear and anxiety. Banks were hoarding liquidity, trust had dried up, and trading, the lifeblood of the financial system, was threatening to freeze. No one knew when and how the crisis might end.

Dousing the fires

Those tremors in Western markets reverberated around the world, including India. In the RBI, we did several things over the following few weeks and months, some of them unconventional, to minimize the contagion on our financial system and our economy. We were guided by three objectives: we must calm markets by dousing the system with liquidity, keep financial markets functioning and maintain the flow of credit to productive sectors of the economy.

Compounding our anxiety in those dreary months were the dastardly terrorist attacks in Mumbai on 26 November 2008. Mumbai shut down, but the world around us did not. Even as the security forces were battling the terrorists and the police were engaged in arresting fear and panic from spreading, some of us, the senior management of the Reserve Bank and essential staff, were back in the office ensuring that we were ready to react and respond to both domestic and external developments. Crisis management meetings on the eighteenth floor of the Reserve Bank central office in downtown Mumbai, even as we could look out of the window and see the onion dome of the iconic Taj Mahal Palace hotel in Colaba belching out smoke, will forever remain etched in my memory as a reminder of that gloomy period.

There were many challenges and dilemmas in managing the crisis. I have already written about them in my book[*] recounting my RBI experiences, and I will not rehash them. Here I want to dwell on only one challenge that was somewhat unique to me: How could I, a greenhorn governor, lead the RBI through this extraordinary crisis?

The credibility question

My main problem was that I lacked credibility, or rather was denied credibility, and for three reasons.

---

[*] Duvvuri Subbarao, *Who Moved My Interest Rate?* (Penguin Random House India, 2016).

First, I was an unknown quantity. I was finance secretary to the Government of India one day and governor of the Reserve Bank of India the following day. As civil servants, we were trained to be anonymous, a dictum that I tried to follow all through my career. But now, as a result of being catapulted from Delhi to Mumbai, within twenty-four hours I had turned from being an unknown unknown to a known unknown.

But it is not acceptable for the governor to be an unknown quantity. The markets and the media need to understand him, to be able to interpret his style and stance, his personality and his verbal and body language. It would take at least six months to reach an equilibrium in that relationship. Because of the crisis, that 'getting to know each other' time was denied to me with the result that the market was nervous about whether I would be able to steer the financial system through this crisis. When people have no confidence in you, even the right actions will fail to work. I faced that threat.

The second reason for my lack of credibility was the circumstances of my appointment as governor. I was not on most people's shortlist of potential candidates. For sure, there were finance secretaries who had become governors in the past, but that had happened after a gap. I was the first serving finance secretary to be appointed governor—in Delhi's North Block one day and on Mumbai's Mint Street the following day. The general surmise was that the government was sending one of its trusted civil servants to the RBI so that he would do their bidding without making too much of a fuss about central bank autonomy.

What complicated matters was that during the crisis, all around the world, governments and central banks were not only acting together but were bending over backwards to demonstrate that they were acting together. The Western media periodically carried pictures of finance ministers and governors attending a crisis management meeting or giving a joint media conference, setting aside their normal relationship of distance. This was all an attempt to calm markets at a time when they were very edgy.

But here in India, if I went to Delhi to meet the prime minister or if I got a call from the finance minister, the surmise was that I was 'getting instructions' from Delhi. I had, of course, to dispel the perception and show that I was my own man, but that would take time. The crisis denied me that time.

My biggest concern, and the third reason for lacking credibility, was that I was an unknown entity even to much of the senior management of the RBI. I had been around for barely two weeks when we were plunged into this crisis and were called upon to do unconventional things. For instance, we provided special lines of credit from the repo window to support NBFCs and mutual funds. I cut the interest rate by a full percentage point whereas the norm until then was half a percentage point if not even smaller. Every decision I took was, of course, based on staff analysis and after discussing matters with them. But at least a few of them were not comfortable with this aggressive easing because 'it was not the way monetary policy was done'. Some of them may have thought that I was acting out of fear and nervousness, and that didn't help to establish my credentials at a difficult time.

Won the battle but the war went on

Given these credibility challenges at the very start of my tenure, it was gratifying that the broad thrust of the media evaluation of the first hundred days of my governorship in December 2008 was that I had handled a turbulent period with intelligence, professional integrity and exemplary calm. Even more gratifying was the one-year evaluation of my governorship in the media in September 2009 where the broad consensus was that the Reserve Bank under my 'mature and reassuring' leadership was bold, swift and imaginative in its response to the crisis and that, in an uncertain time, I had brought clarity and candour to the central bank.

What was most comforting to me was that some of the very same commentators who had earlier criticized me for surrendering to Delhi's instructions had now written that I meant business, didn't bend under pressure and had steered the Reserve Bank with calm determination and quiet confidence during a time of great tumult. Writing in the *Business Standard* of 1 February 2010, Sanjaya Baru said: '[Subbarao's] leadership at the central bank through the difficult months of 2009 has, without doubt, been exemplary. As he led his four deputy governors into the boardroom last Friday, he exuded the kind of confidence that only being in charge and in control gives.'

Universal endorsement is perhaps too much to expect in a public policy job. In the midst of this wide appreciation, some analysts were more grudging and said that even if I may have passed the test as a crisis manager, that success didn't say anything about my competence in the bread-and-butter business of central banking—fighting inflation—and that the real test for me was yet to begin. As later developments would show, this summing-up was prophetic.

Don't just do something. Just stand there.

During a financial crisis, when the public is worried and edgy and the markets are panicky and nervous, there is pressure on policymakers to keep acting—to keep doing something or the other just to reassure the public that they are at the wheel and have not gone to sleep. This, even if it is sensible for the government or the central bank to just stand still.

Albert Edwards of Société Générale has an interesting analogy from football to illustrate this.

'When there are problems, our instinct is not just to stand there but to do something. When a goalkeeper tries to save a penalty, he almost invariably dives either to the right or the left. He stays in the centre only 6.3 per cent of the time. However, the penalty taker is just as likely (28.7 per cent of the time) to blast the ball straight in front of him as to hit it to the right or left. Thus, to play the percentages, goalkeepers will be better off staying where they are about a third of the time. They would make more saves.

'But goalkeepers rarely do that. Because it is more embarrassing to stand there and watch the ball hit the back of the net than do something (such as dive to the right or left) and watch the ball hit the back of the net.'

The Reserve Bank is like a football goalkeeper. It knows that the best option sometimes is to 'do nothing'. But in the midst of a crisis, when there is pressure on the central bank to do something all the time, that's hardly ever a practical option.[*]

---

[*] Drawn from an article by Vivek Kaul in *DNA* on 7 August 2013. This dilemma is also captured in a creative video presentation featuring a boxing match between Keynes and Hayek (https://www.youtube.com/watch?v=GTQnarzmTOc). Keynes asks Hayek what he would do when unemployment is rising. Hayek trots out a few long-term prescriptions. But in the short-term, he says, he would like the government to just stand still.

15

May You Live in Interesting Times

Five Turbulent Years in the Reserve Bank

The Chinese have a saying: 'May you live in interesting times.'

I can't complain on that account. As governor of the Reserve Bank for five years, I had interesting times, indeed much more than my share. My term began with managing the once-in-a-generation global financial crisis in 2008–09. Even as we were recovering from that crisis, we were hit by an extraordinary and stubborn bout of inflation for over two years (2010–11). That battle against inflation segued into an exchange rate crisis starting in mid-2012 up until the close of my tenure in September 2013 as we were engulfed by the 'taper tantrums' and the rupee crashed massively. And all along, I battled communication challenges and had several skirmishes with the government relating to the autonomy of the RBI.

I've written about the challenge of managing the global financial crisis in the previous chapter. Here, I want to talk about the other challenges during those turbulent years.

Grappling with stubborn inflation

India recovered from the 2008 crisis by the middle of 2009, much sooner than most other countries, but we hardly had any time to celebrate as we were hit by an extraordinary bout of inflation almost immediately. Just as the battle with the financial crisis was winding down, another battlefront opened from the inflation side. Whereas I had run an unconventional and easy money policy over the previous year to manage the crisis, I was now called upon to reverse it. Exiting from the crisis-driven easy money policy in a calibrated manner would prove to be more daunting than I could have imagined, and it was certainly more daunting than external commentators and interlocutors understood.

Several factors—some of them cyclical but many of them structural—stoked inflation during this period. Every time I met him, the prime minister would ask me why inflation was so unrelenting. I would tell him that our inflation was, of course, a problem, but it was in some sense a problem of success. The government's affirmative action programmes such as the Mahatma Gandhi National Rural Employment Guarantee Act (MGNREGA) and expanded subsidies, combined with a more efficient delivery system, had pushed up wages and incomes. The late Subir Gokarn, my valued deputy governor, used to contend that as a result of higher incomes, the food habits of low-income households had shifted from carbohydrates to protein, which was, of course, a desirable trend. But the flip side was that production, and importantly, productivity, had failed to catch up with the rising demand, thereby fuelling inflation.

How rapidly we reversed the easy money stance was critical to reining in inflation. We raised the interest rate by 50 basis points (0.5 per cent) on occasion, but much of the time the increase was in steps of 25 basis points, earning me the moniker of 'Baby Step Subbarao'. Many analysts thought this baby-step approach was too timid and too inadequate in the face of such stubborn inflation, and some of them started to ask whether the governor would ever grow up and take an adult step.

To those who said we were forever behind the curve, my simple response is to recall the context of the years 2010–11. The world economy was still in recession while the much-heralded spring shoots turned out to be a false dawn. The eurozone sovereign debt crisis was pounding the global markets, confidence all around continued to be fragile and markets remained testy. The embarrassment that the European Central Bank had to go through when it raised the interest rates, thinking the crisis was over, and then had to reverse its action in quick order was very much weighing on our minds. My 'baby steps' were therefore a delicate balancing act between preserving stability on the one hand and restraining inflation on the other.

With the benefit of hindsight, of course, I must admit in all honesty that the economy would have been better served if our monetary tightening had started sooner and had been faster and stronger. Why do I say that? Because we now know that we had a classic V-shaped recovery from the crisis, that growth had not dipped in the Lehman crisis year to as low as had been feared, and that growth in the subsequent two years was stronger than earlier thought. But remember, all this is hindsight, whereas we were making policy in real time, operating within the universe of knowledge at that time.

Growth vs inflation—a false dichotomy

To control inflation, central banks typically raise the interest rate with the intent of choking demand, which in turn saps growth. This is often seen as a trade-off between growth and inflation control—an interesting dichotomy but a false one. Any sacrifice of growth is only in the short term; in the medium to long term, low and steady inflation actually helps growth because it encourages investment and improves competitiveness.

Moreover, high inflation acts as a 'regressive tax' in the sense that it hurts poor people more than rich people. If the price of a shirt goes up from Rs 1500 to Rs 1600, I may not even notice it. But if the price of rice goes up from Rs 40 to Rs 42 or the bus fare increases from Rs 25 to Rs 26, poor people certainly notice it. Maintaining low and steady inflation therefore is an anti-poverty measure.

I've said earlier that I was criticized for my baby-step interest rate policy, which some thought was too mild given the raging inflation. But some critics from the other side thought that even that baby-step approach was too harsh. 'Is this man killing growth?' was the dramatic title of an op-ed in the *Economic Times* of 17 September 2011.

When inflation is high, bringing it down to a low and steady rate while minimizing the impact on growth is by far the biggest challenge of monetary policy.

Growth vs inflation—what do people want?

The Reserve Bank of India was set up in 1935, a full decade before Independence. I was privileged to be helming this iconic institution in 2010, its Platinum Jubilee year. As part of the celebrations, we held events across the country mainly with the intent of demystifying the RBI—educating people on what the RBI does and why that is important to their everyday lives.

One such event was a nationally televised town hall meeting in Chennai on the steps of the Egmore Museum. It was early January, shortly before Pongal. Chennai was in a festive mood and so were we in the RBI. The RBI staff and the TV channel hosting the event rounded up about 300 people, literally pulling them off the street as it were, for the town hall. The four deputy governors and I were there on the dais along with the anchor. It was a grand and happy occasion befitting the festival season.

As the show began, Vikram Chandra, the show's polished anchor, asked me to explain the event—why the RBI was in full force there in Chennai and was doing a town hall, something so uncharacteristic of a central bank. So, in a couple of minutes, I gave a capsule reply about what we do in the RBI and what difference it makes to people's everyday lives.

Thereafter the anchor asked us—me as well as the four deputy governors—some questions, after which it was thrown open to the audience. Imagine the scenario. The governor and the four deputy governors out there ready to answer questions from ordinary people. Many in the audience were overawed by the occasion and there was some hesitancy to begin with. But within minutes they warmed up to the occasion, the conversation picked up momentum and we were bombarded with questions.

Here's a sampling of the audience questions that came up that evening:

- I am a pensioner and keep all my savings in a fixed deposit. Why is the interest on deposits so low?
- I want to get an education loan for my daughter who is going abroad to study but the bank is asking for collateral.
- I want to junk my present autorickshaw and buy a new one, but the bank is quoting a very high interest rate. When I go to meet the manager, he doesn't even offer me tea!

Midway through this Q&A session, I had an epiphany of sorts. I requested the anchor to pause the conversation because I wanted to take an audience poll. I first asked, how many in the audience wanted the RBI to keep prices steady even if that meant higher interest rates and possibly lower growth. I knew I was oversimplifying a complex question; nevertheless, I wanted to check the public pulse. About half the hands went up in response. I then asked, how many of them wanted the RBI to support growth by keeping interest rates low even if that meant prices going up. Again, about half the hands went up. In a randomly selected group of people, the division was roughly 50:50. There was nothing surprising there.

But what was surprising, and what struck me visually, was that the hands that went up for inflation control were of the middle-aged, middle-class people who had family budgets to manage. On the other hand, the hands that went up for growth were of the younger lot—the twenty-five to thirty-five-year age group—whose priority was jobs and careers.

What this showed was that in a random sampling of people, there were two constituencies—one for growth and the other for inflation control. How to satisfy both constituencies by judicious policy management is the classic challenge of monetary policy—one that I struggled with as indeed does every governor.

Listening to the voices of silence

An important offshoot of this growth-inflation debate is the extent to which central banks should be concerned with the distributional consequences of their policies. In other words, should they worry that their actions are increasing inequality—hurting poor people while enhancing the incomes and wealth of the already rich?

There is an extreme view, no doubt of some intellectual pedigree, that any such distributional consequences should be of no concern to central banks. Their job—indeed their *dharma*—is to maintain price stability and financial stability, and they should go about that job dispassionately. It's possible that some sections of people hurt more than others as a by-product of central bank policies, but that is par for the course. Taking care of inequality is the task of politics. As an apolitical body, a central bank should stay clear of politics, and by extension, steer clear of any concerns about inequality.

This is best illustrated by a joke I read somewhere. A man is in need of a heart transplant. Says the doctor, 'I can give you the heart of a five-year-old boy.'

'Too young,' replies the man.

'How about that of a forty-year-old investment banker?'

'Nah! They don't have a heart.'

'A seventy-year-old central banker?'

'I'll take it.'

'But why?'

'Because it's never been used.'

I feel distinctly uncomfortable with the view that central banks, especially those of poor countries, should remain indifferent to the impact of their policies on the well-being of the larger public.

It struck me, certainly in real time, and more so after I had moved out of the central bank, that in the RBI, there is a well-honed drill of stakeholder consultations before every policy meeting. The governor and the senior management meet with various interest groups—banks, non-banks, financial markets, economists, corporates and trade bodies—who all, of course, have a legitimate interest in how the economy is managed. All these interest groups are organized, have a platform to voice their views and even get an opportunity to present their view to the RBI. In contrast, the low-income segments of the population, who have an equally legitimate interest in how the economy is managed, in particular those who are hurt disproportionately if inflation is high, are unorganized, have no mechanism to express their view and do not have the privilege of a meeting with the RBI top brass. I always believed that this asymmetry placed an obligation on the RBI to bend over backwards to listen to the voices of silence.

Inequality is not just a poor country issue; it resonates in rich countries as well. A rising tide, as they say, lifts all boats, but many people in rich countries find it unacceptable that it lifts different boats differently. It's not happenstance that Thomas Piketty's *Capital in the Twenty-First Century*, a textbook-like tome on inequality, became a bestseller as if it were a crime thriller. The 'Occupy Wall Street' movement in New York and 'The Occupy St Paul's' movement in London in the aftermath of the global financial crisis were not chance occurrences. They were triggered by a deep-seated resentment that even in mature democracies, the poor don't get to be heard.

Even as inequality is a hot-button issue, the reality is that central banks, especially in rich countries, get criticized whichever way they lean. Ben Bernanke, the US Federal Reserve chair who unleashed quantitative easing (QE) to stabilize the markets during the global financial crisis, was taken to task by the US Senate for 'throwing seniors under the bus'. The charge against him was that his flagship QE policy failed in its main objective of stimulating the economy. Instead, all it did was raise asset prices and depress interest rates. Since assets are typically owned by the rich, they felt wealthier while poor people, including senior citizens who typically put their meagre savings in a bank deposit, were condemned to low returns. In effect, Bernanke had thrown them under the bus.

That was an evocative and metaphorical way of alleging that Bernanke was blind to the equity implications of his policies. Interestingly, his successor, Janet Yellen, was criticized for 'not being blind enough' to the equity implications of her policies. When she said in a speech that her policies were aimed at Main Street, not Wall Street, critics rapped her on the knuckles for stepping into the arena of politics.[*]

Given the vagaries of democratic politics, this debate is unlikely to be settled. But I believe that in a poor country like ours, the RBI can't be insensitive to the distributional implications of its policies. The RBI needs to be hard-headed but that doesn't mean it needs to be hard-hearted.

Rupee tantrums

Dr Rangarajan, my former boss in the prime minister's Economic Advisory Council, often says that no governor's term is 'complete' unless they have had an exchange rate crisis. I was not short-changed on that account; I had a ferocious exchange rate crisis in the last year of my tenure (2012–13) when the rupee crashed 20 per cent peak to trough in just four months, between May and August 2013. India had the dubious distinction of being one of the 'fragile five' along with Brazil, Indonesia, South Africa and Türkiye. Just when we thought inflation had begun to trend down, I was thrown into managing another crisis.

---

[*] Speech on 'Perspectives on Inequality and Opportunity' by Janet Yellen, Chair of the US Federal Reserve, Federal Reserve Bank of Boston, October 2014. https://www.federalreserve.gov/newsevents/speech/yellen20141017a.htm.

The proximate cause for the collapse of the rupee was a statement by Ben Bernanke, then chairman of the US Federal Reserve, in May 2013 that they were considering gradually tapering their QE programme. The global market reaction to this 'taper' statement was swift and brutal. Capital fled emerging markets to return to the home shores of the US while all currencies tumbled relative to the dollar.

The way global financial markets panicked at Bernanke's statement was a big surprise on many counts. First, right from the time QE was launched as an extraordinary measure to restore calm to financial markets during the global financial crisis, it was clear that it would eventually be wound down. Second, any news like this implying that the American economy, the epicentre of the crisis, was showing signs of robust recovery should, in fact, have cheered the financial markets, not frightened them as it did. Third, Bernanke was not saying that they were withdrawing the QE, or even that they were stopping it; all he said was that they were considering 'tapering' it—that is that they would continue QE but at a slower pace. But of course, markets decided to panic, reinforcing the truth that no central banker can 'tell' the markets how to behave.

Bernanke's 'taper' statement was just the proximate cause for our exchange rate crisis. In some sense, we were hardwired for one. We were running a huge current account deficit (CAD) year on year. CAD, by itself, is not bad. After all, CAD represents an inflow of foreign savings, which would augment domestic savings in financing domestic investment and hence help growth. In fact, emerging economies like India should run a CAD but within safe limits. Our CAD went beyond safe limits for three years in a row and was threatening to do so for a fourth year.

A toxic cocktail of factors contributed to the rise in CAD—the rising price of oil, increased import of gold as a hedge against inflation and subdued demand for exports as the rich world was yet to recover from the crisis. Underlying all this was our high fiscal deficit, which spilt over into the external sector. Our full-blown balance of payments (BoP) crisis in 1991 was at heart a fiscal crisis, and so was this near-BoP crisis in 2013.

In normal circumstances, the exchange rate should self-correct to bring CAD in line. But these were by no means normal circumstances. The rich countries were in the midst of unprecedented quantitate easing. That 'quantitatively eased money' looking for quick returns flooded emerging markets far beyond their absorptive capacity. As a result, their currencies appreciated beyond fundamentals. And now, with the hint of a taper from Bernanke, this money was fleeing with equal urgency, causing fierce currency depreciation.

To defend the rupee against a free fall, we in the RBI deployed our full ammunition. We instituted capital controls to encourage inflows and restrain outflows. We sold dollars from our reserves in the market. Market intervention by the RBI is always a game of wits. Speculators are forever trying to guess the timing and extent of market intervention, and the RBI's challenge is to wrongfoot those expectations. First thing in the morning every day, we used to discuss the strategy in the situation room meeting and then leave it to our dealers to opportunistically operationalize it through the day. I had always been impressed by the wisdom and skill of the RBI's financial markets professionals; the experience during this period reinforced my appreciation of their skill and intelligence.

Since gold was a big source of import pressure, restraining gold imports had to be part of the rupee defence strategy. From the RBI side, we invoked our regulatory arsenal to impose restrictions on the import of gold as well as on its use as collateral for loans. The government, on its part, raised the customs duty on gold imports from 6 to 10 per cent, clearly wary of crossing the tipping point beyond which smuggling would become an attractive option.

The most critical challenge for a central bank in exchange rate defence is to maintain its credibility simply because a failed defence can be worse than no defence. Fighting against both appreciation and depreciation of currency is a test of credibility for a central bank, but between the two, the former is arguably a better problem to have because of an important asymmetry that is largely unrecognized.

When a central bank is fighting currency appreciation, it is buying foreign currency by paying for it in the domestic currency. In theory, a central bank can print as much of the domestic currency as it wants. Such a strategy certainly has negative side effects as the oversupply of domestic currency can fuel inflation, cause asset bubbles and jeopardize financial stability. But to the limited extent of exchange rate defence, the market can be in no doubt of the virtually unlimited firepower of the central bank.

Fighting depreciation of the currency, on the other hand, requires the central bank to sell forex from its finite reserves. If the central bank is seen to be losing reserves even as capital continues to exit and the domestic currency continues to bleed, the nervousness in the markets can pull the currency down in a vicious spiral. This is a bigger risk.

RBI's exchange rate policy—walk the talk

As I wind up the discussion of the exchange rate crisis in the last year of my tenure, I want to reflect on two strands of criticism of my record, not so much to offer a defence but to communicate the dilemmas I confronted.

The first major criticism was that I did not buy up dollars from the market when there were huge capital inflows during 2010 and 2011, but simply allowed the rupee to appreciate. Had I on the contrary intervened, the formidable war chest of reserves would have helped fight a future depreciation of the currency like the one that hit us because of the taper tantrums.

Juxtapose my alleged inaction against the stated policy of the Reserve Bank, which is to intervene in the market only to prevent volatility in the exchange rate movement. As I saw it, there was no volatility in the exchange rate between 2010 and 2011 to justify intervention; the exchange rate was, in fact, making a smooth adjustment. I felt obliged to walk the talk. Besides, intervention when there was no volatility would have conveyed the impression that we were targeting a specific exchange rate, and that would have set us up for gaming by speculators.

There were other considerations too behind my relative hands-off approach. As we were gradually liberalizing the external sector, my view was that our market participants, in particular the corporates, should learn to manage exchange rate risks. If the Reserve Bank were to step in every time the exchange rate moved, they would happily outsource their exchange rate risk management to the Reserve Bank. That would be a costly moral hazard. Exchange rate panics are never pretty, but their virtue is that they restore fear and humility to the market.

The second criticism against my policy stance was that even as were in the midst of the crisis, I was emphasizing the need to repair the structural imbalances in the economy. I suggested, for example, that finding a scapegoat in Bernanke's statement, as the government was doing, was politically convenient but, from an economic management perspective, clearly misleading.

My view was that pressure had built up in the exchange rate, and we had to provide outlet valves for the necessary adjustment to take place. It would be futile and costly for the government and the Reserve Bank to stand in the way of that adjustment process. On the other hand, the sooner the exchange rate corrected, the sooner we would be able to make a fresh start. The effort of the government and the Reserve Bank, I thought, should be focused on navigating the adjustment and guiding the exchange rate to its market-determined level. I genuinely believed that acknowledging that a massive correction in the rupee was unavoidable would not only manage expectations but also act as a lesson for the future.

In the event, this did not go down well with the government and even the markets, and was interpreted as being defensive and helpless. After stepping down from the Reserve Bank, I reflected on my efforts at communication during this crisis period. Some people have told me that

I was right on the message but wrong on the timing. In other words, I should have deferred the message till after the pressure had subsided, and focused, during the crisis, only on building confidence. I am not persuaded that this would have been the right strategy. My message was clearly situated in the context of the crisis and aimed at managing expectations. If that message had to be effective, it had to be given during the crisis.

The endgame

After bloodletting for four months, the rupee started stabilizing by early September 2013 helped by several factors. By far the most important was that the adjustment had run its course; second, the risk of a flare-up in Syria had abated; third, the Federal Reserve announced that it was postponing the taper indefinitely. Finally, the scheduled leadership change at the Reserve Bank and the formidable reputation of my successor, Raghuram Rajan, helped restore confidence in the Indian markets. In fact, as chief economic adviser to the government, Raghu was on board all through the exchange rate turmoil and was more actively involved in all the decisions after he was named in early August as my successor.

When Raghu came in as an understudy for a month before he was to take charge, he discussed with the staff and determined that the next steps should be to open a special forex window for oil companies and incentivize our commercial banks to raise Tier-2 capital through their branches and subsidiaries abroad and swap the dollars for rupees with the Reserve Bank at a premium. Raghu was kind enough to offer that I announce these measures before signing off. But I thought that the measures would be more effective if he announced them as the incoming governor. At least on this issue, my judgement worked!

The signal and the noise

Since stepping down as governor of the RBI over ten years ago, I've been asked several times about what I would have done differently. In my view, this is a trick question because people ask it with the benefit of hindsight whereas you were acting in real time within the universe of knowledge available at that time. The right question in my view should be: What would you have done differently if you had known then what you know now? But of course, most interlocutors are not interested in this sophistry and press me for a straight answer. When pushed to the wall like that, I answer that I'd have paid greater attention to communication. All through my career, I believed that effective communication gets you a long way. The RBI experience reiterated that belief. I learnt mostly through my mistakes, though.

One of the nice things about being a central bank governor is that the markets hang on every word you say, treating every syllable, nuance and twitch of the face as a market cue. It can be a big ego trip; it's also an enormous burden.

Experience over the last two decades has shown that central bank communication is a powerful policy tool. But deciding what to say, when to say it and how to say it can be a tricky challenge as I found out—the hard way—through my own experience. Here is one illustration of that challenge.

The governor—an alpha male?

In the course of defending the rupee during the taper tantrums that I've already written about, we realized that excess systemic liquidity was fuelling speculation on the rupee and exacerbating the volatility of the exchange rate. As they say, there are occasions when you have to think the unthinkable. This was one such for me. In order to choke speculation on the exchange rate, in mid-July 2013, I raised the interest rate by a full percentage point.

This was by all accounts an unusual measure. Central banks don't normally use the interest rate tool to manage the exchange rate; even if they do, they are quite cagey about it. But in this instance, not only did we do something unusual, but we were also shouting from the rooftops about it. Our motivation was, of course, to demonstrate the RBI's commitment to stabilizing the rupee even if it required resorting to unusual measures.

But this came at a time when there were concerns about growth. Throw your mind back to that period and recall all the talk about whether we were heading into a stagflation. Unsurprisingly, therefore, on TV shows that evening and in the newspapers the following morning, there was a lot of speculation about how the RBI's action might hurt growth recovery.

There was a media conference the following day and quite expectedly, this was the first question put to me— whether this unusual measure by the RBI would hurt growth and when we might withdraw it. My reply was characteristically forthright. I said that the RBI was sensitive to the concerns of growth but that we had to resort to this unusual measure to curb speculation on the rupee. I added that we would withdraw the measure as soon as the rupee stabilized.

I felt like a student who had aced an expected question. My answer echoed to dot what we had said in our written statement.

My smug satisfaction about acing the response in the media interaction didn't last even a few minutes. The market reaction to my response was brutal and unforgiving. The rupee fell by 2 per cent in the next half hour. I was bewildered and anxious about this sharp and unexpected reaction. Whereas I had thought I would calm the markets with my response, I seemed to have set off mayhem.

I huddled with senior management to discuss what had gone wrong. The first surmise was that I had muffled my communication by admitting to the RBI's concern about growth. What the market really wanted to hear was the RBI's total and undivided commitment to stabilizing the rupee to the exclusion of all other concerns. Instead, I diluted that message by hemming and hawing about all the other worries. The *Financial Times* of 1 August 2013 said this about my statement: 'The governor insisted that he was not trying to defend the battered rupee but only stopping a vicious spiral of one-way bets that could lead the currency to overshoot its fair value.'

The second surmise was that I was too apologetic and hesitant when I should have been confident and assertive. What I said was, '*We will withdraw these measures when the exchange rate stabilizes.*' Instead, what I should have said was something assertive like, '*We will not withdraw these measures until the exchange rate stabilizes.*'

One of the newspapers wrote an editorial saying, 'Markets tend to like uber-confident alpha male central bank governors. Dr Subbarao was not one.'

Alpha male? I googled the term to understand what being an alpha male was, and even to this day, ten years down the line, I am not sure whether not being an alpha male is a certificate of weakness or a badge of honour. I will let the matter rest there.

Agonizing over every word

I have written about oral communication so far but even written communication can be quite tricky. Agonizing over the wording and nuancing of policy statements is a standard item on the job chart of a governor. Let me illustrate.

In the mid-quarter review of September 2010, as part of the forward guidance, we said: 'The Reserve Bank believes that the (monetary) tightening that has been carried out over this period has taken the monetary situation *close* [emphasis mine] to normal.'

There were two communication dilemmas here. The first was whether we should say *'close to'* or *'closer to'*. After much deliberation, we determined that saying *'closer to'* had no additional information content; it would be restating the obvious. On the other hand, saying *'close to'* would convey that there was further room for rate action, albeit a small one.

We in the RBI were not unique in agonizing over how our written word might be interpreted. In his memoir, *The Courage to Act*, Bernanke writes: 'We sweated every word. Should I say that additional rate cuts "may be necessary" or "may well be necessary"? Should I say that we stood ready to take "substantive additional action" or "meaningful additional action"? The absurdity of our discussion did not escape us, but we had learnt through bitter experience that a single word often mattered.'

There are many things I miss about being the governor. One of them is that I can no longer move the markets by my spoken word. Equally, there are many things I enjoy about not being governor. One of them is that I can speak freely without any fear of moving the markets.

How independent is the Reserve Bank?

In the midst of the global financial crisis in mid-October 2008, even as the Reserve Bank was dousing the system with rupee and forex liquidity, Finance Minister Chidambaram suo moto constituted a committee on liquidity management, with Arun Ramanathan, the finance secretary, as the chairman. The Reserve Bank was asked to nominate a representative on the committee.

I was annoyed and upset by this decision. Liquidity management is a quintessential central bank function, and Chidambaram had clearly overstepped into RBI turf. Not only did he not consult me on constituting the committee, but he had not even informed me of this before the notification was issued. Coming as it did amidst a lot of suspicion in those early weeks of my tenure that I was a government lackey sent to the Reserve Bank to act at the government's bidding, the constitution of this committee only reinforced the view.

I called up Chidambaram and let him know in unequivocal terms that his action was totally inappropriate and requested firmly that he dissolve the committee. His argument was that when liquidity management was such a central concern, getting advice from external market participants would help us understand and respond to the ground reality in the market faster and better. I granted that, but if he wanted external experience to be tapped, he could have advised me informally to constitute such a committee rather than taking the Reserve Bank for granted. The call ended with my telling him that the Reserve Bank would not participate in the committee.

This skirmish with Chidambaram, who I believed had pushed my candidature for the governor's job, so early in my tenure upset me greatly. Little did I know that this set the tone for what would be an uneasy relationship between us in the last year of my term.

Why indeed should a central bank have autonomy in setting monetary policy? That's an important question. The core mandate of a central bank is to maintain price stability and financial stability. Delivering on this mandate requires ensuring the long-term sustainability of the economy even if it means implementing measures that might cause pain in the short term. Governments, typically driven by electoral pressures and short horizons, have little tolerance for such pain and tend to prioritize short-term compulsions over long-term sustainability. We have had many examples of economies being driven to disaster because governments took control of the printing press. An apolitical central bank that keeps a hawk eye on long-term sustainability is therefore a systemic counterpoise to a democratic government driven by electoral cycles.

Government–central bank differences on monetary policy are therefore hardwired into the system. Problems arise if they are not resolved amicably and professionally. And problems on that account did arise during my term as governor. Both Chidambaram and Pranab Mukherjee who were finance ministers during that period were vexed by the RBI's anti-inflation stance, which they thought was stymieing growth. The issue became particularly sensitive because the government was continuously being grilled for its 'policy paralysis', and they saw a softer interest rate stance by the RBI as a way out of the quagmire.

In a media interview in July 2013, I remember that Chidambaram had generalized this divide by saying something along the lines of how governments were for growth and central banks were for price stability. This stereotyping was misinformed not just with reference to India but even from a broader perspective. When he was asked in the same interview why he was frustrated by the RBI when all it was doing was pursuing its mandate of price stability, Chidambaram said that the RBI's mandate of price stability must be understood as part of a larger mandate of promoting growth. The clear implication was that the Reserve Bank was mistaken in interpreting its mandate.[*]

I begged to differ. Both in private and public, I argued that the RBI was running a tight monetary policy not because it did not care for growth but because it *did* care for growth. But the government remained unpersuaded.

[*] PTI, 'RBI also needs to look at growth, says Chidambaram', Mint, 29 July 2013, https://www.livemint.com/Politics/BqDYfV633wpM1UXJTiJryL/RBI-also-needs-to-look-at-growth-Chidambaram-says-ahead-of.html.

The net result was that I had run-ins with both Chidambaram and Mukherjee on the RBI's policy stance. Both of them invariably pressed for softer rates although their styles were different. Chidambaram typically argued his case like the lawyer that he so eminently is, while Mukherjee was the quintessential politician. He let his view be known and left it to his officers to argue his case. The net result was an uncomfortable relationship.

In October 2012, shortly after Chidambaram returned as finance minister from the Home Ministry, he set about in earnest to reverse the fiscal profligacy of the Mukherjee regime. Possibly to compensate for the fiscal tightening he was embarking on, he very much wanted a softer monetary regime and put enormous pressure on the RBI to lower the interest rate. On objective considerations, I could not oblige him though.

My refusal to fall in line evidently upset Chidambaram enough to do something very unusual and uncharacteristic— to go public with his strong disapproval of the Reserve Bank's stance. In his 'doorstop' media interaction outside the North Block about an hour after the Reserve Bank put out its hawkish policy statement expressing concern on inflation, he said: 'Growth is as much a concern as inflation. If the government has to walk alone to face the challenge of growth, we will walk alone.'[*]

Sure enough, Chidambaram's ire at having been abandoned to 'walk alone' created quite a flutter in the media. I was on notice, therefore, for the first question

---

[*] Ashok Dasgupta, 'We will "walk alone" if need be: Chidambaram', *The Hindu*, 30 October 2012, https://www.thehindu.com/business/Economy/we-will-walk-alone-if-need-be-chidambaram/article4046910.ece.

that would come my way in the scheduled post-policy media conference later that afternoon. Reluctant to fan controversy during a period of economic stress, I papered over the differences, saying: 'The government and the Reserve Bank have shared goals. Both of them want high growth and low inflation. Differing perceptions on how to achieve these goals are common across many countries in the world.'

Reserve Bank as the government's cheerleader?

Pressure by the government was not confined to the Reserve Bank's interest rate stance; on occasion, it extended to pressuring the RBI to present rosier estimates of growth and inflation at variance with our objective assessment. I remember one such occasion when Pranab Mukherjee was the finance minister. Arvind Mayaram, the finance secretary, and Kaushik Basu, the chief economic adviser, contested our estimates with their assumptions and estimates, which I thought was par for the course. What upset me, though, was that almost seamlessly the discussion moved from objective arguments to subjective considerations, with suggestions that the Reserve Bank must project a higher growth rate and a lower inflation rate in order to share responsibility with the government for 'shoring up sentiment'. Mayaram went to the extent of saying in one meeting that 'whereas everywhere else in the world, governments and central banks are cooperating, here in India the Reserve Bank is being very recalcitrant'.

I was invariably discomfited and annoyed by this demand that the RBI should be a cheerleader for the government. It also dismayed me that the Ministry of Finance would seek a higher estimate for growth while simultaneously arguing for a softer stance on the interest rate without seeing the obvious inconsistency between these two demands. I used to take a firm position that the Reserve Bank cannot deviate from its best professional judgement just to doctor public sentiment. Our projections must be consistent with our policy stance, and tinkering with estimates for growth and inflation would erode the credibility of the Reserve Bank.

Having been both in the government and in the RBI, I can say with some authority that there is little understanding and sensitivity within the government on the importance of central bank autonomy.

It's interesting, even somewhat comforting, that these tensions between the government and central bank are not unique to India or emerging economies. They play out in rich countries as well.

Alan Greenspan, the former chair of the US Federal Reserve, said in an interview following the publication of his book, *The Map and the Territory*: 'In the eighteen and a half years I was there, I got a huge number of letters or notes or whatever, urging us to lower interest rates. On the side of getting letters which say you've got to tighten [raise rates], it was a zero. So, it is a huge political, regulatory asymmetry.'[*]

Fast forward several years. Donald Trump, as US President, was vicious in his attacks on the Federal Reserve. In 2018, after the Federal Reserve had raised the interest

---

[*] 'What Alan Greenspan Learned till 2008—Interview with Justin Fox', *Harvard Business Review*, January 2014. https://hbr.org/2014/01/what-alan-greenspan-has-learned-since-2008.

rate for a third time, he said many things: 'I think the Fed has gone crazy.' 'Boneheads.' 'Pathetic.' An 'enemy' of the United States. 'China is not our problem. The Federal Reserve is.'

These were all the ways he vented his ire at the Federal Reserve. Even by the concessions the world had grown to give to Trump's vicious outbursts, this was taking criticism of the central bank to an altogether new level.

We are fortunate that for all the skirmishes between the government and the RBI, our discourse is far more civilized!

Walking alone

All through my occasional skirmishes with the government over the five years I was at the Reserve Bank, I refrained from taking a confrontational position on the autonomy issue in the public domain. It was only in the Palkhivala Memorial Lecture I delivered on 29 August 2013, a week before I was to step down, which I used mainly to render an account of my experience of leading the Reserve Bank for five turbulent years, that I chose to address the issue. This is what I said:

A final thought on the issue of autonomy and accountability. There has been a lot of media coverage on policy differences between the government and the Reserve Bank. Gerhard Schroeder, the former German chancellor, once said, 'I am often frustrated by the Bundesbank. But thank God, it exists.' I do hope Finance Minister Chidambaram will one day say, 'I am often frustrated by the Reserve Bank, so frustrated that I want to go for a walk, even if I have to walk alone. But thank God, the Reserve Bank exists.'

The standing ovation I received remains one of the most treasured and enduring memories of my time as governor.

Dividend payment to government

Another bone of contention between the government and the RBI is the 'dividend' that the RBI pays to the government every year. It's important to understand that the RBI is not a commercial institution nor is profit-making one of its objectives. Nevertheless, the RBI, like any other central bank, makes a profit in the normal course of its business simply because it has an enviable business model.

The main source of income for the RBI is the seigniorage revenue it earns by virtue of its monopoly over the printing of money. Effectively, this means that the RBI takes cheap money from the government, banks and the public (yes, the currency we hold in our wallets is an interest-free loan to the RBI) and invests that in interest-bearing foreign and rupee assets. The interest it earns on these assets is its revenue. Its main expenditure commitments are the cost of printing currency, the agency commission it pays to banks for acting on its behalf for government transactions, employee costs and the interest it pays to banks on their excess reserves.

The Reserve Bank typically makes a significant 'profit' from its operations, and from this profit, it makes allocations to two reserve funds. The first reserve fund is meant to absorb losses from its market operations and to absorb shocks arising out of variations in exchange rates and gold prices. The second reserve fund is maintained for meeting internal capital expenditure and making investments in the bank's subsidiaries and associated institutions. The 'surplus profit' after allocation to the reserves is transferred to the government. For a government bound by fiscal responsibility and budget management (FRBM) targets, the surplus transfer from the Reserve Bank is a significant source of revenue. For example, in 2023–24, the surplus profit transfer from the RBI is estimated at Rs 874 billion, equivalent to 0.3 per cent of GDP.

The standard view of the government has been that the RBI is far too conservative in estimating its contingent liabilities, is holding back far too much in reserves and can, in fact, afford to transfer more to the government as 'surplus profit'. The RBI on its part pushes back saying that any attempt to eat into its balance sheet can impair market confidence in the central bank and indeed in the larger economy.

Uniquely, I was on both sides of this tug of war. As finance secretary, I pushed the RBI to raise the payment to the government, and as governor, I resisted similar pressures.

This tussle is normally settled internally through some give and take. However, it spilt into the open in 2018 during Governor Urjit Patel's tenure, which eventually resulted in his resignation. That was a decidedly unhelpful development. Nobody came out a winner—not the government, not the RBI and certainly not the larger economy.

The closest I will ever get to a Nobel Prize

For all the stress and anxiety, the governor's job comes with some rare privileges. One such that I treasure was the opportunity to attend the Nobel Prize award ceremony in Stockholm in 2012.

As is well known, the Nobel (Memorial) Prize in Economics was not among the five original prizes established through Alfred Nobel's will in 1895. It was instituted through an endowment in perpetuity set up by Sveriges Riksbank—Sweden's central bank—in 1968 to commemorate the bank's 300th anniversary. No matter that it was a later addition outside of Nobel's will, the winner of the Economics Nobel is chosen and the prize is awarded in the same way as the original five.

In return for the endowment, the governor of the Riksbank, which incidentally is the oldest central bank in the world, gets to invite two special guests for the award ceremony. Stefan Ingvis, my counterpart in Sweden, was kind enough to extend that privilege to me in 2012. So it was that Urmila and I found ourselves in Stockholm on a cold, wet, windy and dreary morning on 9 December. The ceremony is held in the Stockholm Concert Hall on 10 December every year, the death anniversary of Alfred Nobel.

Although Urmila could get away with a sari, I was required to dress in a tuxedo. That wasn't a big problem, though, as there are a number of approved tailors and drapers who rent tuxedos and fit them to your size. The support team of the Riksbank managed the logistics with impressive efficiency.

The Nobel Prize in Economics in 2012 was awarded jointly to Alvin E. Roth and Lloyd S. Shapley 'for the theory of stable allocations and the practice of market design'. While Shapley did some very original work in game theory, Roth took it forward in finding practical applications such as matching marriage partners, new doctors to hospitals and students to schools.

The most notable of the prizes in 2012, though, was the literature prize awarded to Mo Yan of China not because the Chinese government protested but for exactly the opposite reason. The award fulfilled one of the Chinese government's most enduring pursuits: a politically tolerable Nobel laureate. The People's Republic had sought a Nobel Prize in literature so avidly and for so long that it became a national psychological fixation—China's 'Nobel complex', as commentators and television shows often put it. Achieving it was always seen as a referendum on China's cultural development and a measure of its authority around the world. For that reason, the Chinese media had exulted in Mo Yan's win, hailing him as a 'history-making' first Chinese national to win the literature prize.

For exactly the same reason, the Nobel award to Mo Yan became controversial around the world as libertarians thought it violated the principles of its founder and represented a collusion with authoritarian power. The result was that we were witness to demonstrations by conscientious protestors en route to and at the award venue.

The ceremony was a grand ceremonial affair with the King of Sweden presenting the awards as several live orchestras played in turn. The award citation for each prize is read by a member of the Royal Swedish Academy whereafter the prize is given away by the king. The speeches by the laureates, which are widely reported in the media, are separate events outside the main ceremony.

The ceremony was followed by a ceremonial dinner for about 1500 guests in the Stockholm City Hall. While the prize winners and their spouses were seated at the head table with the king, we were all seated around about fifty tables in the large hall. The waiters were youngsters from across Sweden who, we were told, were specially trained and certified for the purpose. That training showed as they tagged me in that large gathering and served my vegetarian meal without a glitch—at the same time as they served all the other guests. This impressive efficiency was quite a change from what I typically encountered: 'Oh! You're a vegetarian. Did you order a vegetarian meal beforehand? Let me go and check in the kitchen.'

The following evening there was another dinner hosted by the king, a smaller and less ceremonial affair for about a hundred guests. As we adjourned to the 'cigar room' after the dinner, we were told not to leave because the king, who was holding forth in one corner, might pick some of the invitees at random for a brief conversation over the next hour. Both Urmila and I got slightly nervous about whether we were required to curtsy to the king and how we should address him. When our turn did come, it was a pleasant surprise to find the avuncular king standing there with a glass of liqueur in his hand instantly making us feel perfectly at ease. He told us that he had travelled to Mumbai as a backpacker in his youth and was surprisingly well-informed on Indian agriculture.

This trip to Stockholm would, of course, be the closest I would ever get to a Nobel Prize.

The magic of central banking

'There have been three great inventions since the beginning of time: fire, the wheel and central banking,' quipped Will Rogers, the American humorist.

Notwithstanding all the challenges and dilemmas through five years at the helm of the RBI, it's been my privilege to witness the magic of this invention from within. It's also been my privilege to be associated with the Reserve Bank of India, an institution with a formidable reputation for integrity and professionalism.

You can't tell markets how to behave

I have written earlier that I was perplexed by the savage market reaction to my statement on the exchange rate. As I reflected on that episode several times over the years since then, it struck me that it's presumptuous on the part of central banks to believe that they can predict market reaction.

An analogy from physics comes to mind.

We all know that the two great theories of twentieth-century physics—relativity and quantum mechanics—are inconsistent with each other. All through his life, Albert Einstein could not reconcile to the probabilistic nature of the universe implied by the quantum theory, and famously quipped, 'God does not play dice.' His friend and pioneering quantum physicist Niels Bohr retorted, 'Albert, stop telling God what he can or cannot do.'

Similarly, central bankers can hardly presume to tell markets how to behave no matter the intentions behind their policy moves. If repeated financial crises have taught us anything, it is that central banks have to be humbler about their ability to predict market behaviour.

16

It's Expensive to Be Poor

Poverty and Financial Inclusion

Fifty years ago, when I was a young sub-collector working on the frontlines, parents in villages across India looking for a groom for their girl would make sure that the boy's village had drinking water so they wouldn't be condemning their girl to the lifelong drudgery of fetching water from miles away. Twenty-five years ago, when parents were similarly groom-hunting, they used to check if the boy's house had a toilet. Today, in villages across India, when parents are looking for a boy for their daughter, they ask if the boy has a bank account and a UPI app on his phone. That has been the amazing story of India's financial inclusion.

Deepening financial inclusion has been an institutional commitment of the RBI for several years. When I became governor, I picked up the baton and carried it as far as I could during my tenure. Over the last ten years since I left the RBI, the baton has, of course, moved further on.

The JAM trinity

How the JAM trinity—Jan Dhan Yojana—a bank account for every household in the country, Aadhaar—a twelve-digit biometric identity number for every person in the country, and the Mobile phone together with user-friendly apps—has been a game changer for financial inclusion has been much written about. It's doubtful if any one of these—J or A or M—by itself would have created the magic; it was their coming together that did. For many years, we were saying that we needed a revolution in banking to achieve financial inclusion. With the JAM trinity, the revolution was upon us.

The direct benefit transfer (DBT) that happens every month across states of the country must be the largest one-to-many transfers anywhere in the world. Just imagine this. During Covid, under the Trump and then Biden stimulus packages, American households received money from their government. Much of this was sent through bank transfers, but a significant amount also by mailing debit cards and paper cheques. In India, those transfers happened entirely through DBT. No leakage, no delay, no omissions and no complaints. Also, DBT has furthered women's empowerment. Wages under MNREGA (Mahatma Gandhi National Rural Employment Guarantee Act) are transferred directly to women's accounts as are subsidies.

Stereotypical views about poverty

Out there on the frontlines today there are a plethora of institutions—banks, non-banks, microfinance institutions, fintechs, bigtechs, e-commerce firms—all engaged in financial inclusion through the innovative use of digital technologies. Digital technologies have brought us far along the road to financial inclusion, and for sure will take us farther on. What I want to emphasize though is that as much as digital technologies are a great help, they are not by themselves sufficient. If financial inclusion is to be an effective anti-poverty measure, those engaged in the mission have to understand the sociology of poverty. In particular, they have to disabuse themselves of certain stereotypical views about poverty. It is those stereotypes that I want to focus on here.

'What the poor want is much more than just a safe place for their money'

The first stereotypical view is the belief that what poor people want most of all is an avenue for the safekeeping of their money. In fact, in the past, when we mandated banks to open accounts for low-income households, banks went about the job quite enthusiastically to start with, enticed no doubt by the potential access it would give them to a large pool of low-cost savings, which would improve their business margins.

As the late K.C. Chakrabarty, my colleague in the RBI, known for never mincing his words, would say, banks were on a fool's errand. What the poor want most of all is not an avenue for saving their money; what they want are microfinance and microinsurance. These they didn't get because banks didn't consider them creditworthy. A result of this mismatch of incentives was that bank accounts were opened but remained 'dormant'. Both the banks and the poor were disillusioned.

Back in 2011, I was once in Ernakulam for a meeting with Kerala-based banks. During the conversation, I threw a challenge to Union Bank of India (UBI), the lead bank of Ernakulam district, that they should make it the first district in the country to achieve 100 per cent 'meaningful' financial inclusion—i.e., not only should every household have a bank account, but it should also be using the account actively and regularly.

The choice of Ernakulam was not a happenstance. Ernakulam was the first district in the country to achieve 100 per cent family planning in the 1970s; it was the first district in the country to achieve 100 per cent literacy in the 1980s; achieving 100 per cent financial inclusion in the 2000s would therefore be a logical sequel.

UBI set about the task with impressive diligence, and working along with the state government and the Unique Identification Authority of India (UIDAI), reported by mid-2012 that they had achieved the target of 100 per cent 'meaningful financial inclusion'. We had a big celebration in Ernakulam in November 2012, with chief minister the late Oommen Chandy and Nandan Nilekani of the UIDAI present, to mark the achievement and to also showcase Ernakulam as an example for districts across the country.

A couple of weeks after the event, I asked our staff to conduct a sample survey on how meaningful this concerted effort at financial inclusion had been. The findings were sobering. For sure, Ernakulam was way ahead of the rest of the country but even there a sizeable number of households reported that they were still saving money in chit funds and borrowing from moneylenders because banks didn't consider them creditworthy.

The lesson is that financial inclusion cannot be meaningful if low-income households are forever condemned as non-creditworthy. I gather it's now possible with digital technologies to assess the creditworthiness of an individual even if she doesn't have a footprint in the formal financial sector. For example, if positional data indicate that a woman is in her house at seven in the morning and at another fixed location thereafter for five to six hours, the inference can be that she has a steady job and a permanent address. Similarly, social media activity can give clues to aspiration levels while shopping patterns can give an indication of an individual's attitude to thrift.

In short, turning a person from non-creditworthy to creditworthy must be as much the responsibility of the bank as of the individual.

'Cost of credit matters, but access to credit matters even more'

That allows me to segue into the second stereotype about poverty, which is that the cost of credit matters to the poor more than anything else. The cost of credit matters of course, but what matters even more to the poor is access to credit.

If there is one real-life story that illustrates the management phrase, 'fortune at the bottom of the pyramid', it is the amazing story of microfinance. The remarkable growth of microfinance across the country over the last quarter century, particularly in the southern states, turned out to be a win-win option. It lifted millions of households out of poverty even as microfinance institutions (MFIs) presumably made millions. In the Reserve Bank, we believed that we had discovered the holy grail of last-mile connectivity—the elusive silver bullet that we were looking for.

Until it blew up in our face.

In 2010, there was a deep and widespread agitation in Andhra Pradesh against exploitation by MFIs, ignited in part by the huge premium at which shares were sold in the initial public offering (IPO) of a large MFI. The main grievance against MFIs was that they were exploiting the poor through extortionary rates of interest, resorting to coercive recovery practices and loading poor households with one loan after another, pushing them into the deep end of a debt trap.

The RBI, as the regulator of large MFIs, was in the dock for sleeping at the wheel, for letting this 'exploitation of the poor' flourish under its nose. How we handled the agitation is a separate story, but here I want to focus on the big challenge that I faced—whether the RBI should impose a ceiling on the interest rate that MFIs can charge. Given the root cause of the problem, it looked like the obvious solution; it was anything but.

MFIs were able to penetrate in part because we allowed a laissez-faire regime on the interest rate in the hope and belief that competition among MFIs would keep the interest rates in check. Given this agitation, it was clear that we should come down heavily on malpractices, but was capping the interest rate a part of the remedy? My apprehension was that if we overreacted, we would kill a burgeoning multi-billion-rupee industry that provided livelihood support to millions of poor households across the country and throw them back on the mercy of the even more usurious moneylenders. A classic case of throwing the baby out with the bathwater!

For sure, the rate charged by MFIs—typically around 35 to 40 per cent—looks usurious when compared with the rate commercial banks charge their prime borrowers, which is in the range of 10 to 12 per cent. But no bank would be willing to lend to a typical microfinance borrower—at any rate of interest. In the absence of an MFI, the alternative is not a bank but the moneylender, who would charge in excess of 100 per cent.

Imagine a pushcart fruit vendor who borrows Rs 5000 in the morning and has to repay Rs 5050 in the evening. That's 1 per cent interest per day, and when compounded, would tally to about 500 per cent per year. That is most certainly usurious, but the pushcart vendor will happily take that loan because it's a matter of livelihood for her. Access to credit matters more to her than the interest rate. She has internalized the fact that it's expensive to be poor.

I agonized over whether capping the interest rate on MFI loans would, in fact, be an effective solution to this malady. I appointed a committee under the chairmanship of Y.H. Malegam, a noted chartered accountant and a widely respected member of the RBI board. The committee recommended a formula-based interest rate ceiling to which I yielded, albeit reluctantly.

I am happy to note that the MFI industry has since stabilized, and the RBI has wound down the interest rate ceiling.

'The poor are not like us'

The third stereotype about poverty is that the poor earn regular incomes like us. They don't. The World Bank line for extreme poverty is $2.15 per day per person. But that does not mean the poor earn $2.15 every day; that's the average over time. Not only are the incomes of the poor low, but they are also irregular, uncertain and unpredictable. They have to contend with losing a job, being sick and being unemployed for a long time. They have to contend with illness and death in the family. They have to spend on their children's education and on celebrating weddings and festivals.

Getting a job, getting married, setting up a household, having children and having aspirations for their children are universal human goals. Like the rest of us, the poor too have a today and a tomorrow.

A big challenge for them, though, is to smooth their incomes to meet lumpy expenditures. In designing financial inclusion products, it's important to keep in view that the poor are like us in many ways, but also not like us in many ways.

'What seems irrational to us is actually quite rational from the perspective of the poor'

The last stereotype I want to talk about is the view that the poor don't need to do any financial planning because they don't have much savings. That is wrong. It is precisely because they don't have much savings that they need to do a lot of planning. Studies have shown that poor households, in fact, do sophisticated financial planning.*

---

* Jonathan Morduch, Stuart Robinson and Orlanda Ruthven, *Portfolios of the Poor: How the World's Poor Live on $2 a Day* (Permanent Black, 2010).

A poor woman hiding Rs 5000 in the rice box in the kitchen while at the same time borrowing Rs 5000 at a hefty rate of interest may seem irrational to us. But when your income is low and your ability to borrow on the go is limited, this is very rational behaviour. If her child gets ill and has to be taken to a hospital at two in the morning, it is these savings that are the lifeline.

We will go astray if we choose to judge the behaviour of the poor only through our lens of rationality. Their behaviour is rational too, given their lived experiences.

Financial literacy

It's axiomatic that there can't be financial inclusion without financial literacy. And financial literacy is more than educating the public about thrift, saving and borrowing, financial products and financial institutions and risk management. It's also about lenders, particularly bankers and MFIs, understanding the sociology of poverty and emotionally empathizing with the poor.

The late Ela Bhatt, who became a global icon for women's empowerment through a lifetime of devoted work to improve the lives of women textile workers of Ahmedabad, was on the board of the Reserve Bank during my term. She presented me with a copy of her book, *We Are Poor, But So Many: The Story of Self-Employed Women in India,* which I read avidly. One incident that Elaben related in the book has stuck in my mind.

She took a vegetable vendor to a bank for a loan. The bank manager quizzed the vendor and Elaben, and told them to come back the following week with some documents. When they returned, he quizzed them further and asked for some more documents. This vexatious interrogation repeated over several rounds over several weeks, and the capacity of the banker to invent fresh questions and fresh documents seemed limitless. Elaben says that she then realized that 'financial illiteracy is on the other side of the table!'

17

Pursuing My Bucket List

Post RBI pursuits

As we approached September 2013 when my term as RBI governor would end, what I would do next did cross my mind. But I didn't have the mind space to think too hard about it as I was completely preoccupied with managing the exchange rate crisis. I was clear, though, on one thing: that I needed to move on from public service into private life. I had joined the IAS barely two months after finishing college, and it had been government all the way after that. The government had given me a livelihood, security in my life and career, an opportunity to serve the larger public, and of course, a mix of fulfilment and frustration. I now wanted to live without the crutches of the government.

The prime minister's offer

Prime Minister Manmohan Singh was scheduled to release the fourth volume of the RBI's institutional history on

17 August 2013, about two weeks before I was to step down as governor. In some sense, this event was unique. This volume covered the period when Dr Manmohan Singh was the governor of the Reserve Bank and subsequently the finance minister, and was going to be released by him as prime minister. In the Reserve Bank, we wanted to organize the event on a big scale, but the prime minister asked that it be low-key. So it was that the function was held early in the morning at 7 Race Course Road, the prime minister's official residence in Delhi, with just about fifty guests.

As I was getting ready for the event, I got a call from the prime minister's office to ask me to see the prime minister fifteen minutes before the function. I wondered why and got a bit anxious. We had already sent the briefing material to his office. Did he just want a personal briefing? Was he upset that the event was not as low-key as he had asked for? Was he annoyed about some misrepresentation of his period of history? I went to see him with some trepidation because I had not read the full volume myself given my preoccupation with managing the rupee crisis.

It turned out that he asked to see me for a completely different reason. He told me that he just wanted to compliment me for the way I had led the Reserve Bank through a period of enormous economic and political challenges. I was touched by his graciousness. He inquired about my future plans. I told him that I would be relocating to Hyderabad and that I wanted to take about six months off to decide what I would do next. 'Do let me know if you want anything in the government. I will be happy to consider that,' he added kindly. Thinking that it would be discourteous to tell him that I had decided to keep away from the government and live as a private citizen, I thanked him and took my leave.

'Desanitizing' myself

A week after I stepped down from the Reserve Bank, I returned to Hyderabad. The overwhelming feeling was of relief and liberation. I no longer had to worry about inflation, the interest rate and the exchange rate. Someone else, arguably more capable than me, was doing that worrying. I was the master of my time. I could go where I wanted, when I wanted, without seeking anyone's permission and with no frills. I had no conduct rules to obey, only my own sense of values and propriety.

One of the first things I did to actually experience and enjoy this 'liberation' was to go on a long train journey across India. I have always been fond of train travel and, in my younger days, was, in fact, quite familiar with the platforms of all major railway stations in India. In later years, my train journeys became less frequent in part because of the pressure of time and in part also because I was spoilt by the convenience and comfort of air travel. The five years in the RBI were quite travel-intensive, and almost all of it was by air. The only train journeys I recall during this period were a couple of trips from Mumbai to Pune and on one occasion from Bhubaneswar to Sambalpur and back.

The RBI protocol never allowed me to travel freely. Whereas all my life I got in and out of planes by myself, and did so quite competently I believe, while in the RBI, there were protocol officers who helped me navigate the airports. I was deeply conscious that they were all very well-meaning people who were doing this for my comfort and convenience; nevertheless, I found this protocol quite cumbersome and often felt very self-conscious moving around in an airport with a horde of people in tow.

In fact, even before I joined the RBI, as I moved up in my career, my lifestyle got increasingly sanitized. Not having to take public transport, shopping in high-end grocery and department stores, not buying stuff from street vendors often enough; in short, not exposing myself to the rough and tumble of Indian life.

So, by the time I left the RBI, I had a strong urge to 'desanitize' myself. I read in a Sunday paper a few weeks earlier about the Vivek Express, which takes you on the longest train journey in India, from Dibrugarh in the north-east to Kanyakumari in the deep south. Urmila, of course, was never one to miss an opportunity like this.

So we flew to Dibrugarh via Kolkata and boarded the Vivek Express on a cold and rainy night in February 2014. The three days and four nights we spent on the train were a fascinating experience. Among the passengers were a newlywed couple going to Kerala for their honeymoon who quite willingly exchanged their lower berths for our upper ones, a couple of junior army officers going home on vacation, a businessman from Nagaland going to Coimbatore to explore a business opportunity, a group of college graduates going to Bangalore because their friends who were already there had told them of jobs in the restaurants there, a middle-aged Assamese couple who had never until then travelled outside their state going on a pilgrimage to Tirupati and a mother taking her teenage daughter to Chennai for treating a rare heart disease. Interacting with our co-passengers helped us reconnect with life in more ways than I can really express.

The most fascinating part of that journey though, was seeing the ebb and flow of Indian life through the train windows.

The bucket list

In my farewell speech at the RBI, I drew up a bucket list as it were. I let my imagination fly. I said I wanted to learn salsa dancing, travel in the interior of the country and study mathematics and linguistics. About six months after I left the Reserve Bank, I ran into Y.H. Malegam, who was a director on the RBI board during my tenure, at Bengaluru airport one morning. With a mischievous glint in his eye, he asked me if I had got started on the bucket list. I drew a blank. He said to me: 'Like you, I too had a wish list when I retired from active practice more than ten years ago. I haven't been able to tick even one box so far.'

Malegam's experience turned out to be true in my case as well. Now, ten years after leaving the RBI, I should say my post-career life went in a different direction. In the couple of months after I left the RBI, I had a few offers from reputed universities in the US to come as a visiting fellow, almost all of them prompted by some academic I had gotten to know during my Reserve Bank tenure. To foray into academia at this stage of my life looked quite attractive. My value proposition was my long practical experience in an emerging economy, and frontier universities across the world were increasingly looking for 'professors of practice'.

Rewarding sojourn in Singapore

Even as I was weighing my options, Sanjaya Baru called to ask if I would be interested in going to the Lee Kuan Yew (LKY) School of Public Policy in Singapore. Sanjaya himself had spent a couple of years at the LKY School after leaving his job as media adviser to Prime Minister Manmohan Singh and highly recommended it. Things moved quickly thereafter. Kishore Mahbubani, the dean of the LKY School, called and arranged for me to visit the school, give a couple of talks and meet the students and the faculty. At the end of the week-long visit, they were quite keen that I should join them as a visiting fellow.

I too was enticed by the proposition. Singapore is just four hours away from India in contrast to the US, which was a day-long journey. In a pinch, I could travel to India over the weekends if need be. Importantly, the logistics of living in Singapore were much simpler. The university was providing me with on-campus housing, Singapore's public transport is excellent, and importantly, there was so much of India in Singapore. 'Singapore is the best city in India,' as someone said to me.

But the LKY option unravelled as quickly as it materialized. They wanted me to teach a regular course from the word go. I was not prepared for that. I said I was open to giving guest lectures in other faculty's courses and giving a one-off seminar but didn't want to be tied down to a course schedule over an entire semester, which would cut my flexibility in many ways. Even as that impasse persisted, Bernard Yeung, the dean of the National University of Singapore (NUS) Business School, whom I had met at one of my talks, offered me a visiting fellowship in the Business School meeting all my requirements.

So it was that I became a part-time 'Distinguished Visiting Fellow' at the NUS in 2014 with a concurrent appointment in the NUS Business School and the Institute of South Asian Studies (ISAS). The contract required me to spend six months in a year on the campus with complete flexibility on when I would come and go. They were also very generous on the deliverables. I gave guest lectures in some of the courses where the faculty so requested, gave seminars and participated in panel discussions. The work pressure was high enough to keep me stimulated but not so high as to make me feel overwhelmed. I spoke on issues in public finance, central banking, the global economy, the Indian economy and dabbled in leadership in the public sector.

Asia's great convergence—myth or reality?

NUS aspires to position itself as the academic hub of Asia and therefore lays great emphasis on looking at issues from an Asian perspective. I was familiar with the Indian economy and had some understanding of issues in the global economy. I had worked on East Asia while in the World Bank, but my knowledge was scanty. This fellowship at the NUS gave me an opportunity to weave together an Asian perspective on global issues from the vantage point of the academia. It turned out to be a rewarding learning experience.

As I studied, thought, wrote and spoke about Asian economic prospects, I was able to focus on one overarching issue. Since the days of Marco Polo, the world has waited for the 'Asian Century'. Has it finally arrived?

For sure, Asia's emergence from subsistence levels of poverty to middle-income status and widely shared prosperity is one of the most remarkable success stories of the last half-century. The Asian growth story has inspired many analysts and commentators to predict that the twenty-first century will be an Asian Century, characterized by Asia's convergence with Western standards of living and the shift of the global economic centre of gravity to Asia.

Over the last fifty years, Asia has produced several growth miracles—the mesmerizing Japanese miracle (1970s), the dazzling East Asian miracle powered first by 'the tigers' (Hong Kong, Singapore, Taiwan and Korea in the 1980s) and then 'the cubs' (Indonesia, Malaysia, Philippines and Thailand in the 1990s), then over the last two decades (1991–2015), the astonishing Chinese miracle, with the country clocking double-digit growth on the trot for over two decades, and over the last decade, the tantalizing prospect of an Indian miracle.

In Western minds, Asia, once strongly associated with poverty, backwardness and lethargy, is today associated with prosperity, success and dynamism.

If Britain, with its industrial revolution and colonial power, defined the nineteenth century, and America, with its free-market ideology and innovation culture, defined the twentieth century, will Asia, with its own version of state-led capitalism and unique Asian values, define the twenty-first?

That is an exciting prospect, but it is also a contentious view with opinion sharply divided. The Asian optimists argue their point from a variety of strands. For some, Asia's inexorable rise is only morally right since it will just be Asia regaining the dominance in the global economy that it had enjoyed until the mid-nineteenth century. Others draw their inference by extrapolating recent trends while for many it's plain wishful thinking. On the other side of the argument are the sceptics who contend that Asia simply will not be able to live up to its promise because of the geopolitical and economic headwinds.

I was motivated enough to start writing a book on 'Asia's Great Convergence—Myth or Reality'. It's still a work in progress, but hopefully, I will complete it soon enough.

Who moved my interest rate?

I did write a book though—on my experiences as the governor of the RBI. The motivation for this was the urging by the faculty and students at NUS who heard my talks and lectures to put my ideas, thoughts and experiences into a book. Dean Bernard Yeung attached so much weight to the scholarly pursuit of a book that he readily agreed to free me of other obligations to allow me to focus on writing. I began writing in mid-2015 and the book was released in August 2016—just over a year from start to finish. Earlier governors had written books about their RBI experiences but *Who Moved My Interest Rate?* was the first memoir of a former RBI governor covering his entire tenure.

Antifragile Singapore

Living in Singapore was comfortable, relaxing and hassle-free. Everything works. The public transport is efficient, the city is squeaky-clean, information is easily available, people are by and large honest, services are reliable, there are huge parks for walking and recreation, and you are spoilt for choice on eating out options from iconic hawkers' markets to high-end restaurants. What I found comforting and interesting was that in Singapore, contractual obligations are honoured. For example, if I order an Uber or Ola taxi in India, I am uncertain until the cab actually arrives because there is always the likelihood that the driver will cancel the trip; in Singapore, you can be absolutely certain that the cab will arrive, and on time.

If you are going to the airport, taxi drivers typically ask you if you have remembered to carry your passport, phone and wallet. I was once in a taxi and the driver took a wrong turn. It meant our doubling back for about a kilometre because of all the one-way traffic regulations. The driver told me he was switching off the meter so that I wouldn't have to pay for his mistake!

At a dinner once, I ran into a consular officer from the Japanese embassy in Singapore. He told me that over his career, he had worked in several Japanese consulates around the world. The Japanese, as is well known, are avid travellers. Some of them lose their passports and come to the consulate with an SOS plea. Finding lost passports, he told me, was one of his important tasks everywhere. He added, 'In Singapore though, I don't worry about it so much. I sit on the complaint for a day, fairly certain that the passport will be returned to the consulate.' An illustration of the trust and order in Singaporean society.

Is there a downside to such a patronizing state and orderly society? That's an interesting question. On the week-long exploratory trip to the LKY School that I wrote about earlier, they had arranged for a liaison officer to chaperone me from one place to another and one meeting to another. She was a Singaporean, about forty years old, smart and well-groomed. We became quite friendly. She had lived in the US and Europe for fifteen years and had just returned home for good the previous year. I asked her how it felt to be back in Singapore after a long gap. She gave the familiar answer: 'It feels wonderful to be home. Home, after all, is home.' Then, she thought for a moment and added, 'Living in Singapore though, you lose the edge. You are not prepared to meet an unforeseen contingency or a non-standard situation.'

That afterthought resonated with me. If you have to go to the airport and the taxi always comes on time, you are never prepared to handle a situation when the taxi doesn't show up. I told her jokingly that the solution to that problem is to have Singaporeans, in lots of ten thousand maybe, spend a couple of weeks on their own in India. That India exposure would prepare them for every possible contingency in life!

That conversation brought to mind Nassim Nicholas Taleb's concept of antifragility where he argues that 'antifragility' is quintessential for dealing with those rare, unpredictable events for which we can never be fully prepared. At best we can locate the fragility in the system and abridge it. Taleb points out that many things demand some kind of stress or irregularity to function well, such as our bodies. If the environment is too disinfected, we lose the ability to resist infection. Vaccines introduce a little of what is harmful to build resistance to disease.

Perhaps Singapore would be more antifragile if there were a bit more of India in it, and India would be less fragile if there were a lot more of Singapore in it.

My Singapore appointment lasted for five years from 2014 to 2019. The contract was not extended as the university had a five-year rule for visiting fellows. It was just as well because I was getting too much into my comfort zone.

The challenge of staying relevant

I then began looking around for other opportunities in academia. I explored the option of the Indian School of Business in Hyderabad, but we could not reach a mutually agreeable arrangement. It was now six years after I had left the RBI, and I was no longer as hot a commodity as I was earlier. Whereas when I had just left the RBI in 2013, several universities had enthusiastically invited me, now they were lukewarm. Groucho Marx, the famous American comedian said, 'I wouldn't want to belong to any club that would have me as a member.' I could relate to that. I didn't want to go to places that would have me, and places that I wanted to go to wouldn't have me.

I had a long-pending invitation to spend a few months at the Centre for the Advanced Study of India (CASI) at the University of Pennsylvania. I went there in October 2019 even as I was exploring longer-term opportunities. I am happy I did because it gave me exposure to a broader range of academia than did the NUS. I gave lectures and talks, participated in seminars and panel discussions and interacted with faculty and students from across the university. Just as the university and I were in negotiation for a longer-term arrangement, Covid hit, and I returned home to an uncertain future like almost everyone else on the planet.

Surprisingly, the Covid lockdown period turned out to be busier and more productive than I would have imagined. As Zoom events proliferated, I had my share of talks, webinars, panel discussions and teaching sessions. The *Times of India* asked me to write a monthly column; I've been doing that although I've found it difficult to maintain the monthly periodicity. I struggle to find topics to write on, am apprehensive about whether I am saying anything new or different or just rehashing what's already been said, agonize over the writing and obsessively edit my drafts.

As Covid ebbed, Syed Akbaruddin, a retired foreign service officer, who had taken over as the dean of the Kautilya School of Public Policy in Hyderabad, invited me to talk to his students. That introductory talk in February 2022 led to a longer-term arrangement. I now go about once a month to Kautilya to lecture and interact with students in closed sessions. I like going there for many reasons, including the fact that Akbar works very hard to position Kautilya as a leading school of public policy in India. In between I also taught at the Asia School of Business in Kuala Lumpur, and I go occasionally to the S. Rajaratnam School of International Studies in Singapore.

The Yale sojourn

Sometime in late 2022, I was exchanging e-mails with Stephen Roach on an op-ed he published in the *Financial*

Times. Steve had previously served as the chief Asia economist at Morgan Stanley and is considered a leading expert on China. I first met him at a panel discussion at the IMF, and he also visited the RBI for a seminar when I was governor. Steve is now a senior fellow at the Yale Jackson School of Global Affairs at Yale University. During that e-mail exchange, he asked me if I'd be interested in spending a few months at the Jackson School, and when I said I was open to the idea, he connected me to Jim Levinsohn, the dean of the Jackson School. Jim invited me to visit them when I was next in the US.

So, when I was in the US visiting my elder son, Mallik, in Washington DC during Thanksgiving of 2022, I went to New Haven and gave a talk at the Jackson School, which I believe was well received. They asked if I could spend a full year at the school but we settled for a semester as I wasn't inclined to be away from India over an extended period.

Getting all the paperwork done and getting a J-1 visa took a few months, and that long-planned assignment in the Jackson School finally materialized in the fall of 2023. On a Sunday morning in mid-September, Mallik drove me from Washington DC to New Haven, settled me in my apartment, bought me groceries, and as he was leaving to drive back, he said, 'OK, Baba, I will go now. Take care of yourself. Try and avoid walking around after dark.' That was an echo of what I said to him when Urmila and I left him at his IIT hostel a quarter of a century ago. How life turns!

My apartment on Chapel Street on the edge of the campus is in a Yale-managed building. So, when I went to the school on my first day, I checked with Kelly, the administrative officer, on how to pay the rent. 'Why don't you write a cheque in favour of Yale?' she said. Write a cheque? I don't recall having written a cheque in India for the last ten years, and here in America, I have to write a cheque? A reminder to me how far India has moved into digital finance although I am conscious how much further we have to go to achieve financial inclusion in its entirety.

The Jackson School requires its senior fellows to teach a course in addition to meeting and interacting with students individually and in groups. Over the last ten years since stepping down from the RBI, I've spent extended periods on university campuses where I gave occasional lectures and participated in seminars, panel discussions and other outreach activities. This is the first time I am having to teach a regular course.

We agreed that I would teach a course on central banking in emerging economies. Preparing for the course, including sourcing and compiling the reading material, turned out to be a daunting task, but it was also a huge learning opportunity.

The Jackson School is located on Hillhouse Avenue, and virtually everyone associated with the school has told me proudly that Mark Twain called the oak-tree-lined avenue 'the most beautiful street in America'.

What struck me most of all about Yale students has been how clear and focused they are on what they want to do. My thoughts invariably go back to what President Kennedy said during his commencement address at Yale in June 1962: 'I have the best of both worlds, a Harvard education and a Yale degree.'

Walking around the Yale campus, I see a lot of student activity, including pro-Israel and pro-Palestine protests on either side of the street. In general, I've been struck by how liberal the campus is. For example, in a form I had to fill in connection with something, there were six choices to identify my gender! When I checked with colleagues, I was told that this has, by and large, been the trend across US college campuses. When I was first on a university campus, over forty years ago, I worried about being socially awkward. Now, I worry if I will be politically incorrect!

I find the Yale campus, including its paved walkways and delightfully extravagant architecture, quaint and beautiful. During conversations with colleagues, I learnt that this 'fake' Gothic architecture for buildings constructed in the 1930s came in for some criticism too. In recent decades, Yale has tried to make a new architectural statement by allowing some modernist buildings on the campus. I'd have thought such an architectural mismatch would have riled conservatives. On the contrary, I am told it was a deliberate move to promote the notion that a forward-looking Yale is not locked into backwards-looking architecture.

One other titbit I gathered is Yale's India connection. The university is named after Elihu Yale, a rich Boston merchant, who in the early 1700s donated nine bales of goods to the college, the sale of which yielded £560, a substantial amount of money at that time. Yale himself made his fortune as the first president of Fort St George in Madras, which was a part of the East India Company, largely through secret contracts with Madras merchants that were illegal under the Company policy. In 2020, in the wake of protests around the world focused on racial relations and criminal justice reform, the #CancelYale tag was used on social media to demand that Elihu Yale's name be removed from Yale University because of his association with the slave trade. But the name survives!

More recently, Yale issued a formal apology for its early leaders' involvement with slavery, accompanied by the release of a detailed history of the university's connections to slavery and a list of initial steps to make some amends.

And as I sign off on this book draft, typing away in my apartment on Chapel Street on the edge of the Yale campus, my thoughts are also on the course I am teaching. We are midway through now, and I am eagerly awaiting the student feedback at the end of the course in December.

Being continuously challenged and craving for success in everything I do has become a way of life.

Winning a Lottery in Fiji

In May 2015, some two years after I left the Reserve Bank, I received an invitation from the Fiji Banks Association to give the keynote address at their annual conference later that year.

I am quite fond of travels that take me off the beaten track and was quite excited at the prospect of visiting Fiji on an all-paid trip. While in the World Bank in the early 2000s, I had worked on the Pacific Islands and had gone on mission travel to Papua New Guinea (PNG) and the Solomon Islands several times. Understanding the economy of these far-flung islands against the backdrop of their sociology and anthropology was a rewarding learning opportunity.

While travelling outside the country, I am given to playing a mental game—how long can I be on the streets of a foreign city and not see another Indian? Even in the most unlikely places, deep Latin America, for example, it wouldn't be more than half an hour. On one occasion, I spent six days in the Solomon Islands without running into another compatriot. I thought I was setting a new record only to spot an Indian family in the departure hall of the Honiara International Airport on my return journey.

* * *

I was excited about visiting Fiji because, unlike PNG and the Solomon Islands, which are Melanesian, Fiji is Polynesian with deep historical and cultural links to India. Back in 2007, when I was finance secretary in the Government of India, the finance minister of Fiji along with a few members of their parliament had visited Delhi, and I happened to participate in the bilateral discussion between the two finance ministers. Chidambaram, then finance minister, hosted a dinner for them, and that was a wonderful opportunity to learn things about Fiji that you don't find in tourist brochures.

* * *

A few weeks after the first exchange of emails, the Fiji conference hosts inquired about my speaking fee. Speaking fee? I emailed back saying that what they were offering me was a wonderful holiday, and I was not expecting any speaking fee beyond that.

Urmila and I travelled to Fiji as scheduled. The hosts sent a car to the Nadi International Airport on the main island of Viti Levu to take us to the hotel, which turned out to be more than an hour-long journey. The driver was quite chatty, telling us about his country, and very soon thereafter also about himself and his family. This again was a better way of understanding a country, its culture and people than hearing a tour guide spitting out the standard fare like machine-gun fire.

Within ten minutes of beginning our car journey, the driver asked me about my schedule for the next three days as he was exclusively assigned to us for the trip, airport to airport. I told him about my speaking commitments but added that I would not know my full schedule until I met with the hosts later that evening.

The driver said that was all right, but he wouldn't be available during some specific slots and could I work my programme around that? I thought it was rude of him to impose such a constraint, especially on a foreign guest, and even more so when he was being paid. But then I reminded myself that I must be more understanding. Maybe he had to take an ailing family member to a hospital? Perhaps write an exam? I asked him why. 'I have to watch the Sevens,' he said. Sevens? It turned out Fiji was playing in the Rugby Sevens World Series, and he couldn't miss those games. Hailing from a country where cricket is a religion, I could hardly complain.

In my keynote speech, I spoke about the leadership challenges I had confronted as the RBI governor, and it was well received. The hosts also organized several small group meetings for me, but they did leave sufficient free time for Urmila and me to go around and savour the ambience, culture and food of the wonderful Fiji Islands.

* * *

On the final day of the conference, there was a grand banquet in the evening with about 500 guests. As guests entered the banquet hall, they were asked to drop their business cards into a cane basket for a lottery, which would be drawn at the end of the dinner. Sure enough, the banquet was a grand affair with lots of food, drink, song and music.

And then the grand finale, the lottery draw. The master of ceremonies (MC) worked up a lot of enthusiasm and invited the finance minister of Fiji to come on the stage to give away the prize. The finance minister picked a card from the basket and handed it to the MC, who then with a flourish announced, 'And, the prize goes to . . . Duvvuri Subbarao, former governor of the Reserve Bank of India!' I was invited to accept the brand-new Samsung Galaxy S6 handset from the finance minister.

I was stunned; the draw was so obviously fixed.

But within moments, I realized that the organizers were on the inside of this match-fixing. It was their fun, good-natured way of saying 'thank you' and giving me something in lieu of the speaking fee.

But the hosts didn't know something I knew. I hadn't dropped my business card in the basket! My chance of winning the lottery was not one in 500, but zero.

* * *

Now note this.

In Harare in January 2000, Fallot Chawaua, the master of ceremonies of a promotional lottery organized by the Zimbabwe Banking Corporation, was excited to draw the winning ticket for a grand prize. The lottery was open to all clients who had maintained a deposit of at least Z$5000 in their bank account all through the previous month, December 1999.

'Master of Ceremonies Fallot Chawaua could hardly believe his eyes when the ticket drawn for the Z$100,000 (USD 2600) grand prize was handed to him and he saw His Excellency R.G. Mugabe written on it,' the bank said in a statement.

Of all the tens of thousands of people who were in the draw, the jackpot had gone to the country's rapacious President, who just the previous year had awarded himself and his cabinet salary hikes of up to 200 per cent!

'The prize would represent a considerable amount of money to most people in Zimbabwe, where minimum wages start at less than Z$1,000 (USD26) a month, and where half the workforce is unemployed,' the BBC said in a report.

* * *

The rigged lottery in Fiji was fun for me and the conference hosts. The rigged lottery in Zimbabwe reflected a complete absence of trust in one of Africa's impoverished and extortionist states.

18

Letter to My Mother

Leadership lessons I learnt the hard way

Dearest Amma,

It's been many years since you have gone away. The grief is gone but the void you left behind remains. Even after all these years, when I see or hear something that I know you will find interesting, I say to myself unconsciously, 'I must go home and tell Amma about this,' only to realize instantly that you are no longer around.

After you went away, I moved along in my life and career. Urmila and I are now retired. Mallik and Raghav still recall fondly the love and affection with which you used to give them lunch in our Pandara Road apartment when they got home from school while Urmila and I were away in the office. They are both grown-up young men now, married and settled with two children each of their own. Money-wise, I am more comfortable than when you left, but I want you to know that my lifestyle has not changed a bit.

I still remember our everyday routine. You'd read the newspaper and ask me to explain why the government had done something or the other. I used to struggle in part because even though I was working in the government, I couldn't explain *everything* that the government did. I struggled also because governments are not infallible. They make mistakes, although they too, like us humans, find it hard to admit them. That everyday experience with you made me realize in my later career the importance of governments reaching out to people and explaining to them in plain, simple language the rationale for their policies and actions. This is especially important in a low-income, low-awareness society like ours where government actions matter much more to people's lives and livelihoods than in richer, more literate countries.

Demystifying the Reserve Bank

You were, in fact, the inspiration behind one of the goals I set for myself when I became governor of the Reserve Bank—to demystify the RBI. Most people, even educated people, don't understand what the Reserve Bank does. Many think of it as just a currency-printing office. That it is, but it is also much more. What the RBI does affects people's everyday lives. For example, I remember you being miffed about the low rate of interest on your fixed deposit. At the same time, when Lakshmi Prasanna, your friend and our neighbour, complained that the interest rate on her home loan was way too high, you thought the bank was being greedy. You, like most people, didn't see the connection between the two—that the bank couldn't give you a higher rate on your deposit without charging an even higher rate on our Prasanna aunty's home loan. Importantly, banks' decisions on interest rates—the interest they charge on the loans they give and the interest they pay on the deposits that they take—depend on what the RBI does. I thought it important to explain this and many other things on the RBI's job chart to the larger public in plain, simple language so that they not only understand how the RBI impacts their lives but also hold it to account for results.

Leadership lessons I learnt the hard way

You will be happy to know that I've just completed writing a book on my life and career. These are not memoirs in the conventional sense; just some notes arranged in roughly chronological order. As I was writing the book, I recalled the many lessons that Baba and you taught us when we were children, some by example and some by exhortation. I related to them much more when I encountered real-life situations. In fact, one of my favourite topics when I speak to students these days is 'leadership lessons I learnt the hard way'. I thought you might be interested to know how what you taught me blended with my life's journey.

Do whatever you have to do with passion and commitment

Baba and you always told us that in life we have to do certain things—like homework—even if we don't like them. You also told us that whatever we do, we must do with full attention and dedication. I realized the import of this lesson when I was posted as Officer on Special Duty for arrack bottling by the NTR government in the mid-1980s. My job was to set up plants for bottling government-supplied liquor in every district of the state. When I got the posting order, I was despondent. Why me? There are 300 IAS officers in the state, and why did they have to pick me? You join the IAS with ambitions of 'changing the world', and you end up setting up liquor bottling plants!

But then I remembered what you taught us—do whatever you have to do with passion and commitment. I dove into the task with all the energy and enthusiasm I could muster. Not only did I accomplish the job, but now, many decades later, I recall that assignment as a particularly rewarding career experience. I've written about it in detail in the book but felt like telling you about it in this letter because it meant so much to me.

Dare to fail

My experience with arrack bottling also connects with another thing that Baba and you repeatedly told us: pursue success but don't fear failure. Honestly, I didn't understand it then, but in later life, I realized the value of this advice. For sure, everyone wants to succeed in everything they do but you can't be so stuck on success that you become risk-averse and hold yourself back for fear that you will fail. The raw truth is that failure is a part of life. It's how we grow, learn and become better. If you live so cautiously that you never fail, then you might as well have not lived at all.

You visited me several times when I was in the Sainik School. You also probably heard Commander Almeida, our principal, tell us, 'In life, don't avoid hurdles. That's for cowards. Real men and women dare to cross the hurdles. You may trip and fall but you will be a winner in the game of life.'

In thinking about success and failure in life, I found J.K. Rowling's (of Harry Potter fame) 2008 Harvard commencement address particularly interesting. In a speech that is full of wisdom and wit, and drawing from her own lived experiences, Rowling talks about the many lessons one can learn from failure, including the biggest one—the confidence that one can survive failure and bounce back.

When I was given the arrack bottling assignment, my initial thought was that I was being set up for failure because it looked like an impossible thing to accomplish within the time frame. My first instinct was to duck the posting by applying for leave. But then I remembered what you told me: it's better to attempt and fail; not attempting will be a bigger failure. I plunged headlong into it, and in the event, succeeded. That was a big confidence booster. In hindsight, I know that had I ducked it, the low self-esteem would have killed my confidence for the rest of my life.

For sure, I had my share of failures in my life and career, some big, some small, but I never held back from doing something that I believed was part of my job for fear that I'd fail. I believe I achieved much more that way than being focused on 100 per cent success.

You learn something every day

While on the subject of learning, Baba and you always told us, like probably every parent in the universe, that learning is a lifelong endeavour. You learn something every day. It's a truism of course; no one can really contest it. But I must confess that I found it difficult to put myself in a learning mode all the time.

When I was around fifty years old, I was once on a morning flight from Mumbai to Hyderabad. Sitting next to me was a young woman, maybe thirty-five years old. You know that I am the silent type. I don't normally speak to people sitting next to me on a flight. I was studying my papers, and she hers. When they started serving breakfast, we had to put our papers away. Seeing a window for conversation, she asked me what I did. I told her. Likewise, perhaps out of sheer courtesy, I inquired about her. She was working in the investment banking side of ICICI and going to Hyderabad in connection with a power project. We continued our conversation until the flight landed about forty-five minutes later.

As we were getting off the plane, she said to me, 'Sir, I hope you didn't mind my disturbing you. In my job, I travel a lot. I've decided that I will talk to the person next to me on a plane. It's a great way of learning.'

What she said resonated with me. On a flight, you come across a random person. She could be a prawn exporter, a space scientist or a mother worrying about a mentally challenged son. Striking up a conversation with your neighbour on a plane can be a great educational experience.

That sort of willingness to use every opportunity to learn and expand one's horizons is important for everyone, but especially so for IAS officers who are expected to bring a holistic world view to bear on policy decisions. I have since consciously tried to be open to learning opportunities, but I am not sure I have succeeded.

Keep your ear close to the ground

Baba, who served under many IAS and IPS officers, held them in high esteem and used to tell us at mealtimes about his experiences with them. I recall that he particularly admired officers with a frontier spirit—those who ventured out into the field to see for themselves how ordinary people lived and to understand their problems and grievances. In management phraseology that I picked up later, this is called 'keeping your ear close to the ground'. Let me tell you a little story about this.

When I was appointed governor of the Reserve Bank in September 2008, I went to call on Prime Minister Manmohan Singh in his South Block office. The meeting lasted just about fifteen minutes. During that brief conversation, I asked him if he had any advice to give me since he himself had served as governor of the RBI earlier. Characteristically, he demurred. He just said, 'You've been an IAS officer. You know the country and the people. As finance secretary here in Delhi, you've interacted with the RBI and are familiar with what the governor's job entails. I am sure you will do well.'

Shortly thereafter, I stood up to leave. He graciously walked me to the door, and literally at the doorstep, put his hand on my shoulder and said to me, 'Subbarao, you asked for my advice. Let me give you just one piece of advice. You are moving from long experience in the IAS to the Reserve Bank. That's a big change. Unlike in civil service jobs, in the Reserve Bank, you risk losing touch with reality. Your mind will become so cluttered with numbers like inflation, interest rate, money supply and credit growth that you will forget that there are real people behind those numbers. Please be watchful of that possible blind spot.'

In short, the prime minister was saying the same thing that Baba always admired in successful people—keep your ear close to the ground. I related to this advice particularly during my long fight against high and stubborn inflation for over two years during my RBI tenure. Inflation hurts everyone but it hurts the poor disproportionately. I remember how Baba and you used to struggle to manage our household budget on a low middle-class income when we were growing up. Bringing inflation down from say 7 per cent to 5 per cent is not just a numbers game; it means providing comfort to millions of poor households in the country. I have written about this in the book under the title of 'listening to the voices of silence'. But I am mentioning it here just to let you know that many things that you told us when we were growing up meshed with my life experiences.

Character matters

I chanced to see Richard Attenborough's *Gandhi* at a film festival a few months ago. Seeing it again after forty years was a totally different experience.

There is this scene in the movie when Gandhi is brought to a magistrate's court. As he enters the box, the scattering of people in the court hall who were chattering stand up and do namaste to him. Following that, the half a dozen lawyers there stand up one by one in deference to the Mahatma. And then the court staff and the police personnel follow suit. The atmosphere is sombre, and by this time, the only person who is remaining seated is the bewildered magistrate, unsure about what he should do. What happens then is very touching. With just a slight hesitation, he gets up in a stiff half gesture, locks his eyes with Gandhi's just for a moment, bows ever so slightly and sits down.

This must arguably be one of the most poignant scenes in the history of cinema. When I talk to students about leadership, I talk to them about this particular scene and try to parse it. Personality-wise, Gandhi was an unlikely leader. It was his character that made him one of the world's greatest leaders.

Follow your dharma

The reason I am talking to you about the *Gandhi* movie is because Baba and you emphasized the importance of character although you put it in different words—when in a dilemma about what is the right thing to do, always follow your dharma. But I want you to know that in my life and career, I encountered many situations where I couldn't even figure out what my dharma was.

You know that, like you, I've always been interested in the Mahabharat. I therefore read Gurcharan Das's *The Difficulty of Being Good* quite avidly. The book is actually subtitled 'On the Subtle Art of Dharma', and draws on the tales and characters of the Mahabharat to explore a fundamental human quandary: Why should we be good in a world so full of evil? And is it at all possible to be good? Let me quote some instances I am sure you'd relate to.

Bhishma sat in silence even as Draupadi was being disrobed, torn between his conscience and his abiding loyalty to the king. We think of Yudhisthir as the epitome of compelling, uncompromising dharma. But he lies when he says: 'Ashwatthama (the elephant) is dead.' There was smug satisfaction that technically he didn't lie, but the intention to deceive was there. Yudhisthir's chariot, which had always floated a few inches above the ground, sank back to the earth to mark his moral downfall. If you think about it, every major character in the Mahabharat is morally flawed and every character faces a dilemma about following dharma. In fact, when the Pandavas won the war, they had no joy or any sense of triumph. Instead, they were overcome by gloom and remorse, not just because they had to kill their kith and kin but more because they knew theirs was a hollow victory won through guile, deceit and cunning.

Well into the eighth decade of my life, I am still struggling to understand what dharma is and whether it is at all possible to always adhere to it. Perhaps it is meant to be an unending struggle.

Just a mercenary?

Before I close, I want to tell you a little bit about the title of this book: *Just a Mercenary?*. You know I agonize a lot over important decisions, and unsurprisingly, I agonized over this too. I considered several alternatives and eventually settled on this. If you read the entire book, you will perhaps see why, not so much from the text but from the subtext.

We are all prone to complaining about our country—how it is unfair, unjust and unequal. I complain too. But when I look back on my life and career without any bias, I realize that this country has given me so much. I am privileged to have studied in a Sainik School with a government scholarship, to have received an IIT education, also with a scholarship, and to have served in the IAS. And I rose to become governor of the RBI. This was possible because, warts and all, there are still opportunities for merit in our country.

I am quite clear that all through my career, I've tried to do my best. I am conscious too that my best may not have been good enough on occasion. But the question that constantly runs in my mind is what motivated me. Was it just a sense of duty—an obligation to do your best just because you are getting paid for it? Or was I driven by a higher calling—the need to give back to society for all that I have received?

In short, was I just a mercenary? Or, was I more? The judgement will perhaps remain reserved forever.

Amma, this letter has become much longer than I thought. I know that had we been conversing, I wouldn't have gotten this far. You'd have interrupted me so many times with your doubts, comments and questions. I miss you for all that and much, much more.

Wherever you are, I hope you get a chance to read my book and enjoy it.

I love you always.

Subba

Scan QR code to access the
Penguin Random House India website